"Arka Chattopadhyay's *Posthumanism: Politics of Subjectivity* conducts an extensive theoretical and cultural critique of the normalized anthropocentric subject of modernity, calling for its replacement by a transversal nomadic and plural subject co-constituted by the nonhuman. The ethics and micropolitics of such a replacement are imperative for our time, given the colonial expansion of the human footprint to geological and ecological dimensions in this, the Anthropocene era, resulting in the revolt of the earth, the disruption of the biosphere and the global dystopia of culture wars. Just as human identity can no longer be centered in the independent wholeness of the *cogito*, ethics can no longer be centered in humanism and politics can no longer be the conservation of a representative state. Chattopadhyay points out that a planetary ethics and politics demand a decentering of the human through relationality with its others - cultural others, animals, plants, technical objects, other nonliving entities and the earth. In five chapters and a Coda, he considers posthuman subjectivity in its co-constitution with these others through a wide-ranging and current theoretical engagement along with incisive discussions using telling literary examples. Along with being a rejection of anthropocentrism the book rejects ultra-technological transhumanist fantasies and caste-based social hierarchies. Instead, following Rosi Braidotti, it makes a case for the epistemic praxis of minor sciences, where minoritarian subjectivities challenge mainstream classificatory divisions in favor of blurred boundaries and machinic assemblages of hybrid identities."

Debashish Banerji, Haridas Chaudhuri Professor of Indian Philosophies and Cultures, Doshi Professor of Asian Art, Dept. Chair, East-West Psychology, California Institute of Integral Studies

"Who are We? With eyes wide open, this book shines light on posthumanist subjectivity, showing how the wisdom of an antelope and the predictive models of big data are part of our collective unconscious. A rigorous, eloquent and visionary study."

Francesca Ferrando, Adjunct Assistant Professor, Liberal Studies, New York University

LITERARY/CULTURAL THEORY

POST
HUMANISM

Literary/Cultural Theory provides concise and lucid introductions to a range of key concepts and theorists in contemporary literary and cultural theory. Original and contemporary in presentation, and eschewing jargon, each book in the series presents students of humanities and social sciences exhaustive overviews of theories and theorists, while also introducing them to the mechanics of reading literary/cultural texts using critical tools. Each book also carries glossaries of key terms and ideas, and pointers for further reading and research. Written by scholar-teachers who have taught critical theory for years, and vetted by some of the foremost experts in the field, the series Literary/Cultural Theory is indispensable to students and teachers.

Series Editors

Allen Hibbard
Middle Tennessee State University

Andrew Slade
University of Dayton

Herman Rapaport
Wake Forest University

Imre Szeman
University of Alberta

Krishna Sen
University of Calcutta

Scott Slovic
University of Idaho

Sumit Chakrabarti
Presidency University, Kolkata

Also in the series

Psychoanalytic Theory and Criticism	**Queer Studies**
Feminisms	**Marxist Literary and Cultural Theory**
Jacques Lacan	**Frantz Fanon**
Dalit Literature and Criticism	**Mikhail Bakhtin**
Ecocriticism	**Deconstruction and Poststructuralism**
Postsecular Theory	**Edward Said**
Nations and Nationalisms	**Diaspora Theory and Transnationalism**
Periyar	**Subaltern Studies**
Popular Culture	**Postcolonialism Now**
Life Writing	

LITERARY/CULTURAL THEORY

POST HUMANISM
POLITICS OF SUBJECTIVITY

Arka Chattopadhyay
Indian Institute of Technology Gandhinagar, Gandhinagar

Series Editor
Sumit Chakrabarti
Presidency University, Kolkata

Preface
Udaya Kumar
Jawaharlal Nehru University, New Delhi

Orient BlackSwan

All rights reserved. No part of this book may be modified, reproduced or utilised in any form, or by any means, electronic or mechanical, including photocopying, recording or by any information storage and retrieval system, in any form of binding or cover other than in which it is published, without permission in writing from the publisher.

POSTHUMANISM: THE POLITICS OF SUBJECTIVITY

ORIENT BLACKSWAN PRIVATE LIMITED

Registered Office
3-6-752 Himayatnagar, Hyderabad 500 029, Telangana, India
Email: centraloffice@orientblackswan.com

Other Offices
Bengaluru, Chennai, Guwahati, Hyderabad, Kolkata, Mumbai,
New Delhi, Noida, Patna

© Orient Blackswan Private Limited 2025
First published 2025

ISBN 978 93 5442 782 4

Typeset in Aldine 401 BT 10.5/13 *by*
K. Divya, Hyderabad 500 060

Printed at
B.B. Press, Tronica City, Ghaziabad, UP 201 103

040161

Published by
Orient Blackswan Private Limited
3-6-752, Himayatnagar,
Hyderabad 500 029, Telangana, India
Email: info@orientblackswan.com

The publisher has endeavoured to ensure that the URLs for external websites referred to in this book are correct and active at the time of going to press. However, the publisher has no responsibility for the websites and can make no guarantee that a site will remain live or that the content is or will remain appropriate.

To books:

the dear objects that offer quiet company...

Contents

Preface   xi
Udaya Kumar

Acknowledgements   xiii

Introduction   xv

1. Anti-human, Nonhuman and Posthuman   1
2. Posthumanist Ethics and Politics   36
3. Posthumanist Tropes of Machines and Animals   75
4. The Human in the Object: Literature and Posthuman Object-Independence   114
5. Posthuman Ecologies   145

Coda: Posthumanist Subjectivity   179

Glossary   186

Further Reading   189

Preface

This elegant and compelling short monograph – rich and wide-ranging in scholarship, nuanced in philosophical analyses and lucid in exposition – is motivated by the ethical need for a new conception of the post-humanist social subject. Differentiating himself from both humanist ideas of the subject and a 'subjectless posthumanism', Arka Chattopadhyay develops a fascinating account of issues, pathways and prospects of thought to advance the figure of an empathetic subject that is not exclusively human, and renounces claims to species supremacy and anthropocentric privilege. Addressing students and scholars alike through a clear review of theoretical developments and philosophical debates, the book differentiates hierarchical humanism, poststructuralist antihumanism, and diverse developments in post-humanist thought. Chattopadhyay persuasively pitches an ethico-political posthumanism as a vantage point from which a critique of capitalist transhumanism may be pursued. The relationships of the human with the animal, with things, and with machines form avenues for the development of this argument. The book concludes with reflections on the environment by advancing a posthuman idea of layered multi-species ecologies.

While reading Chattopadhyay's book we engage with the ideas of species-being in Marx; the debates between Derrida and Lacan on the animal; Stiegler's thinking on technology; the thing theory of object-oriented ontologists; and Dipesh Chakrabarty's reflections on the consequences of the Anthropocene for our conception and experience of being human. These theoretical excursions are imaginatively interwoven with astute micro-readings of literary and film texts and socio-political discourses, thus deftly animating the book's analyses through variations in style and level.

The book traces the genealogy of posthumanism not only in the increasing prominence of artificial intelligence, recent developments in biological research and ethical responses to anthropogenetic climate change, but also in poststructuralist and postcolonial critiques of the human subject. Chattopadhyay locates post-humanist enquiries in relation to the fascinating intellectual and political history of debates around subjectivity and agency over the past century, traversing boundaries between academic disciplines and geographical locations – especially the Indian and the global contexts – with thoughtful ease.

In his discussions – be they on the importance of matter or plants, animals or machines, things or technics – Chattopadhyay's primary aims remain political and ethical. He sees in post-humanist conceptions of the subject a move beyond the contemporary biopolitical constitution of human bodies as sites for the government and disposal of life. This allows him to connect with the Dalit question and highlight its deep relationship with contemporary politics of death and, through attentive readings of Ambedkar and other Dalit thinkers, to inflect Indian posthumanism with anti-caste thought.

The deep ambition of this book, to which it is steadfastly committed, is to seek the avowal of agency within the posthumanist reconstitution of the subject, 'to combat subjectless posthumanism and preserve what is human in the posthuman' (xvii, in this volume). The seeming paradox in this formulation and the insistence with which its consequences are pursued attest to the complex challenges that frame the task of thinking the posthuman affirmatively, which is perhaps amongst the biggest philosophical questions of our times.

Udaya Kumar

Acknowledgements

Acknowledgments are almost always like a letter of gratitude you mean to write and yet never quite end up writing! They better be unfinished and incomplete! Nevertheless, let me thank my father Dr Kuntal Chattopadhyay, who transmitted to me the love of literary and conceptual thinking early on; my partner Dr Anuparna Mukherjee, who refused to read this manuscript after hearing tons of discussion on it over calls, burning midnight oil! A big shout out to colleagues at IIT Gandhinagar, Dr Nishaant Choksi and Dr Ambika Aiyadurai, with whom I organised a conference and edited a volume that helped shape many ideas of the nonhuman and the ecological presented in this book. My dear old friend and colleague Dr Sourit Bhattacharya deserves a special mention for reading parts of the manuscript and commenting on it. Thanks to Orient BlackSwan for publishing this book; Dr Sumit Chakraborti, Sumit-da (with the informal Bangla honorific), for giving feedback at different stages in the making of this book; not to mention Namrata and Sreenath for their editorial guidance and care. Other friends and foes who remain unnamed are acknowledged in silence. A book only co-exists with other books just as our ideas co-exist with others (both human and nonhuman) who enrich them.

Introduction

The day of my visit to IIT Gandhinagar (where I currently work) as a faculty candidate, I saw a nilgai ('blue bull'; considered the largest Asian antelope) in the parking area of the academic blocks. I had never seen one before and certainly not inside an academic space. A soon-to-be colleague told me how auspicious it was to see a nilgai right away. I ended up getting the job and it threw the question of 'auspiciousness' open. Human beliefs like these we project on nonhumans, act like a smokescreen between 'us' and 'them'. We make them a part of our world, but is it for us to incorporate them? Do they not have the same right? Is there an 'us/them' in the multi-species earth, we inhabit? In my early days of living inside the IIT campus, I heard stories about the fast-running nilgai and how, if one was unfortunate enough to be in their way, they were a goner! Encountering the nilgai, I had the feeling that we were both positively scared of each other. Whenever the antelope saw a human nearby, it would move away, keeping an eye on them. On the other hand, a human like me would fix my gaze on the nilgai and observe its movement with caution. Who was in whose land? Who wanted who out of the land? Are these the right questions? I wondered what the mutual fear between the nilgai and I said about human–nonhuman relations on this shared planet. Could we consider this mutual, attentive gaze as an act of care rather than scare, whereby both the nilgai and I were respecting each other's territories. Was I looking at the nilgai from a human vantage? What was the nilgai thinking about me? These questions led me to contemplate the human being's position among other sentient and non-sentient beings in the world.

When red ants create masterful, artistic patterns in the kitchen with food traces, invisible to my human eye, or the terrace is regularly littered by the 'peaceful' pigeons, I reflect on our coexistence with other life-forms and the joys and frustrations that shape this co-belonging. I think about objects around me. How often have I felt the company of the overcrowded bookshelves? How much do I like my favourite coffee mug? I think about how a visitor once told me that the sound of water boiling in the kettle is the sound of human happiness. How is my relationship with the ants and pigeons different from all the inanimate things that lie around me? I have bought some of these things to use while others were present from before. Can I step out of myself and see them for what they are? These questions arise from my subjective experience. They have driven this book in different ways.

The reason to begin with these lived experiences is that I strongly feel the ethical need to ground a posthumanist social subject with lived experiences that enmesh the nonhuman. Unlike the populist avatar of a subjectless posthumanism, from one end of this book to another I have attempted to construct a posthumanist subject through philosophy, literature, and brief references to cinema. But how different is the posthuman subject from human and humanist subjectivity?

'Are we human' is a question about our subjectivity that invades everyday digital life. Our laptop often asks this question when we are browsing, just to check if we are not bots. In the name of digital data security, we must prove our humanity to machines by spotting zebra crossings and cars in pictures; keying in the right numbers; making sure we know basic maths like $8+4=12$, and so on. In India, each time we order food on Zomato or make an online purchase on Amazon, there is an OTP that authenticates our human identity. The random digits of a unique code feebly represent our subjective uniqueness in the nonhuman register. The other day, a friend who came back to social media after ages was telling me how it thinks he is a bot because he doesn't have a profile picture or too many friends in his new account.

The digital predicament of continuously proving our humanity to machines is the condition of 'posthuman capitalism', to quote the titular expression from Yasmin Ibrahim's 2021 book. As she argues, the digital surveillance capitalism of 'big data' constitutes a posthuman form of global capital in which human beings are always in the process of becoming kinetic data. Does this mean, there is no human subjectivity possible in the current world? How do we resist this subjectless process of digital capitalism? Ibrahim is hopeful about subjective resistance and the agency to change this 'datafied world' (Ibrahim x). She talks about data activism, for which we need data activists. But are these activists not human? To resist, we need a resisting subject of posthumanism. But how is the resistant subject posthuman? The posthuman subject will not be exclusively human. If at all, it would be residually human. This subject would certainly not believe in the supremacy of the human species but wouldn't forget human empathy and ecological care. The posthuman subject wouldn't see itself as the centre of the world but as an embedded object in its margins. It can only participate in a play of larger nonhuman entities existing in the world. As it becomes obvious in the current global climate crisis, the human is only one of many planetary players, responding to a call for action that emanates from what lies beyond itself.

The way multiple species co-inhabit the earth, without hierarchy, theory and text commingle in the flat world of this book. It is meant to be an explicatory exercise to reach out to students and scholars in the field. Yet, in its positing of theoretical linkages among different philosophical systems of thought and active practical examples of posthumanist literary readings, the book stakes an argumentative claim of thinking through posthumanist subjectivities.

The opening chapter tracks diverse developments of posthumanisms in the plural (there is no one posthumanism), from classical philosophical ideas of hierarchical humanism, to anti-humanism and poststructuralism. The aim of this chapter is to chart the transition from humanism to posthumanism, claim the urgency of this thought in the here-and-now, and identify the important thematic sites of technology, animals and things that recur across the chapters. Each interpretive site is marked by an illustrative micro-reading of literary narratives and poetry (Brian Evenson, Ted Hughes, and Wallace Stevens in this chapter).

The second chapter enters the core conviction of the book that posthumanism is an ethico-political way of thinking by foregrounding a new notion of subjectivity. This subject must go beyond human life and consider other life-forms, including plants and inanimate matter, as self-generating flows of energy. This chapter wants to establish Indian socio-political markers for a posthumanist practice of thought, beyond the silos of academic disciplines.[1] It uses Ambedkarite discourse to inflect Indian posthumanism with the axiom of caste justice. Encompassing posthumanist embodiment, the chapter develops ideas on thinking politics beyond the human through philosophical frameworks, Object-Oriented-Ontology (OOO) and Actor-Network-Theory (ANT) to zoom in on three literary case studies from South Asia: Saadat Hasan Manto's short story 'The Dog of Tetwal'; Salman Rushdie's novel *Shame*; and Indra Sinha's novel, *Animal's People*.

The third chapter furthers the ethico-political strand by positioning posthumanism as a critique of capitalist transhumanism. It makes a theoretical and practical study of two posthumanist sites of interpretive engagement: technology and machines on the one hand, and nonhuman animals on the other. The philosophical literature in the field on these two themes is invoked here alongside illustrative practices of reading contemporary novels like Iain Reid's *Foe* and Don DeLillo's *Zero K*. With Bernard Stiegler as our guide for a use of technology that doesn't lapse into transhumanism, and the Lacan–Derrida debate on the existence of an animal unconscious, we advance a political ethic that emerges from posthumanism. A Lacanian response to Derrida's critique is mobilised to expose the nonhumanity or animality of the so-called human body. Exposing the constructedness and impossibility of the human is a radical ethical task for posthumanism. To deconstruct the human–animal binary, the chapter uses three world-literary sites of interpretation: Paul Auster's *Timbuktu*; Marie Darrieussecq's *Pig Tales*; and Perumal Murugan's *Poonachi or The Story of a Black Goat*.

In the fourth chapter, we focus on objects without a necessary dependence on the human. Though politics in the explicit sense takes a backseat here, the ethic of shifting the human subject toward a reconfigured posthuman object underwrites the chapter. Thinking through the autonomous ontology of objects, devoid of human meaning, produces a philosophical and literary construction of posthuman objects in Roland Barthes and Alain-Robbe Grillet, as well as navigating the contemporary thing-theory of Tristan

Garcia and Graham Harman. The analysis of literary works by John Banville and E. L. Doctorow ramifies these notions of posthuman objects. We notice the lethal materiality of hoarded objects and the haunting spectrality of things that recoil from the human activity of pumping meaning into their existence. Objects protest in this act of inflicting injury or withdrawal. In this implicit way the chapter engages with an 'objectal' dimension of politics.

The fifth and final chapter gives rightful place to environment as we move toward the posthuman idea of layered multi-species ecologies by examining the works of Timothy Morton, Claire Colebrook, and constructing an ecological unconscious from Lacanian psychoanalysis. Ethics and politics become central as we go into eco-Marxist evocations of the 'metabolic rift', connecting it with the human as an ecological entity. The anchorage on Dipesh Chakrabarty's Anthropocene work reinforces the Indian contextualisation of posthumanism running through the book. The chapter uses two novels – Anna Kavan's *Ice* and Wyl Menmuir's *The Many* – to demonstrate the literary implications of posthuman ecologies. As the readings show, these texts – in their overt environmentalist dimension – intersect with governmental biopolitics of controlling the human. The brief conclusion at the end is a critical space to think about a way forward with agency, to combat subjectless posthumanism, and preserve what is human in the posthuman.

NOTE

1. As I write this, a new volume of essays, *Posthumanism and India: A Critical Cartography* covering a diverse set of topics from brahminism to music and from philosophy to literature is all set to be published.

REFERENCES

Banerji, Debashish, Monirul Islam, and Samrat Sengupta. *Posthumanism and India: A Critical Cartography*. Bloomsbury India, 2024.

Ibrahim, Yasmin. *Posthuman Capitalism: Dancing with Data in the Digital Economy*. Routledge, 2021.

Chapter One

Anti-human, Nonhuman and Posthuman

FROM HUMANISM TO POSTHUMANISM IN PHILOSOPHY: ANIMALS, OBJECTS AND TECHNOLOGY

This chapter offers an overview of posthumanism through a brief history of the idea from 'humanism' and 'anti-humanism' to the current 'post'. To define posthumanism, we must first understand humanism and differentiate it from its popular use as 'humaneness' or 'generosity'. The philosophy of humanism offers a human-centric world view. The academic term for it is 'anthropocentrism'. 'Anthropos' refers to the human species and anthropocentrism is a world view that puts the human species at the centre of everything. In this hierarchical view, human beings are considered the most intelligent and placed at the top of the species network or the 'great chain of being'. What comes after humanism or the 'post', as a temporal prefix attached to humanism, performs a dissolution of this human-centric way of looking at the world. When I say 'world', I mean both the life-world of multiple species and the world of things, usable and unusable. A philosophical outlook that displaces the human from the centre of the world and abolishes hierarchies among species and matter is our initial working definition of posthumanism. To add a cautionary note, just like humanism itself, posthumanism is not one consolidated theory but a set of diverse discourses that critique hierarchical humanism. In this chapter, I will introduce the fundamental tenets of posthumanism by tracing the idea through important moments in the history of philosophy and by surveying contemporary literature on posthumanism. We will begin with a discussion of three foundational themes of the posthuman (technology, animal and object), look at its currency in terms of environmentalism, and examine the implications of 'posthumanities' as a trans- and inter-disciplinary turn. We will end with a critical question about the existence of posthumanist subjectivity. All these argumentative threads run through the book and the present chapter serves as an initial purchase on these notions. I include micro-readings of literature to situate posthumanism not only as theory, but also as a practical and conceptual tool for reading texts. These readings, though often approaching particular microstrands within a text and not the entire text, will become gradually elaborate across the chapters.

To start with a significant historical-political example of hierarchical humanism in western philosophy, in *Economic and Philosophic Manuscripts of 1844*, German political economist and thinker Karl Marx makes a distinction between the human and other animals in terms of their labouring practices: 'The animal is immediately one with its life activity. It does not distinguish itself from it. It is *its life activity*' (Marx 73; emphasis original). However, he observes that '[m]an makes his life activity itself the object of his will and of his consciousness. He has conscious life activity. It is not a determination with which he directly merges' (73). This gulf between self and labour marks the special value of human consciousness for Marx and translates into what he calls the human 'species-being': 'Conscious life activity distinguishes man immediately from animal life activity. It is just because of this that he is a species-being' (73). The difference between the human and the nonhuman animal boils down to the point that the human is free and conscious of its being but the nonhuman animal is not. The hierarchy is clear. Marx doesn't consider the nonhuman animal to have a species-being because they cannot universalise their species and raise it to the level of a collective experience: 'Animals are unable to combine the different attributes of their species, and are unable to contribute anything to the common advantage and comfort of the species' (125). Contrary to this inability of animals, human rationality and conscious intellectual labour has the power of universalisation. Human beings can construct themselves as a species and study their own selves as objects of their consciousness. The Marxian discourse solidifies hierarchical humanism in this way. It places the human in a position superior to that of the nonhuman animal on grounds of intellectual labour and reasoning. The supremacy of the human becomes evident in a resounding statement Marx makes in the same text: 'An animal produces only itself, whilst man reproduces the whole of nature' (74). The animal labour of reproduction is aimed at producing only itself but the human being produces and reproduces the entire world or nature through their intellect and consciousness. We will return to the Marxian idea of nature in Chapter 5 while discussing ecology. But as we can see here, for Marx (and for many other humanist thinkers), the distinguishing factor between the human and the nonhuman is self-consciousness.

Going further back in the history of western philosophy, we find Hegel in *Elements of the Philosophy of Right* (1821), subscribing to the same hierarchy: 'An animal can intuit, but the soul of the animal does not have the soul, or itself, as its object [*gegenstand*], but something external' (Hegel 74; emphasis original). For Hegel, the key difference between the human and the nonhuman lies in the former's capacity to have itself (the human) as the object of its own intuition and the latter's lack of the same. It is not that the animals don't have intuition but they do not have their self as the object of their intuition. In other words, for Hegel, animals don't have self-consciousness.

Displacing the human from the top of the species chain leads to a flat, non-hierarchical ontology in which the human subjects are positioned as objects or agents in a larger network. It flattens out the distinction between the inanimate object and the human object. By implication, this posthumanist objectification of the human is diametrically opposed to Marx's vision of human objectification. In the *1844 Manuscripts*, Marx talks about the estrangement of the human through the labour that objectifies the labouring subject. His idea of objectification is morally negative and representative of capitalist alienation, whereas the posthumanist would champion objectification as an egalitarian process. And yet, the two points

Marx makes are relevant to our posthumanist idea of objectification: 'the object as such presents itself to consciousness as something vanishing' and 'the alienation of self-consciousness [...] posits thinghood' (Marx 142). The first thesis underlines that an object can never be properly captured by human consciousness. It simply vanishes. This is an invitation to think the object as itself outside the self-consciousness of the human. The second thesis that follows from the first, asserts that the alienating self-consciousness produces the human as an estranged object of its own labour. Though Marx remains a species-humanist, in these two theses, there is a way of reading him as posthumanist if we see these postulations in the light of the object beyond the human (thesis one) and the human as object (thesis two).

To stay with the object and travel back to ancient Greece – the breeding ground of western philosophy – in Plato's radical idealistic framework, the phenomenal world of things is not real. What is real is the idea of the object in the human mind. In this philosophy, objects have no independence in relation to the human. Real objects are turned into human ideas and made completely dependent on human cognition. Hegel reflects in *Elements of the Philosophy of Right*: 'When I think of an object [*Gegenstand*], I make it into a thought and deprive it of its sensuous quality; I make it into something which is essentially and immediately mine' (Hegel 35). The object in human thinking becomes a thought-object and loses its materiality. It becomes a human possession, as Hegel suggests. From a humanist perspective, the 'thing-in-itself' – as Immanuel Kant would have it – remains outside the purview of human consciousness. The human consciousness can approach the ideational representative of the thing but not the *thing as such*. For Kant, we cognise the world of things as 'objects of experience' but not as 'things in themselves' (Kant 115).

The progress of modern scientific technology has revealed how the human being is hardly accessible beyond technological filtering and simulation. What we often consider human is little more than a technologically-mediated virtual body, digital image or cognitive data. Be it computers, artificial intelligence, robotics, or Web 2.0, with interactive social media, the human being is created by the order of what Martin Heidegger would call *technē*. In the famous 1954 essay 'The Question Concerning Technology', he argues that technology is a coming forth of Being (*Dasein*) itself. In this sense, the human being does not simply use and invent technology, but technology invents the human in a dialectical process. Bernard Stiegler, one of the most important thinkers of technology in the twenty-first century, maintains (following Heidegger) that the human being is co-constituted by the technological apparatus: 'the human *is* technics' (Stiegler 35; emphasis original). According to Stiegler, we cannot understand the human being without understanding human technology. He gives the example of the ant in the anthill and the importance of observing it within the anthill. For him, the social, the technical and the psychic are all intrinsic to the formation of the human, as is the animal. These are only artificial differences because 'you don't have a psychic individual without a society, and you don't have a society without technics' (35). Following Stiegler, we propose that the human being is not just technologically mediated but technologically *invented*, in a radical sense.

The status of the human is a foundational question in the movement from humanism to posthumanism. The conceptual critique of the human subject in posthumanism has moved in three principal directions:

1. The subversion of the human–nonhuman hierarchy.
2. The foregrounding of the material world of inanimate objects.
3. The constitution of the human by technological processes.

Why Posthumanism Now? Anthropocene and the Decolonial

So far, we have discussed paradigms of posthumanist philosophy that go back to the classical and leap forward into the contemporary period. The theorisation of the human as species, agent and subject, have comprised a core area in philosophy, biology, and planetary science across the ages. There are ways of reading this theorisation in a posthumanist way. Posthumanism is a mode of engagement or a method of interpretation. There is nothing epochal about it; these concerns have been there for centuries. For example, in fourth century BC, Aristotle composed *History of Animals* with a keen eye for species biology. However, if there is a timeless interest in the human, the nonhuman, and the thing in their hierarchical and non-hierarchical arrangements in different versions of the humanities and sciences, there is no denying that there exists another strand of posthumanism that is more epochal and contemporary in its preoccupations. We must ask why posthumanism has gained currency in the late-twentieth and early–twenty-first centuries. Why has it emerged into prominence in this era?

The first response to this question could be that the three aforementioned aspects – the hierarchy of the human over animal, matter, and technology – has been undercut by scientific modernity and the postmodern age in such a way that it has made it imperative for human beings to think beyond their species. With the progress of science and technology, we have been able to cut through the mirage of human dominance. We have seen how the very idea of the human is dictated by technology, nonhuman life worlds, and inanimate matter. In a dialectical sense, the human can only be defined relationally. If we cannot separate the human from nonhuman animals, things and simulations of technology, we cannot define or know it. We have increasingly realised that the things we consider exclusively human are not human. Artificial intelligence and Emotion AI (artificially constructed emotional intelligence in bots) have reconfirmed that neither rationality nor affect is an intrinsic human property. They can be simulated in nonhuman agents and constructions.

ChatGPT as the writing avatar of Open AI has stormed the educational world in 2023, raising ethical questions about the authenticity of human creativity and research. If AI can write poems, novels, make paintings and conduct research on its own, how does that impact old-style humanism that considered creativity and research to be exclusive human privileges? If ChatGPT takes over, we stare at job losses in many sectors, including education. It puts pressure on the idea of human originality, not to mention issues of copyright breach and plagiarism. If a scholar writes an essay with the help of ChatGPT, who is the writer of the text – the human or AI? Can AI claim authorship? Is it ethical to pass off an essay written by AI as ours? Since it is a 'generative' form of AI, the human subject and the technological entity can co-create knowledge together,

Anti-human, Nonhuman and Posthuman   7

placing the ethical question in a fine balance. Digital technology and its ethics become crucial in these contemporary leaps beyond the human. We will return to the ethics of posthumanism in the next chapter but let us continue with the temporal question. Have we always been posthuman or is it that we are becoming posthuman in the twenty-first century?

Biology has exposed the nonhuman nature of the human body as an organism. As early as 1920, the late Freud of *Beyond the Pleasure Principle* uses animal biology to situate the cellular play of life and death in the body. Freud has to approach the human body in its animal form to address the question of drives. He must admit that '[t]he present development of human beings requires, as it seems to me, no different explanation from that of animals' (Freud 36). For him, the idea that the human being is exceptional among all species of life at creating a path of intellectual perfection is nothing short of a 'benevolent illusion', and he is unwilling to 'preserve' it. In a posthumanist take on Freudian psychoanalysis, Judith Roof writes that for Freud, 'life can illustrate the principles of life because all life is connected' (Roof 110). While we will return to the status of human unconscious in psychoanalysis to ask if it is truly human in later chapters (Chapters 3 and 5), let me point out here that Freud appeals to animal biology for grounding the notions of life and death drives. Most of the human body is comprised of nonhuman phenomena and life-forms like bacteria, viruses and proteins. This bio-environmentalist conception makes us think about the fact that the 'human' is nothing but a cultural name for the corporeal. The human body has nothing inherently human in it.

To continue with the environmental strain, our contemporary climate crisis acts as a significant context for the consolidation of an epochal posthumanism in the twenty-first century. This context is double-edged. As Dipesh Chakraborty has argued – taking a cue from planetary sciences – the epoch of the Anthropocene sees the human subject as a geological agent, capable of changing the climate. This is called anthropogenic climate change. As humans become geological agents who can significantly impact the environment, we see a newfound emphasis on the power of the human. It risks solidifying species hierarchy and an old-style humanism of domination, but the

Anthropocene attributes the climate crisis to the human. It advocates something that approximates the posthumanist ethic of a flat life world without species hierarchies. Global warming, unprecedented natural disasters like floods, earthquakes, cyclones, and melting glaciers, all make it incumbent upon human beings to take more responsibility and think out of the supremacist species-box that has caused ecological damage. The climate crisis of the Anthropocene creates a contemporary trigger for the posthumanist understanding of multi-species interaction in a non-hierarchical ecology.

Within the Anthropocene debate, Chakraborty urges us to look away from humanist histories for any actions that constitute reparation. Critiquing Wilson's idea of human leadership in thinking a collective future through the self-understanding of the human species, he reflects, 'We humans never experience ourselves as a species. We can only intellectually comprehend or infer the existence of the human species but never experience it as such. There could be no phenomenology of us as a species' (Chakraborty 220). This line of thinking is in direct conflict with the aforementioned Marxian (and Hegelian) idea of a humanist species-being. While Marx and Hegel championed the human ability to position itself as the object of its own analytic consciousness for Chakraborty the human species cannot experience itself as a species. The untenability of a human species-experience makes humanist reparation impossible. If there is a way out of the climate crisis, for Chakraborty, it must first renounce a humanist notion of history. As he argues, human beings are only one among many examples of the concept of species and not 'the' species in any paradigmatic sense: 'Even if we were to emotionally identify with a word like *mankind,* we would not know what being a species is, for, in species history, humans are only an instance of the concept species as indeed would be any other life-form. But one never experiences being a concept' (220). To address the problem of climate degradation caused by the human, we must think of a multi-species ecology that abandons any belief in the species-superiority of the human. In this multifocal way our times have called out the species-humanism of orthodox thinking. It has led us onto a diverse set of ideological thoughts that can be clubbed together as posthumanism.

The flourish of posthumanist discourse in the late-twentieth and early–twenty-first centuries also owes itself to the decolonial moment. The anti-colonial and postcolonial projects have championed a critique of humanism as the 'civilizing mission'. The imperial logic that justifies colonising a particular race is based on a thesis that certain races are culturally and ethnically superior to others, and that the inferior races better be 'civilised' out of their savagery by the superior ones. The evolutionary humanism of social Darwinism (the struggle for species survival and survival of the fittest at the racial and social level) acted as an ideological justification for the colonial enterprise. The strategy of animalising and dehumanising the colonised subject only to justify colonial re-humanisation through practices of control and slavery, are cases in point. Therefore, decolonisation means taking a critical position vis-à-vis imperialist humanism. Rosi Braidotti goes back to decolonial thinkers like Franz Fanon and Aimé Césaire to situate the posthuman. In an essay on posthumanism and postcolonialism, Monirul Islam shows how both discourses go against a majoritarian orthodoxy and share a strong interest in the Other, be it colonial or nonhuman alterity (Islam 120). Mignolo and Walsh in their book, *On Decoloniality* (2018), see humanism as constitutive of colonialist discourse and colonial modernity. For them, the 'invention of the human' consists of 'coloniality of knowledge (epistemology) constitutive of coloniality of being (ontology)' (Mignolo and Walsh 170). In other words, humanism could be considered a colonialist invention in knowledge that wants to colonise the entire species-network of beings. By appealing to Braidotti's work and questioning the western stakes within humanist universality, they push us to think posthumanism beyond a Eurocentric lens (171–72).

Mark Jackson, in the introduction to a volume on posthumanism and postcolonialism, insists that the two projects must draw out implications from the crisis in the concept of the human that binds them together (Jackson 5–6). As he shows, the Anthropocene debate opens up a bridge between the postcolonial and the posthuman by expanding the eco-political question beyond Europe and by bringing in the colonialist history of environmental abuse (19–62). Achille Mbembe, in *On the Postcolony* (2001), implies a different set of relations between the posthuman and the postcolonial that becomes a double bind. On the one hand is the racist dehumanisation of the African race, and on the other is the polemical reaffirmation of Black humanity (Mbembe 12). In Mbembe's analysis, for colonial discourse, the coloniser exists as a human (only a human can exist) while the colonised just *is*, like a rock that is in the world (187). Humanism gets implicated here in the colonial project by insisting on an ontological difference between being and existence. Postcolonialism, by dint of the same implication, demands a posthumanist ethic. As we can see, both the Anthropocene debate and the decolonial discourse are contemporary triggers for a discussion on posthumanism.

From Poststructuralism to Posthumanism: Critique of the Humanist Subject

To trace the historical progress of posthumanism, let me now discuss some of the foundational works that theorise the posthuman. For this we must return to the discourses (loosely called 'poststructuralist') prevalent in the second half of the twentieth century, especially in 1960s France and Europe. It is in the works of thinkers like Michel Foucault, Jacques Derrida, Jacques Lacan, Roland Barthes and Louis Althusser, that we find a systematic critique of humanism. Neil Badmington, in the introduction to *Posthumanism* (2000), comments that 'posthumanism inherits something of its "post-" from poststructuralism' (9). There are other important anti-humanists from this era like Georges Bataille and Maurice Blanchot, but the poststructuralist criticism of the human subject is crucial in paving the way for posthumanism. Despite many granular differences, poststructuralists are united in declaring the death of the human subject in the human sciences. For Foucault, the human subject is nothing but an effect of discourse. The human is displaced by the mechanics of language and eclipsed in the working of the signifiers for Lacan and Derrida (though what they mean by the signifier remain different). As Barthes would have it, we are spoken *by* the words that we speak, while for Althusser the human is a cultural construction. As we have seen, Marxism and psychoanalysis anticipate tenets of the posthuman. Lacan returns to Freud by inflecting psychoanalysis with language as much as Althusser goes back to Marx through the structuralist and poststructuralist lens of ideological discourse theory. Badmington, in the aforementioned introduction to posthumanism, narrows down on Marx and Engels and the need to adopt a 'theoretical anti-humanism' in their book *The German Ideology* (Badmington 5). As we have seen above, Marx has a degree of ambivalence regarding humanism. On the one hand, he is a species-humanist but on the other, Marx opens up a discourse of capital in its agency over the human and advocates a class-dispossession of the human in the name of the proletariat.

Badmington also mentions Freud's critique of human exceptionalism and credits psychoanalysis with a 'rethinking of what it means to be human' (6). He quotes Lacan's remark that due to the Freudian discovery of psychoanalysis, 'the veritable center of human beings is no longer at the place ascribed to it by an entire humanist tradition' (qtd. in Badmington 7). The psychoanalytic subject is not the humanist subject of rationality but the animalist subject of drives. Though Badmington does not mention Gilles Deleuze, the latter is a towering influence with his notion of the 'becoming-animal' and remains a major reference for the notable contemporary posthumanist thinker Rosi Braidotti.

Roland Barthes's brief piece on a mid-1950s American exhibition of photographs in Paris titled 'The Family of Man' raises an important critique of classical humanism as a universal theory of the human that blurs the distinctions of ethnicity, race, nationality, caste, class, gender, and so on. For Barthes, classical humanism eclipses history with nature whereas a truly 'progressive humanism', as he reminds us, must 'establish Nature itself as historical' (Badmington 12). In *The Wretched of the Earth* (1961), Frantz Fanon – the French–West Indian psychiatrist and philosopher – advances a non-European view of the human that does not imitate a western and Eurocentric humanist discourse. In what Fanon calls a new humanity, the idea of a homogenising human universal is questioned. In *Order of Things* (1966), Michel Foucault declares the death of the human as a historical category of thought that dissolves when the discursive focus on language comes back to the so-called 'human sciences'. For him, the establishment of the modern *episteme* (knowledge) at the end of the eighteenth century was founded on a retreat of language and discourse. In the second half of the twentieth century, when language and discourse return, the idea of the human is bound to disappear.

Jacques Derrida considers humanism as a metaphysical philosophy of 'ontotheology' that places the human as a unitary ontological subject in the form of 'full presence, the reassuring foundation, the origin and the end of play' (Derrida 370). The deconstruction of metaphysics in Derrida's project has implications for humanism and signals a transition toward the posthuman sphere where the human is devoid of metaphysical presence. It becomes a figure of absence in the differing and deferring logic (signs make meaning via difference and meaning gets deferred across the signs) of language. If humanism becomes the replacement for a religious discourse or 'theology' as Derrida suggests, it cannot remain faithful to its atheistic promise.

Putting a spin on this, let me turn to the Indian writer-philosopher Rabindranath Tagore, whose vision of 'religion of man' is an attempt to displace institutional religion with a religion of universal humanity. He was formulating these ideas from a different tradition of thought imbued by Upanishadic philosophy. In the Hibbert Lectures delivered in the 1930s, Tagore posits a universal human spirit that is immortal. His project is not to discard the religions of the world, but to redirect them on this spiritual humanist path. Tagore occasionally slips into species hierarchy, for instance, in the expression 'primitive poverty of the animal life' (234) that is used to criticise human individualism. What I want to highlight here through Tagore is different – a comment on the 'post', implied within his transcendental discourse of humanism. The human spirit Tagore describes is not *given*. It is a soulful, kind, and universal spirit of the human that he urges us to kindle. This human universal is a potential to be cultivated by humanity. It is an axiom to be worked upon – a posthuman future envisaged for the human from within the humanist discourse. As Tagore comments, echoing the Upanishad's idea of the 'super soul', this is a universal humanity which has renounced all narrow concerns of the self

Anti-human, Nonhuman and Posthuman 13

(28). This 'super-personal man' (226) can only come into being by surpassing the human in its petty existing form. It is a posthumanist, axiomatic and futuristic humanism that we encounter in Tagore. Let us return to poststructuralism and 1960s Europe after this brief but necessary evocation of Tagore, who reminds us of a different avatar of egalitarian humanism and marks the paradox of a posthumanism axiomatically contained within humanism as its future. Louis Althusser's *For Marx* (1965), identifies the Marxist diagnosis of humanism as an ideology and not as truth. He shows that the Marxist notion of the human, as either individual or universal, falls prey to either empiricism (empirical individuality) or idealism (essentialist universality) respectively. In Althusser's structuralist reading, both these positions are essentialist and homogenising. For him, Marx in his 'theoretical anti-humanism' keeps inventing new concepts like the forces and relations of production to take the discourse away from the human. Apart from the poststructuralist denunciation of the Cartesian human *cogito* as a stable and unified rational subject, the postmodernist thinker Jean-Francois Lyotard appeals to cosmic thought after the human body's death (Badmington 130–33). Another postmodernist, Jean Baudrillard, problematises the idea of the human body in the wake of cybernetics and medical simulation (Badmington 34–41). In Lyotard's notion of the 'inhuman', we have a temporal unfolding in which the human slowly turns into the nonhuman and the cosmic, but there is also a social process of regulative pedagogy that transforms the human into the nonhuman (Lyotard 4–5). Lyotard envisions the postmodern condition of the human as a 'vehicle' for techno-science (53) and this is where it must 'de-humanise' itself. In Lyotard's thought of the late 1980s, we see the emergence of a planetary system of complexity that takes the emphasis away from the human. He observes that humanism considers language as a human instrument, but in another view, 'the real "user" of language is not the human mind *qua* human, but complexity in movement, of which mind is only a transitory support' (72). What takes precedence over the human here is a physicist's view of complex and dynamic planetary matter. As Lyotard says, the life-form is 'human because [it is] earthly' (9). In this argument, the human is human only because it is planetary. It is planetarity that determines and thus overpowers the human.

This stress on the planetary is enhanced by Gayatri Chakravorty Spivak who subverts the 'global' of globalisation with the notion of planetarity: 'The globe is on our computers. None lives there. It allows us to think that we can aim to control it. The planet is in the species of alterity, belonging to another system; and yet we inhabit it, on loan' (Spivak 72). As opposed to the familiarity of the globe created by the human, the planet is a zone of alienation and Otherness. The human is not in charge of planetarity. The planetary could be the locus of the posthuman. As Spivak reflects, 'If we imagine ourselves as planetary subjects rather than global agents, planetary creatures rather than global entities, alterity remains underived from us; it is not our dialectical negation, it contains us as much as it flings us away' (73). This Other is the nonhuman space of the planet, but not simply a negation of the human. As an entity, it remains underived from the human. The human is not the centre or the *telos* anymore. Planetary Otherness has taken over.

Jean Baudrillard in *The Consumer Society* (1970) gives the movement beyond the human a Marxian political slant of capitalist objectification that we mentioned earlier in this chapter. For him, late-capitalist consumerist society is punctuated with a profusion of objects and the consumerist 'man' is taken to be a universal though it is not. The guise of universality is used to hide the historically conditioned market relations that reduce the human to an object: 'The whole discourse on consumption aims to make the consumer Universal Man, to make him the general, ideal and definitive embodiment of the Human Race. [...] But the consumer has nothing of a universal being about him: he is himself a political and social being, a productive force' (Baudrillard 85).

For Baudrillard, spontaneous and genuine human relations are lost and socially engineered as signs in the symbolic economy of consumerism (161). This social engineering leads to a point where the notion of the human is 'hounded out of existence by productivist society' (181). The posthumanist subject emerges from the productivist society. It is a discursive product of market networks that go beyond the human. But does this leave no agency for the posthuman subject? We will come back to this question in the following chapters.

To evoke gender in posthuman subjectivity, the feminist thinker Donna Haraway dwells on the species admixture of the human, nonhuman, and technical in her conception of the cyborg in 1985. The cyborg is presented as a mythical figure from science fiction (for example, *Blade Runner*) and pop culture of the 1980s (for example, *Star Wars*) that is perversely resistant to socio-political norms. They are a 'cybernetic organism' (Badmington 69); a hybrid of the human, animal and machine. They go beyond a binary conception of gender – 'a creature in a post-gender world' (71). For Haraway, this posthumanist imagination of the cyborg is a 'postmodern collective and personal self' that 'the feminists must code' (79). The cyborg is imagined as a disruptive figure that militates against the palpability of a unidimensional, perfect communication. It creates noise and ambiguity. In its transgressive agency, the cyborg shows us 'how not to be Man, the embodiment of Western logos' (81). As Paula Rabinowitz, Judith Halberstam and Neil Badmington suggest, Haraway's work has opened an important connection between posthumanism and feminism that deconstructs simplistic gendering of bodies and asks questions about posthumanist femininity.

Karen Barad, a feminist posthumanist philosopher of science especially of inanimate matter as studied in physics, offers a definition of posthumanism in *Meeting the Universe Halfway* (2007) that questions the very act of boundary-making between human and nonhuman and between nature and culture. How do we make these distinctions and why? For her, it is the task of posthumanism to critique these boundaries: 'Posthumanism does not presume that man is the measure of all things. It is not held captive to the distance scale of the human but rather is attentive to the practices by which scale is produced' (Barad 136). Her posthumanism – while being critical of postmodernism, poststructuralism and Haraway's cyborg-feminism – focuses on the formation of the human–nonhuman division. In what she calls a relational ontology of 'agential realism', all matter 'is produced and productive, generated and generative' (137). The human being is by no means the centre but only an element in the entanglements of matter and mattering as an active process that Barad envisages, taking her cue from Niels Bohr's quantum physics. For her, posthumanism is a 'critical naturalism' (331) that embeds humans in the wider world of nature where matter is always self-generating. From poststructuralism that admonishes the humanist subject and repositions it as an effect of structure and discourse, we arrive at posthumanism that critiques the centrality of the *anthropos* as a unitary ontological subject and posits the human as an embedded multi-species constellation.

POSTHUMANISMS: THEORETICAL DEVELOPMENTS WITH LITERARY ILLUSTRATIONS

This section will discuss posthumanist theory with a focus on themes like technology, animality and academic disciplines. We will return to these themes throughout the book. The aim here is to introduce these ideas and have an initial figuration for them. The section will interpenetrate theory with short demonstrative readings of literature, establishing posthumanisms in a heuristic field of literary reading.

Technology and a Literary Micro-Reading

Katherine Hayles' *How We Became Posthuman* (1999) is the first major book at the turn of the century to discuss posthumanism as a cultural and literary phenomenon. She starts from another literary theorist (and postmodernist) Ihab Hassan – perhaps the first to use the term 'post-human' still with a hyphen (Hassan, qtd. in Hayles 1). Hayles de-hyphenates the posthuman. She begins with mid-twentieth century robotics, cybernetics and pulp sci-fi culture and concentrates on the human body merging with the machine, becoming virtual, and information taking over its materiality. The development in cybernetic systems from the 1940s to 1980s ends up with virtuality that marks a twin point of information on the one hand and corporeal materiality on the other. She develops an 'informatics' of the 'flickering signifiers' in electronic data, expanding Lacan's idea of the unstable and 'floating signifier' (Hayles 29–30) in print mechanisms. She pushes the presence–absence dialectic of print signifiers toward the electronic flicker, distributed between pattern and randomness. For Hayles, the posthuman suggests a new link among embodiment, materiality, culture and language, encoded into the machine. The cyberpunk tradition of Andrew Gibson's *Neuromancer* (1984) is her example for literary informatics and Italo Calvino's *If on a Winter's Night a Traveler* (1979) becomes a site to study the relation between the text-body and cybernetic information flow. Hayles's argument cuts across cybernetics, computational and neuro-cognitive theories of information and engages with the cyborg subjectivity of the posthuman as an epochal development. As discoveries of cognitive science like the embodied and extended functioning of the mind make cognition more interactive, systemic and environmental than human, they push us toward an idea of the posthuman. Hayles attends to these advancements in her almost exclusive cybernetic focus, sifting through inaugural figures like Norbert Wiener, and moving to Humberto Maturana and Francisco Verala's postulation of 'autopoiesis' (self-reproducing systems). Her reading of Bernard Wolfe's 1952 dystopian novel *Limbo* focuses on the author's deliberate use of cybernetics to construct a technologically posthuman subject. Cybernetics becomes a tool to transcend the liberal humanist subject but, as Hayles shows, it also re-inscribes liberal humanism by situating a human observer in relation to self-consciousness (143–47). Hayles engages with Foucault's archaeology of disembodiment via discourse to bring back the material body *qua* the voice in the trope of audio technology and recording in William Burroughs's cybernetic trilogy – *The Ticket That Exploded*, *The Soft Machine* and *Nova Express* – in the late 1950s and 60s. Her study establishes posthumanism as a technologically mediated notion of the human in a residual, embodied form that is not without the vestiges of the liberal humanist subject. There remains a transitional dimension in her conception of the posthuman in this early intervention.

Let me give a brief literary example of techno-scientific posthumanism from the contemporary American writer Brian Evenson's story 'Any Corpse', part of his 2016 collection *A Collapse of Horses*. The story problematises language processing in artificial intelligence and offers a critique of technocratic transhumanism (more about this term soon). In the post-apocalyptic storyworld, folks eat human meat and a woman is looking for a recently slaughtered full body. The furnishers, who are not human beings but machines with AI, ask her if 'any corpse' will do. When the lady says yes, the furnishers kill her to have her corpse. The problem lies in the processing of the signifier 'any'. The universal signifier includes the consumer for the AI-run furnishers but the irony is that they will never be able to survive as an economy if they cannot differentiate between the consumer and the commodity. If they kill the consumer, turning her into the product, there will be no one left to buy the product. The furnishers have a problem in understanding time as well. They cannot differentiate between the present and the future and as a result see the woman as a future corpse. The relation between language and time is compromised in artificial cognition and hence the murder. I will not go into the latter half of the story where this act gets repeated with a man who buys the woman's murdered body. The story suggests the problems of an exclusive technological transhumanism by equating it with violence. The posthuman and the transhuman lock horns as the story-world recedes into the austerity of the ancient cave-dwelling humans, roasting meat over fire.

Animality and a Literary Micro-Reading

Of the three major posthuman themes (technology, animality, and object/matter), it is technology that takes precedence in Hayles. Let me now move toward animality in what Cary Wolfe calls 'zoontology' or a study of the animal's being. We must consider the nonhuman animal as an independent entity that does not need to be defined in relation to the human. A major symptom of classical humanism is to see the nonhuman animal almost always as an extension or a negation of the human. There is an anthropomorphic gaze that converts the animal into the human. We find many literary texts in which animals are personified, such as George Orwell's political satire *Animal Farm* (1945) in which human community and state politics is allegorised, or Eugene Ionesco's play *Rhinoceros* (1959) where the surreal disease that turns human beings into rhinos becomes a symbolic representation of Hitler and Nazi politics. In

Sukumar Ray's *Abol Tabol* (*Absurd and Bizarre*, 1923), we see hybrid, unnameable and phantasmatic animals that populate the world of non-sense verse. Bengali words like 'hashjaru' (a combination of duck and porcupine) are invented to name some of these animals. These creatures incarnate a critique of human language and represent a grotesque absurdity that militates against human rationality. They are vehicles of laughter, though as Simon Critchley reminds us, according to Aristotle, animals do not laugh themselves (Critchley 25). Whether animals laugh or not, they often inhabit the human narrative of jokes. They are used as metaphors of offense and abuse in cuss words (for instance, the sexist 'bitch' abuse) that reveal the hierarchy of human exceptionalism.

Literature often turns animals into symbolic tropes standing for something other than themselves. In posthumanist animal philosophy on the other hand, we must grant animals an autonomous selfhood and consider animal subjectivity with their intrinsic rights. Peter Singer – a contemporary Australian philosopher of animal rights – holds, following Bentham, that if animals have the capacity to suffer and *feel* the suffering, it makes them eligible to have rights as subjects (Singer 154). Animals have the right to be considered equal because they can register suffering, unlike a stone that does not suffer and hence cannot be granted rights. Singer critiques what he calls 'speciesism' – a formation like racism, sexism or casteism. For him, the human use of animals for scientific experiments and consumption of animals as food are two common forms of speciesism. Cruelty toward animals or human exploitation of animals are important practices that mark speciesism.

As Cary Wolfe argues, language is central to the way animals and humans are usually distinguished in philosophy. Human beings can talk but animals cannot. For him, Derrida's late work on the animal question generates an ethic of the Other where the Other could well be nonhuman. Wolfe highlights Derrida's deconstruction of Heidegger's humanistic hierarchy of thinking that the object cannot form a world, the animal has a half-formed, poor world, and the real world-forming creature is the human being alone. Derrida shows how traditional philosophy has habitually reduced animals to 'animot' or a mere signifier ('mot' means 'word' in French).

Anthropocentric philosophy turns animals into discursive objects. Human discourse homogenises the multiplicity of the life world: 'the Word, logos, does violence to the heterogeneous multiplicity of the living world by reconstituting it under the sign of identity, the as such and in general—not "animals" but "the animal"' (Wolfe 2003, 23). For Derrida, language cannot be the differentiating factor between humans and animals; the latter may not have human speech at their disposal but they are not bereft of language. Animals have complex ways of communicating through codes that often lie beyond human understanding.

Wolfe notes that, in his 1999 interview 'Eating Well' Derrida coins the term 'carno-phallogocentrism' which combines the eating habits of humans with a tradition of knowledge that equates rationality with the masculinist order of the phallus (phallus + *logos*). It is under this regime of the human being's well-being that animal meat becomes a mass market product in global capitalism, produced in increasingly greater numbers through artificial insemination. Wolfe goes to Maturana and Varela (majorly mentioned in Hayles, as we have seen) to bridge their thesis of autopoiesis in relation to language with Derrida's idea of linguistic tracing that goes beyond the human. Derrida critiques the Lacanian distinction between the human and the animal that the former can pretend, lie and even speak the truth via lying but the latter cannot do so. Though this is a much more compelling distinction than saying humans have language and animals don't, for Derrida, that a trace can always get permanently erased does not mean that either the human or the animal could deliberately erase their traces (Wolfe 2003, 31). A trace may get erased for contingent reasons that lie beyond the control of the human or the animal. So, even if Lacan is correct to maintain that the animal cannot respond by lying the truth (truth-telling through a lie) whereas the human can, it does not mean that the erasure of the trace (erasure is another kind of tracing for Derrida) is an exclusively human affair. Animal traces can get erased too, either wittingly or unwittingly.

Derrida accuses Lacan of a tacit anthropocentrism that sees animals as reacting without being unable to respond (Wolfe 2003, 125). In Derrida's reading, the animal in Lacan is square-bracketed within the Imaginary order of instincts and cannot make the cut into the Symbolic order of language or the ineffability of the Real. This works in tandem with Derrida's citation from Lacan to the effect that the animal is deprived of the unconscious because it does not have access to the Symbolic (124). Animals may have a fixed code but they don't have the mobility of language (124). There is no denying that the Lacanian mirror stage is a thesis dominated by ethological examples of the animal infant getting sexually excited by its mirror image. To cite Lacan's own example from the essay on the mirror stage, 'The experiment nevertheless acknowledges that it is a necessary condition for the maturation of the female pigeon's gonad that the pigeon see another member of its species, regardless of its sex' (Lacan 2006, 77). There is an ocular prevalence of the Imaginary here but it is equally important to acknowledge (this is missed in Derrida) that the mirror stage offers Lacan's thesis on the human ego that demonstrates how the human subject misrecognises the mirror image as the ego. The animal is thus made to become a homology for the human. But does Lacan afford any ontological autonomy to animals?

Derrida admits that his arguments are limited to Lacan's *Écrits*, and not the seminars or his late teachings (Derrida 134). To put Derrida's argument into a Lacanian perspective, let me say that the unconscious in later-Lacan is more Real than Symbolic. The unconscious goes beyond the Symbolic and creates a discordance between speech and body. It is an effect of the body as a substance of enjoyment or *jouissance* (pleasure as pain and vice versa, not to mention excessive stimulation that becomes a torture). The human being doesn't just enjoy their body in a conscious way, but the body has its own ways of enjoying the human as well. The body enjoys the human through the modality of speech in an unconscious way. Later-Lacan replaces 'language' with 'speech' in the domain of the human, and calls the unconscious a 'speaking-being' or *parlêtre* (punning with para-being or what remains beside being in a fluid ontology). The unconscious is embodied and environmental insofar as the Real is the Real of matter. The Real cannot form a world by itself. If it could, it would become reality. But the Real is that which is rejected by the reality of the world. It is a refuse of the world. In this sense, the Real unconscious contains a fragmented refuse of the material world. As we know, the Lacanian unconscious is inter-subjective: a cut between the subject and the Other, and this Other could be a nonhuman and inter-species entity. It can certainly be a nonhuman animal. We could consider Freud's famous case study of little Hans who had a phobia of horses. His unconscious affect was evidently the result of an inter-species interaction.

It is obvious that psychoanalysis works on the human subject in the clinic. A dog or a cat won't come to the couch. Even if they sit on it, they won't get into the analytic process. Human speech is the only mechanism psychoanalysis can use to work on what stumps speech, that is, the Real unconscious. Speech produces a disturbing enjoyment as it happens on the body. When it comes to this *jouissance* of speech as a body-event, Lacan is open to the speculation about an animal unconscious. As he reflects in the 1974 talk 'La Troisième' or 'The Third', 'if there is something that gives us the idea of "enjoy yourself", it is the animal [...] that seems to be implied by what one calls the animal body' (61). The body that enjoys is the animal body in Lacan. This suggests that the human unconscious, not at the level of the Symbolic but at the level of the Real of *jouissance*, has a proclivity toward animality. The animal body knows *jouissance* without a complex access to the Symbolic. The Real of the animal body duels with the human Symbolic and produces an unconscious that is neither exclusively human nor wholly animal. It is a posthuman unconscious that partakes of both animal *jouissance* of the body and the human order of language. I will further elaborate on the posthuman implications of the Derrida–Lacan debate in Chapter 3 while discussing animals.

Before moving on to the disciplinary ramifications of post-humanities as a post-disciplinary field, let me demonstrate animality in a poem by Ted Hughes, the Irish writer who has composed intriguing poems on particular animals. In 'The Howling of Wolves' from *Wodwo* (1967), the poet follows the sounds of the wolves to understand their meaning. This humanist desire to know what the animal voices mean is backed up by the opening comment of the poem that the wolves' howls are 'without world' (Hughes 404). In a Heideggerian articulation, as we have seen above, the animal (unlike the human) experiences a poor version of the world due to their limited capacity to cognise and construct a world. Going one step ahead, Hughes's poetic voice declares the animal sounds being devoid of any world whatsoever. Their eyes are compared to steel and it is said that 'they must live/Innocence crept into minerals' (404). The mineral image objectifies them to the core of inanimate matter. These are traces of species-humanism operating as a hierarchical gaze on the wolf. The voice struggles to guess if these are howls of joy or agony. Though the human project of decoding the animal fails, its humanism is intact. This humanist strain in the treatment of the animal changes in the latter half of the poem as the signifier 'earth', with its planetary nuances, comes to overpower the 'world.' When 'world' gets displaced by 'earth', we move registers from the human to the posthuman: 'The earth is under its tongue' (404); 'The wolf is living for the earth' (405); and again, 'The night snows stars and the earth creaks' (405). The climax of the poem lies in the acknowledgment of this growing intimacy between the animal and the planet. The quest for human meaning vanishes and the animal is finally treated as itself, for its own sake – as a planetary creature, underived from the human and released from the shackles of human meaning. The voice admits that the wolf lives for the earth, so much so that it carries the earth under its howling tongue. The last sentence of the poem makes the wolf disappear. All we have is a nonhuman ecology of matter or the planet itself: 'The night snows stars and the earth creaks' (405). Hughes's poem marks this shift from the humanist wish to impose meaning on the animal voice to a failure of this quest that leads to the emergence of a posthumanist planetarity. It subsumes the animal under the close-knit ecology of the nonhuman earth.

Posthumanities: A Trans-Disciplinary Movement

Cary Wolfe in *What is Posthumanism?* (2010) considers the cyborg variety of techno-posthumanism as 'transhumanism'. For him, this transhumanism may tend toward the posthuman but it hasn't become posthuman as yet. In Wolfe's words, transhumanism is 'an *intensification* of humanism' while posthumanism 'is the *opposite* of transhumanism' (Wolfe 2010, xv; emphases original). Wolfe juxtaposes cognitive science with deconstruction and critically navigates the domain of the bio-ethics of justice, as it defines the shared embodiment, mortality and finitude of the human and the nonhuman as fellow creatures in the world. In an attempt to understand how approaches to posthumanism themselves can be humanist or posthumanist, Wolfe works through Martha Nussbaum's Aristotelian take on the human as a 'political animal', in which the animal body of the human becomes as important as their political and social proclivities. Though he appreciates Nussbaum's project of seeking dignity in the animality of the human (Wolfe 2010, 68), Wolfe eventually stages an encounter between this justice tradition of bio-ethics (that equates ethics with life without considering death) and the Derridean paradigm of deconstruction in which the impossible relation of the human with death becomes a yardstick for the ethical experience (93–94). The Derridean ethical experience is an experience of irreducible Otherness or difference that cannot be appropriated by the (humanist) self.

Wolfe takes up the question of discipline formation to argue for post-humanities as a transdisciplinary movement. For him, any discourse that 'takes account of the constitutive [...] nature of its own distinctions, forms and procedures' in a way that is different from the 'critical subject of humanism' can be called posthumanism (2010, 122). He imagines such a discourse to have two observers instead of one. The first is the one who uses the forms and procedures within a discourse, while the second critically surveys the blind spots in the same procedures. The two cannot be identical; while the first may be human, the second must be nonhuman. Any discourse that satisfies this condition lays claim to posthumanism. Wolfe bridges animal studies with disability studies by discussing the works of Temple Grandin, an animal science doctorate who has lived with autism all her life. She is the designer of a large number of livestock facilities in the United States. In her work, Wolfe finds a connection between animality and disability and goes on to deconstruct the supremacy of sight in the sensorial hierarchy, typical of humanism. Grandin shows an acute sensitivity to touch, for instance, that links autistic perception with the way animals sense things. The autistic and animal subjects share a limited access to standard human language. This closes the so-called linguistic divide between the human and the animal. Wolfe's analysis is not founded on one simple opposition between the human and the nonhuman, but on multiple lines of fracture and heterogeneity (139).

In her book, *The Posthuman* (2013), Rosi Braidotti focalises the disciplinary move beyond humanities and the formation of post-humanities or 'posthuman humanities' (143) in the era of after-theory. Though she agrees that the human being is not the subject of the so-called 'humanities', Braidotti also affirms the need to defend the 'humanities' as a multi/inter/transdisciplinary constellation. This defence is important in the utilitarian era of capitalist scientism (science as dogma or the only claim to truth) and the digital pedagogy of online education. She prescribes a method of doing theory in the wake of posthumanism that would be geopolitically specific, self-reflexive, critical as well as creative, and non-linear (163). Braidotti envisages an egalitarian 'multi-versity' (173) as the university of posthuman times. This quasi-digital institution must think globally but act locally, be linguistically and culturally diverse, intermingle the academic and civic responsibilities, and provide free access to academic materials. Braidotti's posthumanism is finally a 'becoming-posthuman' (193) that does not let go of deep post-species humaneness and empathy. In the next chapter, we will go deeper into her transdisciplinary idea of major and minor sciences and illustrate the potential of post-humanities in the Indian context.

Is there a Posthumanist Subject in Multi-Disciplinarity?

Is there a subject in posthumanism or does it offer a subjectless ontology? This is the question Rosi Braidotti's *The Posthuman* addresses in a frontal fashion. The ethico-political consequences of this question will inform the present book from one end to another. Braidotti wants to cement a posthumanist subject that does not fall prey to the totalitarian and fascist political possibilities of a subjectless world (102). She constructs a politics and an ethic of the posthuman by restoring the subject. As she writes, '[a]dvanced capitalism and its bio-genetic technologies engender a perverse form of the posthuman' (7). Critical posthumanism must resist this capitalist posthumanism. Tracing a genealogy of posthumanisms,

Braidotti traverses the terrain we have covered above – from Marxist humanism to poststructuralist anti-humanism in post-War European philosophy. From the unitary subject of humanism, we come to the anti-humanist subject that is 'relational' – 'framed by embodiment, sexuality, affectivity, empathy and desire as core qualities' (26). This relationality of the subject is affirmative, unlike the shared vulnerability created by globalised networked subjectivities. Braidotti considers the deconstruction of masculinity and the post-secular turn (the acknowledgment that the death of the human and God often lead to atheistic dogma in the name of the secular) as intrinsic to the posthuman. For her, Black and postcolonial theories are not squarely secular and it is their post-secular dimension that keeps Eurocentrism away from posthumanism. She advocates a minimal, residual form of humanism as the need of the hour in the twenty-first century, unlike the mid-twentieth century anti-humanism.

Braidotti divides posthumanism into three categories:
1. Reactive (coming from moral philosophy)
2. Analytic (coming from science and technology studies)
3. Critical (coming from anti-humanist philosophical traditions).

She identifies herself with critical posthumanism. The first (reactive) responds to humanism and the second (analytic) examines the technological control of *bios*, or what is called biopolitics. The third mounts a critique of not only classical humanism but also the proto-fascist subjectless posthumanism of military robotics and war-mongering. The ethic of critical posthumanism is an ethic of incessant becoming that considers life beyond the human (not *bios* or human life but *zoe* or life in its diverse forms). Braidotti's posthumanism is post-anthropocentric in imagining this general politics of *zoe* in a vital materialism that takes its inspiration from Spinoza and Deleuze (Barad is not far behind).

There are three ethics of becoming in her critical posthumanism: 'becoming-animal', 'becoming-earth', and 'becoming-machine'. None of these three becomings are deterministic. They present Deleuzean visions of fluidity. There is no becoming one animal, one machine or one earth. If there is any oneness, it is a oneness of process and change. The monism of becoming is founded on what Braidotti calls a principle of the not-one or difference (100). In theorising becoming-animal (67), she proposes a *zoe*-egalitarianism that marks the human–animal interaction. If there is a critical becoming-animal of the human, there is a corresponding becoming-earth (81) in the eco-logic of posthumanism. This geo-centred posthumanist subject is one (in a Spinozist monist ontology) with the self-organising vital materiality of the planet. The ethic of posthumanist becoming-machine (89) depicts the fusion of human consciousness with the general electronic network.

Braidotti offers a positive view of posthuman 'necro-politics' as a subversion of *bios* by *zoe*. She articulates a politics of *zoe* that effectively obliterates the difference between life and death, and opens up a posthuman philosophy of death that is anything but anthropocentric. Building on Achille Mbembe's insights into necro-politics, she talks about posthuman warfare that creates new, machinic ways of dying. '"RISE", a six-legged robo-cockroach that can climb walls' is an agent of what Braidotti terms 'techno-bestiary' (124). She notes that while political thought around bio-power continues to proliferate and diversify, the concept of death remains frozen as a 'unitary' and 'un-differentiated' phenomenon (128). With a materialist and vitalist turn to *zoe* as endless cosmic energy, Braidotti constructs an affirmative ethic of death from necro-politics. Personal death is subsumed within a larger flow of *zoe* as life force. Her central claim rests on the 'productive differential nature of *zoe*' as a continuum of life and death (132). According to her, the desire to live and die are two aspects of *zoe* and there is no tension between Eros and Thanatos. Death is the mark of the inhuman that passes into never-ending *zoe* as an immanent flow of intelligent and autopoietic matter. Braidotti's argumentative move is to incorporate death in the energetics of life as *zoe*. She suggests that within the desire to live, our 'innermost desire is for a self-fashioned, a self-styled death' (135). This is not a nihilistic death wish but an affirmative desire to style, craft and stage one's own death. The uniqueness of each life rests on the singularity of how the person dies. Life and death are not a binary formation in this posthumanist necro-politics. In the form of death, the trace of the inhuman saturates life as the life–death boundary becomes imperceptible. It is this becoming-imperceptible of death into the cycle of life that is posthumanist for Braidotti.

In *Philosophical Posthumanism* (2019), Francesca Ferrando produces a diverse taxonomy and genealogy for posthumanisms. She differentiates the transhuman from the posthuman insofar as the former locates technological transformation as yet another, albeit radical phase, of human development (Ferrando 33). For certain schools of transhumanism, as Ferrando observes, technology may become a god-like power but for posthumanism, technology is neither an Other nor a divine omnipotence. It is 'an external source which might guarantee humanity a place in post-biological futures' (39). She discusses anti-humanism as a response to Renaissance humanism and places the Nietzschean idea of the 'overhuman' (Übermensch) as a complex combination of species-humanism and anticipatory posthumanism. Unlike anti-humanism, posthumanism does not rely either on the death of the human or the death of God. In 'philosophical posthumanism' and post-anthropocentrism, Ferrando highlights post-dualism which enacts a deconstruction of absolute forms of fixed dualisms that have traditionally discriminated between subject and Other, man and woman, human and animal/machine/object, and divided matter into static binary oppositions.

Ferrando posits the human as 'humanizing', that is, a process and a project through the feminist ideas of becoming-human, taken from Simone de Beauvoir to Luce Irigaray and Judith Butler (68–72). Humanising as a process, never to be completed, is further intensified through the notion of the 'anthropological machine' picked up from the Italian philosopher Giorgio Agamben (73). For Agamben, the human species is constructed as machinery to create recognition for the human. Ferrando goes through colonialist versions of exclusionary humanism and, beyond humanist rationalism, urges us to take spirituality into account in tracking the history of the posthumanist idea. She asks whether the selection-based idea of humanism is not inherently biased (87). A deconstruction of life and death is furthered by the arrival of biological AI (artificial intelligence in a machine's body that has biological neurons) that questions the possibility of life as purely human or animal. Her analysis positions posthumanism against the capitalist brand of transhumanism and genetic engineering that produces designer babies. She mobilises perspectivism (harking back to Nietzsche) that allows a plurality of points of view and connects it with Jainism's doctrine of *anekantavada* or 'non-absolutism' (148). The Indian philosophy of Advaita offers a non-dualistic view of the world resonating with the post-dualism of the posthuman way: 'the inner essence of an individual (Ātman) corresponds to the transcendent existence (Brahman): no frontal dualism between immanence and transcendence can be established' (156).

Ferrando's book ends with a turn to the New Materialisms of the twenty-first century: string theory and the multiverse hypothesis that argues for multiple parallel worlds, especially Max Tegmark's argument about a mathematical multiverse. She inflects the mathematico-physicist notion of the multiverse with a posthumanist post-dualism in which the gulf between multiple worlds and the border between the subject and the Other disappear. In the thought experiment of a posthumanist multiverse, she envisions a Bruno Latur-like actor network in which human beings will be part of a larger rhizomatic (a-centrist) structure. They will be actors subjected to a vastly nonhuman platform of connections. Finally, she advocates posthumanism as both thinking and praxis, and insists on keeping a residual notion of the human in the posthuman, much like Braidotti who writes an energetic preface to Ferrando's book. Her approach to posthumanism highlights the ontological questions of being and existence. She asks how we can exist as posthuman creatures in a society that is itself undergoing a posthuman transformation. We will discuss this ecologically entangled and creature-like posthumanist subjectivity in more detail in the following chapters.

Posthumanist Objects and a Literary Micro-reading

After technology and animality (and an initial figuration of posthumanist subject as multi and post-disciplinary post-humanities), let us come to the third posthuman theme of the object. Though we have touched upon it above with matter and planet, let me focus on object here, concentrating on a twenty-first century school of philosophy – Object-Oriented-Ontology

(OOO hereafter) as a posthumanist version of object-philosophy. As Ferrando writes, this school hinges on the ontological 'autonomy of the object—to be considered not in dependence from the subject, nor in relation to other objects' (163). She sees OOO in tandem with posthumanism. OOO is post-anthropocentric and post-dualistic vis-à-vis the subject–object duality. Graham Harman, the founder of OOO as a philosophical movement, builds his idea of the object from Heidegger's discussion of the tool; Quentin Meillassoux's critique of correlationism (a claim that we can only access thinking and being together in correlation and not apart from one another) of subjects and objects; Tristan Garcia's thing theory; and Bruno Latour's idea of actor-network. OOO remaps the human being from a sovereign position of subjectivity to being just another object among many other objects. Harman considers objects to be actors but it does not mean they cannot exist without acting. He critiques fetishising objects as agents. For him, objects do not necessarily need human mediation: 'A truly pro-object theory needs to be aware of relations between objects that have no direct involvement with people' (Harman 6). This is where OOO shows posthumanist tendencies.

Tristan Garcia, in *Form and Object* (2011), presents a flat ontology in which things are always in the world. For him, the meaning of things is just to be in the world, much like human beings. The meaning that things have is no more and no less than just being-there in the world. He flattens the distinction between the human and the object: 'When I comprehend a thing, being a thing myself, I limit this thing, and I make an object of this thing (Garcia 147). Garcia's definition of the object is posthumanist: 'A thing is nothing other than the difference between *that which is in this thing* and *that in which this thing is*' (13; emphases original). This definition is differential. It avoids what Harman calls the 'undermining' (reducing an object to its components) and 'overmining' (reducing it to its relation with other objects) of objects in traditional philosophy. The object is treated here as a difference between its undermining and its overmining.

Garcia, like his fellow thing-theorist Levi Bryant, posits a formal notion of equality among objects. This is a structural democracy of objects, staying frozen in their immovable slots. But the history of human use tampers with them and dislodges this democracy. Bryant notes that '*the Democracy of Objects* attempts to think the being of objects unshackled from the gaze of humans in their being for-themselves' (Bryant 19; emphasis original). For Bryant, this democracy does not exclude but only decentres the human subject. Garcia has a similar notion of 'accumulation'. Objects accumulate and create networks of meaning and this accumulation 'denotes the hierarchy between things' (Garcia 96). He agrees with Bryant that 'the formal condition of the accumulation of objects is its opposite: the equality between all things' (96). For Garcia, things become objects when they accumulate. Things are on the side of being while objects acquire signification in their network with other accumulating objects.

Like the animal trope, objects often become humanised in literary narratives. Either they stand as symbols for something else or they get imbued with a meaning projected onto them by a human subject. Their thingness is compromised in the process. Wallace Stevens, the great twentieth-century American poet, often makes an attempt to take the objects of the world out of the human economy. As Cary Wolfe reflects in his book on posthumanist ecopoetics, Stevens' poetry revolves around a 'tension' between portraying 'things as they are' (to quote the poet himself) and how the poet's imagination constructs a world of things (Wolfe 2020, ix). This is a tension between anthropomorphism and posthumanism. In some of his poems, Stevens writes the world of objects as they are, and not as symbols invested with human meaning. In the poem 'Note on Moonlight', this is what he calls 'the mere objectiveness of things' (Stevens 589). In another poem, 'Man Carrying Thing', we see the human turning into a thing rather than the thing being humanised. The poetic voice cannot visually pinpoint or subjectivise the things, it sees

> A brune figure in winter evening resists
> Identity. The thing he carries resists
>
> The most necessitous sense. Accept them, then,
> As secondary ... (406)

Neither the human subject nor the thing they carry can be specifically named and remain thing-like in their obscurity. The poetic voice admits that it is secondary to subjectivise them. The poem continues:

> (parts not quite perceived
>
> Of the obvious whole, uncertain particles
> Of the certain solid, the primary free from doubt,
>
> Things floating like the first hundred flakes of snow
> Out of a storm we must endure all night,
>
> Out of a storm of secondary things) (406)

Let's observe the repetition of the signifier 'things'. These are fragmentary objects that resist human signification. They cannot be perceived clearly. They are full of 'uncertain particles' and keep floating like countless snowflakes in a storm of other 'secondary things'. What we see here is a disconnected and distant human observer, looking at the play of things. Things relate to other things in this object-storm while the human being is reduced to a mere bystander. These are autonomous objects that do not require human mediation to connect with other objects.

To conclude, this introductory chapter aimed to start a conversation about what is human, what is anti-human, and what is posthuman in a philosophical sense. As we have seen, one can retain empathy for a fellow human being and yet be against the species superiority of the human race. Posthumanist philosophy builds a post- or anti-anthropocentrism that looks at the world without putting the human species at its core. Once we see the human subject as an ecological entanglement, it widens the scope and we begin to encounter the nonhuman life worlds of animals and material objects like never before. In this chapter, I conducted a philosophical, history-of-idea survey of posthumanism. We travelled from classical humanism that supports human exceptionalism, to poststructuralist anti-humanisms that reduce the human to discursive effects. Finally, we came to settle on a posthumanist vision that doesn't see the human subject either as cause or as effect of material discourses and practices of the world, but as an embedding in the larger world of matter, ecology and discourses. We will extend this discussion of posthuman subjectivity in the chapters that follow. Considering the literary readership of this book, the chapter was interspersed with micro-readings of the posthumanist idea in poetry and fiction. There will be more detailed literary readings in the coming chapters. We observed the currency of the posthumanist moment for our urgent times and surveyed crucial posthumanist themes like animals, objects, technology and environment, all keyed into conceptualising posthuman subjectivity. These are threads I will be deepening in the subsequent chapters. In the next chapter, I will establish the ethico-political foundations of posthumanism that have to do with a remapping of human subjectivity. This will allow us to intensify posthumanism as a contemporary movement of thought that cuts across disciplines.

REFERENCES

Aristotle. *History of Animals*. Translated by Richard Cresswell, George Bell and Sons, 1883.

Badmington, Neil, editor. *Posthumanism*. Palgrave, 2000.

Barad, Karen. *Meeting the Universe Halfway: Quantum Physics and the Entanglement of Matter and Meaning*. Duke UP, 2007.

Baudrillard, Jean. *The Consumer Society: Myths and Structures*. Translated by Unknown, Sage, 1998.

Braidotti, Rosi. *The Posthuman*. Polity Press, 2013.

Bryant, Levi. *The Democracy of Objects*. Open Humanities Press, 2011.

Chakraborty, Dipesh. "The Climate of History: Four Theses". *Critical Inquiry*, vol. 35, no. 2, 2009, pp. 197–222. *JSTOR*, https://doi.org/10.1086/596640. Accessed on 12 November 2021.

Chakravorty Spivak, Gayatri. *Death of a Discipline*. Columbia UP, 2003.

Critchley, Simon. *On Humour*. Routledge, 2002.

Derrida, Jacques. "Structure, Sign, and Play in the Discourse of the Human Sciences". *Writing and Difference*, translated by Alan Bass, Routledge, 2001, pp. 351–70.

Evenson, Brian. *A Collapse of Horses*. The Text, 2016.

Fanon, Frantz. *The Wretched of the Earth*. Translated by Constance Farrington, Grove Press, 1963. Print.

Ferrando, Francesca. *Philosophical Posthumanism*. Bloomsbury, 2019.

Foucault, Michel. *Order of Things*. Translated by Unknown, Vintage, 1994.

Freud, Sigmund. *Beyond the Pleasure Principle*. Translated by James Strachey, Norton, 1990.

Garcia, Tristan. *Form and Object: A Treatise on Things*. Translated by Mark Allan Ohm and Jon Cogburn, Edinburgh UP, 2014.

Haraway, Donna. "A Cyborg Manifesto". *Posthumanism*, edited by Neil Badmington, Palgrave, 2000, pp. 69–84.

Harman, Graham. *Immaterialism*. Polity, 2016.

Hayles, N. Katherine. *How We Became Posthuman: Virtual Bodies in Cybernetics, Literature and Informatics*. U of Chicago Press, 1999.

Hegel, G. W. F. *Elements of the Philosophy of Right*. Translated by H. B. Nisbet, edited by Allen W. Wood, Cambridge UP, 1991.

Heidegger, Martin. *The Question Concerning Technology and Other Essays*. Translated by William Lovitt, Garland, 1977.

Hughes, Ted. "The Howling of Wolves". *Collected Poems*, edited by Paul Keegan, E-book, Faber, 2012, pp. 404–05.

Islam, Monirul Mohammed. "Posthumanism: Through the Postcolonial Lens". *Critical Posthumanism and Planetary Futures*, edited by Debashish Banerji and Makarand Paranjape, Springer, 2016, pp. 115–30.

Jackson, Mark, editor. "Introduction: A Critical Bridging Exercise". *Coloniality, Ontology and the Question of the Posthuman*, Routledge, 2018, pp. 1–18.

Kant, Immanuel. *Critique of Pure Reason*. Translated by Paul Guyer, edited by Allen W. Wood, Cambridge UP, 1998.

Lacan, Jacques. *Écrits*. Translated by Bruce Fink, Norton, 2006.

---. "La Troisième/The Third". 1 November 1974. Translated by Ellie Ragland and Yolande Szczech, https://freud2lacan.b-cdn.net/LA_TROISIEME-bilingual-5cols-new.pdf. Accessed on 12 November 2021.

Lyotard, Jean-Francois. *The Inhuman: Reflections on Time*. Translated by Geoffrey Bennington and Rachel Bowlby, Polity Press, 1991.

Marx, Karl. *Economic and Philosophic Manuscripts of 1844*. Translated by Martin Milligan, Progress, 1959.

Mbembe, Achille. *On the Postcolony*. Translated by A. M. Berrett, et al, U of California P, 2001.

Mignolo, Walter D., and Catherine E. Walsh. *On Decoloniality: Concepts, Analytics, Praxis*. Duke UP, 2018.

Roof, Judith. "From Protista to DNA (and Back Again): Freud's Psychoanalysis of the Single-Celled Organism". *Zoontologies: The Question of the Animal*, edited by Cary Wolfe, U of Minnesota P, 2003, pp. 101–20.

Singer, Peter, and Tom Regan, editors. *Animal Rights and Human Obligations*. Prentice-Hall, 1976.

Stevens, Wallace. *The Collected Poems of Wallace Stevens*. E-book, Vintage, 1990.

Stiegler, Bernard. "This System Does Not Produce Pleasure Anymore: An Interview with Bernard Stiegler". *Krisis*, no. 1, 2011, https://edepot.wur.nl/194315. Accessed 12 November 2021.

Tagore, Rabindranath. *The Religion of Man*. George Allen and Unwin, 1922.

Wolfe, Cary. *Ecological Poetics; or, Wallace Stevens's Birds*. Chicago UP, 2020.

---. *What is Posthumanism?*. U of Minnesota P, 2010.

---, editor. *Zoontologies: The Question of the Animal*. U of Minnesota P, 2003.

Chapter Two
Posthumanist Ethics and Politics

EMANCIPATION FROM THE HUMAN: BEYOND *BIOS* WHERE PLANTS MATTER

The first chapter explored a variety of philosophical positions like anti-humanism, transhumanism and posthumanism through the most prominent extant literature on the subject. Contrary to a common perception about posthumanism being an apolitical theory of machines, animals, environment and things, as we could glimpse, it takes a strong political and ethical stance about each of these dominant arcs of posthuman transformation. The change from human to posthuman forms of subjectivity is a socio-political and ethical change. If critical posthumanism has a political task to counter the inhumane capitalist discourse of transhumanism (for example, machine fetishism), it is founded on an ethic that goes against species-humanism and promotes an egalitarian care of the life world. This ethics and politics has a pedagogic implication once we consider post-humanities as a post-disciplinary congregation.

When we say posthuman ethics and politics, it is not to be confused with biopolitics, which is the nation-state's way of controlling human bodies and the entire field of *bios* (human life). In fact, posthuman ethics and politics must combat biopolitics with something we discussed in the last chapter – Braidotti's idea of a politics for all lives (*zoe*-politics). In what follows, I will analyse the ethico-political positions that emerge from the post-humanisation event in the humanities with the purpose of locating this discursive turn in the South Asian literary-philosophical context. As we shall see, whether it is the Dalitisation of the posthuman subject or studying macro-political events like the Partition of 1947 and the Bhopal gas tragedy, the Indian context is useful for politicising posthumanism and the posthuman embodied subject as a resisting agent of social change.

If we look at politics and ethics in their orthodox incarnations, the foremost posthumanist move is to uncouple these two fields from their traditional human-centric thinking. Classically speaking, both ethics and politics have been square-bracketed with human affairs as if they couldn't exist without the human. It is human moral behaviour, decisions, choices and dilemmas that have been placed at the core, while the nonhuman domains have typically been relegated to a place outside ethics. A symptomatic example is the binary belief that counterpoints the instinctive and amoral animal action with the rational and ethical action of the human being. When it comes to politics, the Aristotelian idea of the human being as a political animal has been central to its very ontology. But what if we expand our conceptions of ethics and politics beyond the human species into the larger life world, including plants and inanimate matter? There are two related but different questions here. The first is about the ethical and political implications of posthumanist philosophy. The second is regarding the way in which posthumanism could actively rethink ethics and politics. In this chapter, we will try and address both these questions.

The political ethics of the posthuman can also become a self-critical tool. We notice this argument in Christopher Peterson's *Monkey Trouble* (2018) that examines the scandal called the human at the heart of posthumanism. He sees posthumanism itself as a human desire, and attempts to weaken what he considers a fantasy of completely decentring the human. He weakens posthumanism in an ethico-political project of critique: 'its weakness reflects an ironic power that aims to deflate the ultrahumanism of those posthumans who "know" too much about the human' (Peterson 120). This critique aims to redefine the human in the posthuman, not so much as a margin but more as an entanglement. This is where the ethico-political question around posthumanism throws itself in. Peterson's final vision, following Walt Whitman's poetry, is that of a 'cosmocracy-to-come', modelled on Derrida's infinitely-promised democracy. This democracy is a weak formation in that the promised 'to-come' (Derrida's *à venir*) is always more uncertain and contingent than a solid 'future' (109). This democracy is not restricted to the human and supports a weak utopia of equality, hospitality and justice 'to-come'. Even as Peterson imagines this utopia, he is aware of the human dimension of desire at the core of this imagination. He mentions that it is none other than the human who invites all other species to this cosmic party (120). However, it is the weak, incomplete and unfinishable nature of the 'to-come' that saves this utopian imagination from the ultrahuman fantasy of totally de-centring the human in posthumanism.

In the entry on 'Posthuman Ethics', Patricia MacCormack, in a different key from Peterson's, traces this ethic in line with Nietzsche, Spinoza and Deleuze. For her, a posthuman ethic resists the uncritical fetishisation of technology and cyborgism in transhumanism (MacCormack 2018, 346). As Patrick Hanafin argues, there is a rights framework in posthumanism but Braidotti would critique the humanism of Peter Singer's idea of animal rights on the ground that he is willing to give animals rights only when they are humanised. This is a becoming-human of the animal while the truly posthuman rights discourse would be anchored by a becoming-animal of the human (Hanafin 353). In *The Emancipatory Project of Posthumanism* (2018), Erika Cudworth and Stephen Hobden locate an emancipatory politics in posthumanist thought through the Anthropocene–Capitalocene debate, Latour's actor-network theory, and Marxist thinking on political change. They call for a 'creaturely politics' that 'stresses the bodied nature of the human and our bedding in vital networks with other beings and things' (Cudworth and Hobden 137). This invokes a Marxist idea of emancipation which is not only socio-political but also has a species dimension when Marx considers the manifestation of species-being as the horizon of human emancipation (22). Cudworth and Hobden argue, with recourse to Latour's idea of politics as a relation to nature, that posthumanist political theory sees policy and agency as interventions into a network of the social that is irreducible to the human. The socio-political exceeds the human and to change a complex world (network), the idea of emancipation must go beyond humanity and humanism. A major part of this ethics and politics, as Cudworth and Hobden contend, involves the debates opened up by animal rights discourses that make it incumbent upon the human to remove or minimise animal exploitation for science and market consumption. They cover a range of discussions, from the abolitionist logic that argues in favour of completely removing commercial and consumptive usage of animals as commodity to more moderate measures like having uncaged chickens in poultries. When we choose to buy cage-free eggs, the choice is implicitly ethico-political. Apart from the animal, they also probe a vegetal thinking that turns the gaze to the world of plants. Following Michael Marder, they argue that the plant world is 'politically attractive for they draw no delusional line between self and other' (104). The exuberant and giving plant world may be a useful paradigm to articulate posthumanist ethics and politics. For them, plant life stands up to a future where there would be no humanist individual self, and hence the importance of the ethical turn of becoming-plant (104). Becoming-plant is indeed committed to the idea of endless becoming as a strategy of posthumanising the human subject. It is also consistent with the notion of an ecologically entangled subjectivity. Let us delve deeper into this argument.

Michael Marder's plant ethics in *Plant-Thinking* (2013) advocates vegetal philosophy as an ecological strand within posthumanism. There is a thread that connects the Derridean weakness in Peterson with the way philosophers Gianni Vattimo and Santiago Zabala claim Marder to be an exponent of 'weak thought'. This 'weak thought', as they explain, is an ethical position that wants to create a non-metaphysical politics (Marder xii). Marder positions himself *qua* weak thought by rethinking the ontology of vegetal life against the metaphysical orthodoxy of human ontology. He must pursue 'a weakening of the self's boundaries, commensurate with the powerlessness (*Ohnmacht*) of the plants themselves' (150). If weak thought is the philosophy of the oppressed, as Marder sees it, the plant's silence puts it in a subaltern position. It is their vulnerable finitude that calls for ethical action. Articulating the posthuman ethic of plant life, Marder urges us not just to think about, but more importantly, to think *with* the plant world. He argues for an 'intimacy' with vegetal beings in which the humans give due autonomy to them (181). For him, the ethical lesson is that '*plant-thinking is plant-doing*' (181; emphases original). To think vegetal being is to work with the plants and help in nurturing and reproducing them, privately or publicly. Plants deserve our respect. We have to cultivate them existentially and not think of them as only consumable commodities (fruits, vegetable) or reduce them to inaction (for example, the pejorative use of the term 'vegetative' for inert). If ethics is about relations with the Other, for Marder, the plant Other must ground human ethic.

In a 2014 article appearing in *The Guardian*, Luce Irigaray – the French feminist – sees a fidelity to life in the plant world in their tireless attempts to neutralise air pollution and renew the quality of air:

> The lesson taught by plants is that sharing life augments and enhances the sphere of the living, while dividing life into so-called natural or human resources diminishes it. We must come to view the air, the plants and ourselves as the contributors to the preservation of life and growth, rather than a mesh of quantifiable objects or productive potentialities at our disposal. (Irigaray and Marder)[1]

We see here Irigaray's attempt to locate posthuman ethics in the plant world's actions of purifying the environment. The human is supposed to learn from the plant, this ethical principle of enhancing the life of the Other. This is a reversal of species-humanism.

Sumana Roy, in *How I Became a Tree* (2017), renders some of these questions regarding plant ethics in a creative way. For her, human beings tend to reduce plants to lifelessness as they don't move. Roy looks at the patriarchal language of feminising plants, especially the floral ones, and analyses her own desire to become a tree against that convention. She wants to become a tree to escape noise, as she says (Roy 23). Citing Ellison Banks Findly's work on plant lives in Indian thought, Roy reflects on Upanishadic plant ontology that places the human as cosmological entanglement (213). Though she doesn't have a posthumanist position on plant life, Roy's emphasis on the becoming-plant of the human, instead of the more conventional anthropomorphic becoming-human of the plant, has implications for posthumanism. She reads Nandalal Bose's tree paintings not as anthropomorphisation of the tree (though Roy is all too aware of an anthropocentric inclination in Bose's writings) but as Bose himself turning into a tree. Herein lies the reversal of humanism. Roy's desire to become a tree, in her own analysis, is a need to return to 'slow time' which brings us back to the human in the posthuman (62). To echo Christopher Peterson's above argument, we encounter the difficulty of de-centring the human in Roy's book. The desire to become posthuman remains anchored by a profoundly human desire, for instance, the desire to become vegetal. On the one hand, Roy inverts anthropomorphism by adopting a vegetal perspective, but on the other, her desire to become a tree is a deep human desire to slow down the capitalist time of velocity. This certainly doesn't make her work anthropocentric. Her book offers a posthuman ethic of seeing the human as a vegetal and ecological embedding. This human subjectivity projects its feelings onto the plant world like a humanist but it also locates itself as an extension, and not the centre of vegetal reality. In the final chapter, Roy likens the papaya tree outside her bedroom window to a mother figure and fantasises a physical transformation: 'what would happen if I were able to break my bones and rearrange them into the shape of a tree' (220). This thought experiment once again underlines the desire to be a posthuman subject as a human and humane desire. We notice an important manifestation of posthumanist ethics in this paradox.

In a sardonic turnaround of this pacifist and emancipatory discourse of becoming-plant, we have the imaginative construction of a man-eating plant 'Septopus' in Satyajit Ray's 1961 Bengali science-fiction story 'Septopuser Khide' ('Septopus's Hunger'). A story like this shows how the humanist imagination can position the plant as a threatening Other. When Kanti, the botanist, seeks the narrator's help to eliminate Septopus, he tells the latter that even if he has to kill it, there would be no criminal offence (Ray 31). This line of reasoning makes us think of nonhuman rights. Killing a plant is not considered a crime the way killing a tiger or a lion is. Kanti differentiates plant from animal species by reflecting on how the former, unlike the latter, cannot walk or express their feelings and may not even have a mind (30–31). In Ray's humanistic narrative, it ultimately becomes the responsibility of the botanist who collects and fosters this giant plant to get rid of Septopus. At the end of the story, after the giant plant is shot dead, the scientist decides to research harmless vegetables as he abandons his study of plants that eat animals.

Coming back to Cudworth and Hobden's ethico-political project of posthumanism, by 'creaturely politics' they mean a multi-species politics of relationality in which the human beings will see themselves less as humans and more as animals or creatures like their nonhuman comrades, sharing an ecology. They develop their ideas of ethics and politics beyond the Anthropocene/Capitalocene debate. The Anthropocene, as noted in the previous chapter, attributes climate change to the human being as a geological agent. The Capitalocene makes the historical system of capitalism and its age-old sway over nature responsible for this crisis, beginning in the sixteenth-century culture of environment-making that organises the world of nature in a capitalist way. We could think of the Industrial Revolution in Europe as an important epochal marker. To discuss a politics of life beyond the binary of Anthropocene and Capitalocene, Cudworth and Hobden evoke a third term: Donna Haraway's 'Chthulucene' as the post-Anthropocene era of multi-species assemblages. Instead of taking the planetary path of Gaia that imagines the earth as a living being, they resort to 'terraism' (their coinage) – 'both a commitment to the flourishing of earthly life through action and a commitment to the minimisation of forms of domination' (Cudworth and Hobden 147). This is not a politics that comes from the top, through policy change; it believes in a bottom-up approach.

Following the Frankfurt School thinker Theodor Adorno, they prescribe a way of living that is 'less wrong' and thus an idea of 'negative emancipation' (147). It reminds us of Adorno's 'negative dialectic'. This negative emancipation involves a control on global meat production or population for instance. This is a politics against biopolitical control. The control here should come from the community and not the nation-state. As examples of the posthuman community, Cudworth and Hobden mention various inter-species cooperatives like the human beings, swimming with dolphins for years, or the honey gatherers and the honeyguide bird who indicates the exact location of beehives to the gatherers. These are symbiotic ecological interactions where both sides benefit from direct communication without the mediation of the state. These communities are mutually helpful and non-exploitative. Cudworth and Hobden see them as alternative spaces of political practice that follow Foucault's idea of heterotopia – heterogenous, pluralist and hybridised spaces. These spaces are networked with other spaces beyond themselves. They resist hegemonic spatial formations like the binary of Anthropocene/Capitalocene.

POSTHUMAN EMBODIMENT: BEYOND BIOPOLITICS

How do we see corporeality in the context of posthumanism? Can a posthumanist idea of embodiment resist biopolitics? Hamid Dabashi in *Corpus Anarchicum* (2012) locates the posthumanist notion of human body in the political cultures of radicalism and protest, especially incarnated in the bomber's suicidal subjectivity. This is a notion of the body as disposable waste that does not make a whole. The possibility of explosion is built into this fragmented body. Dabashi charts a movement from the Enlightenment humanist body to the posthumanist body in the era of globalised capital. The context is post-9/11 (the 2001 attack on the World Trade Centre) Islamophobia; America's war on Iraq in 2003; the Arab Spring; Israel–Palestine conflicts; and the American war on terror, that in turn creates a surge of anarchist bodies in global protest cultures. Against the secular framework of humanism, Dabashi proposes an idea of the posthuman body that is not indifferent to the working of religion in the political discourse. For him, the posthuman body is a site of resistance to the state's control over the human body from life to death in instances like the death penalty, battles over abortion, gay and lesbian rights, and so on. The body that self-explodes defines this biopolitical controlling of the state: 'The globalized condition of the posthuman body remains amorphous in correspondence with the amorphous capital and the postmodern state that continues to claim it as the sole site of its self-legitimizing violence' (Dabashi 214). Once again, we see how posthumanism in a political sense could combat ideas of biopolitics. Dabashi invokes Mohammad Bouazizi's act of self-immolation in 2011 as an instance of the radical politics of posthuman corporeality. Bouazizi who killed himself in protest against the autocratic regime and became an important trigger for the Tunisian Revolution of 2011, represents a failure of the Enlightenment body of humanism in all its glorification. This posthuman disposable body, that fails to write humanist liberations on its surface, produces what Dabashi calls a 'countermetaphysics' (214). In his argument, the politics of the posthuman body is transnational. It stumps the nation-state's effort to unify all sites of self-legitimising violence by multiplying the sites of suicidal violence. For Dabashi, what the posthuman body declares 'is the ultimate denial of the state [as] its singular and final site of legitimacy' (6). The amorphous body, created by the amorphous movement of global capital, turns into an anarchic body when the singularity of violence is riven by the multiplicity of the posthuman bodies as waste objects. Dabashi's work offers an important political utilisation and contextualisation of posthumanist corporeality to understand contemporary global politics through anarchism. Let me now come back to the question of ethics in posthumanism to re-approach politics from this vantage point. This ethics however cannot let go of an embodied practice.

In *Posthuman Ethics* (2012), Patricia MacCormack frames the ethical question underpinning posthumanism around cultures of embodiment. The bodily differences between the human and the nonhuman have been key to triumphalist discourses of humanism. It is typical to represent dehumanisation through a corporeal transformation where a human being becomes an animal. The figure of the monster is an archetype. MacCormack studies technologies of 'teratology' or monster-formations in medicine to ground the posthumanist bent toward a love for the monster and a monstrous ethic. The monster as a figure of the unknown is not one particular animal but a conglomerate of many. This indeterminacy is true to the idea of becoming-animal which cannot be reduced to the process of becoming one fixed and particular type of animal.

For MacCormack, the ethics of posthumanism has to be relational. It must reach out to the nonhuman instead of fixating on the human responsibility to be ethical in multi-species interactions: 'Posthuman ethics begins toward the nonhuman with the "I will not" which creates the "I am not all" thus "I am not so the other may be"' (MacCormack 2012, 77). This is not a pathological and compulsive affirmationist ethic (though that does not take away from its positive nature). But instead, it is an ethic of not doing everything for the human (I will not). This posthuman embodied subject sees itself as a non-absolute, non-total form of subjectivity (I am not all). It prescribes action in non-action (I will not) that cares for the Other (so the other may be). Love in its non-orthodox paradigm, such as queer love, becomes a model to discuss this care ethic (101–14). This posthuman subject declares an anti-speciesism or an a-speciesism (abolition of the very notion of 'species') and believes in a grace that leaves the animals alone. MacCormack considers the posthumanist ethic as a vitalist critique of what she calls 'necrophilosophy' (115) or the line of poststructuralist thought that is prompt to declare the death of the human or the divine. She is in agreement with most critical posthumanists in seeing posthuman ethic as a resistance, not only to humanism, but also to anti- and transhumanism.

We will soon turn to caste as a political category that complicates the human body and its social regime of humanisation. But to round off this thread for the moment, let me say that the posthuman body is inter-subjective as well as inter-objective. Subjects and objects could create a collective corporeal chain. There is no binary or even strict differentiation between subjects and objects in this way of thinking. If embodiment is defined as an experiencing of the body, the posthumanist idea of embodiment is to map the human body as a tiny particle of a larger ecological corporeality. It is interesting that we often use the signifier 'body' in popular parlance to designate a corpse more than a living body. It exposes a binary of life and death that is integral to any humanist imagination. French philosopher Georges Bataille writes in *Erotism* (1957) that the corpse as an object of contagion is buried to put it at a safe distance from the living: 'If they have to bury the corpse it is less in order to keep it safe than to keep themselves safe from its contagion' (46). Though we know with the inception of scientific modernity that such a peril is at best a superstition, as Bataille argues, there is something intuitively intolerable about the idea of corporeal decay that puts off those who are alive. As a result, they want to steer clear of the corpse-object.

Contrary to this humanism of the contagious corpse, the posthuman body has to normalise the condition of the corpse and celebrate it as the body's extensible relation with ecology. We have already seen how Braidotti celebrates a unique, self-styled dying as an important posthuman deconstruction of the life–death binary. But here we are talking about the mere facticity of death. The body is posthuman in its capacity to die or to be extended and dismantled across the ecological space. It is death that marks this posthumanisation of the human body. As an example from Indian philosophy, we could consider the theory of *panchabhoota* ('five elements') that conceptualises the body in an environmental way as divided into the five basic elements (*bhoota*): earth/*prithvi*, air/*vayu*, water/*jal*, fire/*agni* and space/*akasha*. The so-called human body is nonhuman or ecological. In death, it returns to its constitutive nonhuman elements. There is no difference at this point between the human and nonhuman animals except that the latter is not always terrified of rotting flesh. That aside, coming to posthuman embodiment, we must get rid of the life–death opposition in the body. This opposition is cemented by biopolitics that wants to decouple death from life to be able to control both. In posthumanism, life and death are part of a continuous, unending becoming. We disrupt this becoming and tend to objectify the corpse as a thing in the humanist mode of thinking, enabled by a notion of biopolitical control. We can control the corpse by making it into a dead object. But the posthumanist thinking of the body will have to accept the future corpse, inhabited by each body that is alive. It is in death that the body becomes equated with its ecological elements, be it through burial or cremation. From there another becoming starts. We will have an opportunity to return to the dead body in the next section but I wanted to mention the *becoming-corpse* here as an ethical axiom of posthuman embodiment.

Beyond Disciplines: Toward a Dalit 'Minor Science' of Indian Posthumanism

In *Posthuman Knowledge* (2019), Rosi Braidotti approaches posthumanist epistemic and educational practices as a move beyond the student–teacher binary by drawing attention to nonhuman mediators like the animal or technological apparatus. The decentring of the human as the subject of humanities expands the horizons of the discipline as we go into a post-disciplinary idea of pedagogy with a subject who is always becoming-Other. Braidotti remains faithful to her Deleuzean roots in suggesting a nomadic subject of endless becoming. This subject is a heterogeneous assemblage of alterities, many of which are not human. She formulates an affirmative ethic of posthumanism to critique cognitive capitalism (neurocognitive paradigms serving the global capitalist market). Instead of just a shared notion of vulnerability, what we have here is an ethic of neo-materialist desiring subjects who take it upon themselves to realise their potential, standing up to structural and systemic violence and injustice. As she writes,

> Heterogeneity, complexity and multiplicities mark this process of becoming, which opens a myriad of possibilities of both resistance and counter-actualization of alternatives. It is this complexity and heterogeneity that constitute posthuman subjectivity, defined as the composition of posthuman subjects who want to know otherwise and produce knowledge differently. (Braidotti 331)

The ethic of the posthuman lies in displacing the *anthropos* and emphasising questions of *zoe* (all life), *geo* (cartography of knowledge production), and technological relations. The posthumanist ethic moves away from any pathological conception of endangered humanity that erases the human violence on other species and the planet. Her attempt is to construct a virtual community that is strung together by the ethical formula: 'we-are-in-this-together-but-we-are-not-one-and-the-same' (345). Braidotti calls this 'transversal subjectivity'. It acknowledges the commonality of the crisis (for example, anthropogenic climate change) as well as internal heterogeneity. This is her key idea of a collective posthuman subjectivity without making the human the leader of such a community. Rather than consolidating the science–humanities binary, she develops notions like major and minor sciences following Deleuze's ideas of majoritarian and minoritarian literatures, in which the latter resists the academic supremacy of the former. Her example of one such minor science is digital humanities. This minor science comes in the wake of the posthuman and rethinks transnational borders to generate a new community platform (349). This kind of platform helps in decolonising media.

The posthumanist ethic is a relational structure that works on linked networks of social injustice: gender, race, empire, ethnicity, caste, and so on. The ensuing politics of the posthuman consists of 'the communal process of composing transversal subjects committed to the actualization of the virtual' (351). This affirmative ethic of subjectivity does not deny negative affects but wants to actively work against them so that the narcissism and paranoia of negativity does not harm the relational ethic of difference and interdependence. Braidotti's ethical system wants to convert negative affects into positive ones. It is an ethic of action and praxis that works on affects in an embodied and embedded way.

If we follow this chain of implications, humanist and posthumanist practices are bound to evince a politics. For example, we could think of the Hindutva brand of politics that dominates the Indian subcontinent now. Among other things, this religious politics is centred on the cow as maternal goddess and human saviour. It utilises the sacred sentiment around the cow in Hinduism in a political way.[2] In the middle of the COVID-19 pandemic in 2020, Indian politicians belonging to the Hindutva fold were invoking the sacredness of the cow and claiming that cow urine will protect us from the virus.[3] This is an act of politicising religious belief regarding human–animal relations. The inter-species relation often has an element of human projection in it. Human beings project human or divine qualities on animals. Animal worship is an old practice in many religious cultures. But when an organised political party uses it, it takes a different turn. On 11 July 2016, in Una, Gujarat, seven members of a Dalit family were beaten up by a group of cow vigilantes for allegedly skinning cows. It is the caste-based division of labour that brings the work of removing dead cattle from the roadside upon Dalit subjects. This is what they were doing when the Hindutva fringe warriors followed them. The Dalits in question were flogged to avenge the way they 'hurt' Hindu sentiments. This is a political crime of caste atrocity that has an intense link with human–animal relations and its partisan politicisation. If we follow the causal links, Dalits are often de-humanised with metaphors of animals.[4] Dalit subjects live in close proximity with animals. As cleaners, they come in direct contact with the dead flesh of the animal and consequently, they are treated like dead meat. It is the discourse of Brahminical humanism that drives this violence on the Dalit community. We will come back to this point.

Dipesh Chakraborty has argued that the Dalit body of the manual scavenger is a planetary body, 'constructed non-anthropocentrically—it is always human with animals, live or dead, and embedded in the world of microbes (with its relationship to waste)' (15). This is a posthumanist conception of the body that entangles the Dalit corporeal subject. But as Chakraborty clarifies (not to lapse into a fetishisation of the Dalit body), this planetary corporeality is not exclusive to the Dalit subject. The Dalit predicament of manual scavenging only makes it apparent that human bodies in general (and especially in the context of the Anthropocene) are not as human as we think: 'we could look upon the Dalit's body as both an acknowledgment and a reminder of all the other living bodies we need in order to keep our human bodies alive' (15). The caste alterity of the becoming-Dalit in this case helps in thinking through the posthumanist, post-anthropocentric subjectivity of environmental entanglements.

Brahminism as an ideology joins hands with a hierarchical species-humanism that turns the cow into a divine figure. Eating beef is made into a big political issue. The right-wing politics of social control across India has staged a veritable onslaught against beef eating. In vegetarian states like Gujarat, one may still get chicken and buffalo, but beef is strictly prohibited. This imposition on food habits and dietary practices incarnates the biopolitics of Hindutva that shuns eating the animal worshipped by Hindus. Though the purview of this prohibitive practice far exceeds the Dalits (so-called 'upper-caste' subjects like myself are also put under the scanner), Dalits are the ones who often have to bear the brunt the most. The Hindutva drive toward vegetarianism may appear to be posthumanist as it bans humans from eating animals, but we can infer from the above discussion on plants that vegetarianism itself is not immune from the same logic of violence involved in eating another life-form like the plant. The Indian political thinker of caste, Babasaheb Ambedkar, shows, in his extensive research on Hindu eating habits (see the 1948 book *The Untouchables*, collected in Volume 7 of his complete works) across the centuries, that Hinduism had no real prohibition on killing or eating cows. It was more of a directive to minimise excessive cow killing (Ambedkar 7: 327). He uses the description of the Yajnas from the Buddhist Sutras to show that Hindus did kill cows and eat beef in the period following that of the Vedas and the Brahmanas (7: 328). He also deduces from Manu's verses that he didn't impose any prohibition on eating cows. Ambedkar reminds us that killing a cow is called nothing more than a 'minor sin' in Manu's works (7: 344).

In the text 'Who were the Shudras?' Ambedkar talks at length about Hindu cosmogonies (theories of origin) that include the origin-stories of animals and other nonhuman entities. His elaborate citations and deductions from the *Rigveda* (the hymn 'Purusha Sukta') and *Yajurveda* ('Vajasaneyi Samhita') highlight a complex humanism built into Vedic philosophy. To give one example, in Ambedkar's deduction, 'Purusha Sukta' states that the animals – aerial or otherwise, wild or tame (with two rows of teeth: horses, cows, goats and sheep) – were created from a universal sacrifice that the gods performed with Purusha, who enveloped the earth with their thousand heads, thousand eyes and thousand feet (7: 22). If Purusha is a manifestation of the earth, the animals are created by a nonhuman and creaturely avatar of cosmic ecology. This interpretation has a slant toward the posthuman, but we do see more than a trace of species hierarchy in the Hindu cosmogony. According to the 'Purusha Sukta', as Ambedkar discusses, the lowest of the four Hindu *varna*s, the shudras, are born from Purusha's feet while higher *varna*s like brahmins, kshatriyas and vaishyas are born from the upper parts of the cosmic body: mouth, arms and thighs, respectively. This is a hierarchical conceptualisation of the body which, in turn, cements caste hierarchy. The lowest caste of shudras are considered the transporters of other castes as they are created from the feet. The cosmogony supports a caste-based division of labour. But more relevant for us is the detail that horses and shudras come from the feet of Purusha and therefore, both are to be transporters (7: 39). The shudras, as the caste-Others, are dehumanised in this horse analogy that activates the human–animal hierarchy. The Hindu cosmogony is too polyvalent and incoherent for Ambedkar (7: 41) in his attempt to find a resolution to the problem of caste inequality. But as we can glean from his discussion, Hindu cosmogony espouses a complicated humanism, dangling between a species hierarchy of body, labour and caste on the one hand, and a posthumanism of ecological species origination on the other.

I would argue that in the Indian context, the political emancipatory project of posthumanism must be inflected with the Dalit discourse as Dalits are the real caste-Others in our society. They are veritably dehumanised by the caste system at both social and political levels. This is what justifies the need for a Dalit posthumanism for socio-political critique. Just as Braidotti appeals to race, gender and minor sexualities in the posthumanist expansion beyond the disciplinary formations of knowledge, I would appeal to anti-caste discourse and the Ambedkarite axiom of annihilation of caste as an important critical tool for posthumanism and post-humanities. The structure of inter-species hierarchy that constructs humanism finds its counterpart in the intra-species hierarchy of the caste system in India. Ambedkar, in his famous *Annihilation of Caste*, (1936) invokes the human–animal species distinction to drive home the inherent inequality of the caste system: 'Men are no doubt divided from animals by so deep a distinction that science recognizes men and animals as two distinct species. But even scientists who believe in purity of races do not assert that the different races constitute different species of men' (Ambedkar 1: 49).

While we may find a trace of species-humanism in Ambedkar's political rhetoric here, the passage makes it clear that the humanist idea of species hierarchy is a correlate of caste hierarchy. Ambedkar's point is that whereas there is a species difference between the human and the animal, there is no such difference between one race and another, between one caste and another. This is what makes the caste system a form of 'graded inequality' (1: 167) to quote the famous expression Ambedkar uses in 'Thoughts on Linguistic States'. It is an ethical imperative for the politics of posthumanism in the Indian context to adopt the anti-caste discourse and maintain its commitment to social justice.

Ambedkar dwells on the practice of manual scavenging that makes for an intimate co-existence between Dalit subjects and animals, especially when they are dead. Caste-Hindus will not touch the dead animal. It is for the Dalit body to inhabit a space shared by the animal carcass. He underlines the divisive affect of disgust, created between the *savarna* and Dalit subjects in this way: 'It is true that this occupation has created a feeling of repugnance against the Untouchables in the mind of the Hindus. [...] why do the Untouchables eat carrion? Will the Hindus allow the Untouchables the freedom to give up skinning and carrying their dead animals? (Ambedkar, 5: 256)

As Ambedkar goes on to reflect, Dalits are forced to skin, carry dead animals and eat carrion; it would be a legal offence if they did not. In a *savarna* way of thinking, the Dalit subject's labour identification with dead matter and animals makes them comparable to the nonhuman.[5] This is the inhumane nature of casteism. The labour of critical posthumanism is to expose this abusive and unjust power dynamic that equates Dalits with dead animals. As seen above, if we are able to celebrate death as a posthuman *becoming-corpse* of the body that returns it to its origins in ecological elements, it will help us de-stigmatise Dalit professions. The caste-based division of labour, as Ambedkar knew all along, intrinsically produces an exploitative division of labourers.

Dalit posthumanism, as a minor science, will allow us to talk about the practices of death, especially the site of the corpse as a posthuman entity. Be it the experience of the Chandal who helps cremate human corpses or the Dalit person who lives intimately with animals[6] and removes dead cattle as their caste-based occupation, Dalit subjectivity contains insight into the body beyond the human that caste-Hindu subjects do not. The point of a Dalit minor science is definitely not to celebrate this caste-based division of labour that becomes an oppressive experience, but to derive posthumanist lessons from the lived social experience of Dalit subjects. These lessons will talk back to caste oppression and social injustice.

Erin Edwards in *The Modernist Corpse* (2018) makes a connection between the posthuman and the posthumous, reading the dead body as a posthuman site to deconstruct the binary of life and death. She distances herself from the deterministic capitalist transhumanism of the body as technological prosthesis and constructs a posthumous posthumanism that rethinks death as part of the continuum of life. This thinking resembles Braidotti's posthuman philosophy of death, as discussed in the previous chapter. But Edwards focuses on the corpse as a phenomenon, wavering between the human subject and the nonhuman object. The corpse shifts from a politics of *bios* to a politics of *zoe* and yet it steers clear of a binary formation between the two (Edwards 18).

Dalit posthumanism as a minor science can connect Edwards's theorisation of the 'posthuman corpse' (33) with the social experience of the caste-based occupational practices of Indian Dalits who cremate human corpses and remove dead cattle. Ambedkar often draws our attention to the different Hindu funeral practices (see "Philosophy of Hinduism" 3: 65) and the role that the Dalit subject is expected to play there (see "Untouchables or the Children of India's Ghetto" 5: 96, 134). For him, the Dalit subjects are always-already socially dead: 'deadened, if not dead' (5: 134). As Ambedkar argues, Dalit revolt must include a mass refusal to handle dead cattle belonging to Hindus. During the 1930 Kalaram Temple entry movement in Nashik, Dalits took up this protest agenda when they refused to carry the dead animals of upper-caste Hindus. There is a social assumption that the corpse (especially animal corpse) is dirty and hence *savarna*s would delegate Dalits to do this 'dirty job' of scavenging, transferring the dirtiness of the corpse to the living Dalit body in the process. Though the human corpse, by the same logic of species-humanism, is not as dirty as the nonhuman, there is still something revolting about it (remember Bataille?). This disturbing labour is offloaded to lower castes like Chandals or Doms. As Ambedkar writes, these are not voluntary but coercive professions.

Dalits do not eat carrion because they like to; they are forced to do it (5: 256). It is for the posthumanist to analyse this three-fold socio-political othering of the Dalit subject, the dead human body and dead animals.

To illustrate the Dalit experiential nearness to dead bodies and the kind of posthuman insight it may generate beyond the dichotomy of life and death, let me mention a moment from the Bengali Dalit writer Manoranjan Byapari's autobiographical memoir, *Interrogating My Chandal Life* (2014). At one point, Byapari describes his work in the Kanker *shamshan* (crematorium) in Chhattisgarh. As he narrates, thanks to the demographic and a robust medical system, people didn't die often in Kanker and when a dead body came to Muktidham, the crematorium, all Byapari had to do was to meet the family, make the preparations, take them to the wood store and sell the wood for the cremation. But this description leads him to reflect that the *shamshan* is not just a place for the dead but also for the living, 'A place where people came to sit quietly in peace and tranquillity' (Byapari 332). Without making this subjective insight caste-exclusive, there is still a way of claiming that the Dalit subject's proximity to corpses and death makes them transcend the binary of life and death. Muktidham becomes a posthuman space in which life and death can and do co-exist in continuous becoming.

Though he doesn't go deep into the human–animal divide, Aniket Jaaware's *Practicing Caste* (2019) ends by touching on the ethical importance of what I would call the basic outline of a Dalit posthumanism: 'We seek an animality that kills only for food, not for abstractions. We seek an animality that lets be, one between "humans" and those creatures that humans call "animals," and again why stop there, perhaps we need vegetational life: slow' (200). This interstitial human–animal self must become the subject of a caste-inflected emancipatory posthumanism.

To reiterate, the posthuman subject must be an anti-caste subject, engaged with the social struggle of emancipating itself and others from caste injustice. It has to become-Other in the context of caste by embracing the Dalit struggle. In a Braidottian way, the posthuman subject would be 'transversal'. They would acknowledge the inequality of social lived experience, take responsibility for the 'graded inequality' of the caste system, and consider themselves to be together with the Other in the crisis.

To situate Dalit posthumanism as a minor science, let us look at another moment, this time from the Dalit writer Baburao Bagul's short story 'Revolt' from *When I Hid My Caste* (2018). Prabhu, a Dalit belonging to the Bhangi caste, finally gets to know on his deathbed that his son Jai has been offered the caste-job of a sweeper, after a wait of two long years since applying for a job. Jai is getting good education and doesn't want to give it up to go back to the inherited caste-job, but his father disagrees. In this battle of generations, the father wants the son to take up the job that comes easier to his caste-identity as a Bhangi. But, the son wants to abolish the rigidity of caste labour if not caste itself. In this duel, we read the following:

> "Where is it written that a Bhangi's son must become a Bhangi?"
>
> "In our poverty. In our dharma. In our country."
>
> "What dharma? If it breaks a person and turns him into an animal, is that dharma? In this country that invests greater significance in a stone than in a human being? I will not heed such a dharma. If it has given us only this poverty, this deprivation, then it behoves us to reject it." (Bagul 76)

The animal trope is notable in the passage above. Caste discrimination is considered a brutal practice of dehumanisation where a human being is reduced to an animal. The animistic belief would give more value to a sacred stone than a human being if they are the Other in the caste system. In Jai's liberating articulation against his father, there is a strong link developed between casteism and species-humanism, that inferiorises the animal and the thing as compared to the human subject. It is this species-humanism that the anti-caste discourse of posthumanism must oppose. The posthuman egalitarian subject must be casteless. It is interesting how the signifier 'animal' comes back in the climax of this story when Jai, in the middle of doing his caste-job of a Bhangi sweeper, kills a carter in extreme anger. As he starts hitting the man, he calls him 'animal' (82). The ironic return of this word marks the presence of the same species-humanism in the Dalit subject who must act like a cog in the Brahminical machine. The ideological slippage suggests how the Dalit cause can also get infected by the Brahminical hierarchy of the human and the animal. Jai resorts to a violence that is marked animal-like in humanist language by the same signifier ('animal') that accompanies his action.

I would posit the anti-caste discourse of Babasaheb Ambedkar as a crucial Indian instance of what Braidotti calls minor science – a transdisciplinary concentration that holds onto the post-disciplinary political ethic of posthumanism. As she maintains, cognitive capitalism doesn't want to privilege the minor sciences as much as they celebrate the major sciences, but we need to advance political post-humanities along the lines of these minoritarian subjects. In the Indian context, if posthumanism is committed to its emancipatory project, it must forward Dalit studies as a minor science that exposes the species-humanism complicit in producing caste hierarchy. The human–animal relation in Dalit dehumanisation; Dalit practices of eating; the proximity with death in the Dalit life world – these and other lines of inquiry ought to become critical threads in Dalit posthumanism as a science of the oppressed.

ETHICS AND POLITICS WITH ANIMALS AND THINGS

Let us continue with our larger discussion on the ethico-political strands of posthumanism. As I mentioned in the beginning of this chapter, apart from looking at the political and ethical implications of posthumanism, we need to rethink political theory from a posthumanist perspective. Magdalena Zolkos in an article on the posthuman turn in political theory concludes,

> The post-human turn in political theory does not simply incorporate animals, plants, objects, and so on within an expanded and more inclusive domain of political community [...] it does not simply assign the nonhumans a place within a polity, thereby rendering them proper to politics. Instead, [...] it critically interrogates the epistemic and political effects of "the unassignable place," which, more than a history of non-admission of animality to human polity, points at the constitutive operations of this "foundational exclusion." (Zolkos 11)

The post-humanisation of political theory is not only about including the nonhuman within the discussion of polity but also about studying why the nonhuman was left out of this conception of politics in the first place. The posthumanist take on politics challenges the very humanist codification of politics and, by extension, ethics. Claire Colebrook, an important posthumanist thinker, wants to expand ethics beyond the human in a way similar to Zolkos: 'The figure of the globe appears to offer [...] an attention to global interconnections and networks would expand responsibility and awareness beyond the figure of the isolated moral subject. Ethics may have to be considered beyond discursive, human and political modes (especially if one defines politics as the practice of a polity)' (Colebrook 60). Here we see an iteration of cosmopolitics or a politics of the planetary that ensures a movement of the ethical that exceeds the human. But, how do we include the nonhuman in ethics and politics? Is it practically possible?

In *What Animals Teach Us About Politics* (2014), affect theorist Brian Massumi takes up the project of constructing an 'integrally animal politics' that is not synonymous with a 'human politics of the animal' (Massumi 2). For him, there is no difference between the frivolous and the serious in the animal world and, as a result, he dwells on the domain of animal play to theorise an animal politics of performative gestures that is non-normative in nature. By play, Massumi refers to any act of expressive and affective gaming among animals, such as fights among puppies; cats hitting each other; mutual taunts of chicks; dogs biting one another, and so on. According to him, the domain of play is the site of difference: '[a] wolf cub who bites its litter mate in play "says," in the manner in which it bites, "this is not a bite."' (4). The play-fight paradoxically declares that it is not a fight. This negation is a mark of difference in the play. To continue with the same example, this play exposes the difference between biting and nipping. If it is not violent combat but play, the wolf cubs will nip in the name of biting. Taking his departure from Bruno Latour's idea of 'parliament of things', Massumi develops an embodied, relational, affective/expressive animal politics of action that backgrounds the state of existence and foregrounds the event of play (40). The ludic politics of animals that he maintains returns to the question of language as the orthodox differentiator between humans and animals. In this imagination of animal politics, 'the instinctive acts of animals' are supposed to 'include language in potential, in their ludic element' (45). This politics makes language into play, overshadowing the former with the latter. It offers an instinct-driven idea of animal language.

Massumi's animal politics is a politics of mutual inclusion of the human and the animal, but it does not disregard the generic differences that exist between the two. Contra anthropomorphism, he claims that this theorisation is 'animo-centric' because it ethically prescribes the human to become animal and not the other way round (52). This politics is not afraid of instinct – a perennially embarrassing notion in humanist–rationalist circles that downplays animal instinct with human reason: 'The self-driving movement of instinct, under the propulsion of the supernormal tendency, is what operationally includes the human in the animal. To think the human is to think the animal, and to think the animal is to think instinct' (54).

In this inclusive pro-instinct view of politics, vital instinct in animals is posited as sympathy which generates an ethic of relation that, in turn, opens up the political. For example, we could think of the sympathy that drives the instinct of pecking among herring gull chicks (when the adult gull places its head close to the chick in a vertical position and moves its bill, the chick pecks at the bill). Human politics of statecraft, characterised by sovereignty, is a politics of 'anti-becoming' (69) in Massumi's words. As opposed to that, he sees his own animal politics as a politics of becoming. For instance, when the child plays with an animal, say a tiger, the mutual inclusion makes a becoming-animal of the child. The task of animal politics is to make this possible for adults as well. This is a politics of all life – a *zoe*-politics rather than a *bio*politics. It provides a way of imagining a non-anthropocentric politics of life beyond the human.

Bruno Latour, who gets more than a mention in Massumi's book, is an important thinker of the nonhuman 'actor-networks' in politics. In *Reassembling the Social* (2005), an introductory book on Actor Network Theory (ANT hereafter), Latour defines politics as 'the progressive composition of the common world' (254). His idea of politics takes its bearings from nature. While the 'political composition of nature' does not exclude the nonhuman, the formation of society does: 'nature assembles non-humans apart from the humans; society collects humans apart from the non-humans' (164). Latour de-hyphenates the socio-political across the human–nonhuman divide. For him, the political as a formation of the collective in nature is a larger domain than the social which is only one iteration of the collective. We have to uncouple the two. As Latour observes, 'if there is a society, *then no politics is possible*' (250). The social as a predominantly human assemblage exists so that there could be no politics to change society. A political actor in the network of nature does not have to be human. Politics goes beyond the human because it is not coterminous with the social but synonymous with a collective of nature. In this way politics comes closer to ecology than anything else. In Latour, politics has 'to trace again and again the paradoxical shape of the body politic in *a political way*' (239; emphases original).

It is needless to say that this body politic is not exclusively human. There are connectors in this network system that are often nonhuman entities. Latour's proposal is to replace '"the politics of nature" by the progressive composition of one common world' and 'to carry out the task of political epistemology forced upon us by the various ecological crises' (254). As the presence of the social makes the politics of nature impossible, it becomes a task for politics to construct a common world or a shared ecology for the human and nonhuman. Both society and nature are premature collectors for Latour and without hyphenating the social and the political, the ethical task of 'political epistemology' is to bring together the assemblages of nature and those of the social. If there is a posthuman subjectivity here, it is a relational, ecological and collective idea of the subject as an actor-network of multiple human and nonhuman elements.

Instead of a two-house collective of nature and society, in *Politics of Nature* (2004), Latour presents a single collective for the political ecology of the nonhuman and the human. In this ecological space, there is a distinction between the human and the subject insofar as the nonhuman is an acting subject in this network. The human and the nonhuman can 'exchange properties' (Latour 2004, 61). For Latour, this is a new way of thinking democracy that includes the nonhuman (223). As he clarifies, this does not mean that we give voting rights to the nonhuman. The question of voting lapses back into a 'metaphysics of nature' whereas it is this very metaphysics that is negated when the two-house collective is unified (60).

In order to incorporate the voice of the nonhuman into this new democracy, Latour postulates the construction of political ecology at a point *before* the distribution of speech across life worlds. We must remember that the speaking–mute binary is artificially framed into the politics of democracy by none other than human players. Life worlds are not necessarily divided into human speech and nonhuman silence. This division is something that the human being has created, and this very creation is an act of speciesism. It is humans who erect a wall of false differentiation between the human and nonhuman in the name of speech. We have to acknowledge that there could be nonhuman beings who may not have what human beings define as speech, but they have their own language and communication system. Latour reflects, 'I have only called attention to a phenomenon that precedes the distribution of forms of speech, which is called a Constitution' (68). This idea of constitution that recovers a time before human beings unequally distributed speech among life worlds, is the backbone of his new democracy. ANT provides a thesis of human–nonhuman entanglement for politics to truly compose a common world. In this regard the political is posthumanist in its very construction. To put it differently, politics is foundationally posthumanist. Humans exclude nonhumans and form the social. The ethical task of posthumanist political theory in Latour's imagination is to recover the foundation of politics in the pre-social intrication of the human and the nonhuman.

What about objects? How do we include them in politics and ethics? In Graham Harman's critique of ANT from the end of Object-Oriented-Ontology (OOO), the former reduces an object to what it does (actor) rather than what it is (Harman 2018, 109). This is contrary to OOO's position on the object. For them, the object is the difference between its constitutive components (downward) and its connections with other objects (upward). According to Harman's example, if Pasteur is an 'actor', ANT can only see him and his work in the actual historical sequence in which it unfolded, leaving no room for counterfactual interpretation. On the other hand, OOO allows us to imagine Pasteur in 'any number of situations other than the ones that actually occurred' (110). Be it *Immaterialism* (2016) or *Object-Oriented Ontology* (2018), Harman engages in a socio-political analysis of historical events using OOO as a heuristic tool. Of course, for him and OOO, a historical sequence of events is as much an object as any inanimate thing is. In *Immaterialism*, his example is the Dutch East India Company and in *Object-Oriented Ontology*, he zooms in on the American Civil War of 1861 to 1865. In both analyses, Harman charts the difference between the events that constituted the working of the colonial company or the war and the effects they had beyond their constituent contexts, forces or events. The interesting part of this analysis is the element Harman calls 'symbiosis' where one object changes another in a larger historical sequence to produce a new object (Harman 2018, 111). The political dimension of Harman's historical engagement lies in the question of change. This is a qualitative change and not a change in degrees. For him, it marks the crucial difference between ANT and OOO. In ANT, the difference between Napoleon losing a scalp hair and winning the battle of Jena is only quantitative or a change in degrees. Symbiosis is not this kind of change. It is a change in substance that generates a new object (134). I am not going into the details of Harman's study of these historical events, but his commitment to change is a significant part of posthumanist politics. It shows an attempt to read a historical sequence not by its human actors but its spaces, places and contexts that go well beyond the human – military tools, forts, company ships, truces, and so on.

For Harman, the politics of OOO is all about pushing the ANT envelope. As he concludes, unlike ANT, OOO can accommodate asymmetrical and non-reciprocal relations among objects in a networked sequence of objects/events. It offers a posthumanist way of interpreting socio-political and historical events in their complex set of relations that transcend human actors. These are events or objects that are not mastered by the human actor. The complex nonhuman assemblage of these evental sequences far outperforms the human. For an Indian contextualisation, let me invoke the solidarity movement against the alleged displacement of local tribal communities for the construction of the Rs 2700 crore Statue of Unity (a statue of Saradar Vallabhbhai Patel as a great nationalist and patriotic icon of the Indian Independence movement) in Kevadiya, Gujarat. On the day of the statue's inauguration in 2018, many protesting Adivasis and local activists were arrested by the police. The chain of protests and arrests continued well into 2019. To study this movement, we must carefully consider the nonhuman network of relations involved – the ecology of the Narmada River; the financial economy of the statue as a fetish object; the local economies of the tribal community and the alleged evacuation of the communities from the area. Some of the questions that drive this movement are:

1. Were the local people forcibly removed from their land for statue tourism?
2. Was the newly made Sardar Sarovar Dam depleting the water resources of the local villages?
3. Were numerous trees felled for the statue project, leading to deforestation?
4. Were the locals actually getting the employment that the government had supposedly promised them from the new statue tourism opportunities?

As we can see, these are not questions about human agents alone. The human is inextricably linked with the nonhuman aspects of ecology and economy. These structural and systemic dimensions become more complex in its human–nonhuman balance once we bring in the political symbolism of the statue as an instrument of the ruling dispensation's Hindu nationalism, Gujarati exceptionalism (Patel's Gujarati identity is important), and so on.

To return to OOO, following Latour's aforementioned idea of a politics of nature, Harman calls for politics as 'coalitions lined up around the boundaries of an issue whose exact nature can never be determined' (Harman 2018, 142). This open and indeterminate idea of the political offers an 'object-oriented politics', a term Latour himself has used. For Harman, this is a politics of truth as dynamic process that emerges from the linings and formation of political publics around a demanded issue or problem. It is not a politics of power or reified knowledge; it is a politics of fluid truths. This object-oriented politics goes against the power struggle of knowledge. It 'rejects all claims to political knowledge' (146). For Harman, Latour's idea of actor-network is mistaken in considering size as strength – the bigger a network of allies is, the stronger it gets. He critiques this point by introducing the term 'political chain' of objects, in a more moderate and minimal form (144). As Harman illustrates: 'adding a fifth guest to dinner often creates the famous "fifth wheel" social problem' (144). The same object can also be engaged in multiple chains but in OOO, unlike ANT, the relations among multiple chains may not be reciprocal.

Differences aside, both ANT and OOO in their different pathways help us conceptualise politics as a more-than-human system of relations and non-relations among human and nonhuman actors and objects. We also realise how we can think of a collective posthuman thread of ecologically entangled, inter-subjective and inter-objective subjectivity.

Posthuman Politics of Embodied Subjectivity: Literary Samples from South Asia

To ground the politics of the posthuman in practices of reading, I will go through a few South Asian literary examples in this section. As we shall see, the South Asian context imports certain ethico-political inflections into posthumanism. Let us look at a short story in which discourses of human speciesism and the companion species of the dog[7] are played out in a specific political context. This story, 'The Dog of Tetwal', is penned by the famous chronicler of the Indian partition, Saadat Hasan Manto. The original text is in Urdu and I will be relying on the 2007 English translation. In the middle of cross-border firings, a dog befriends both the Indian and the Pakistani camps of soldiers when they start feeding it. The dog's only language of response is wagging its tail and it performs this gesture for both camps. The Indian soldiers name it 'Chapad

Jhunjhun' and tie a name tag around its neck, claiming it as a 'Hindustani dog' (Manto 84). When the dog crosses the line, the Pakistani soldiers spot the tag and rename it 'Sapar Sunsun'. They write a fresh name tag that describes it as a 'Pakistani dog' (85). They command it to return to the Indian side and show its new identity to them. When it is about to reach the Indian camp, the Indian soldiers notice that it is coming from the enemy territory, and start firing. When the dog turns around, the Pakistani soldiers fire to instigate it into going back. In this series of firings, the dog eventually dies from an Indian soldier's bullet. As the Pakistani soldiers mourn its death, calling the dog a 'martyr', the Indian soldiers are quick to add, 'He died a dog's death' (87).

Is a dog's death significant? As the speciesist idiom goes, dying like a dog is the most undignified way to death. Manto's story presents a politically contextualised critique of species-humanism that derogates the companion species. It is the desire to master and colonise the dog that leads to its sad demise. The political dimension is strengthened by the debate over the dog's nationality. The partition affects the nonhuman when the humans project their vile political names and identity categories on them. The naming of the dog suggests a colonialist strategy of control. It is also marked by a streak of anthropocentrism. At the end of the story, the dog is caught between two politically-coloured categories of a martyr and a nobody. The animality of the animal disappears under the guise of these two human signifiers. It vanishes between the two names, 'Chapad Jhunjhun' and 'Sapar Sunsun' – between a sacrifice and a nonentity. The dog is neither a martyr nor a nobody but a scapegoat (let's mark the 'goat' in the appellation 'scapegoat') caught up in a human war of identifications. The divisive logic of political nationality overshadows the dog's own self and becomes the cause of its undoing.

As one Indian soldier comments, 'Now, even dogs will have to be either Hindustani or Pakistani!' (83). The only animal-like gesture the dog uses is wagging its tail to accept food from both camps, but this language is not satisfactory for the binary human register of either-or. The animality of the animal has no identification, as Harman Singh, an Indian soldier says, 'This is no identification [...] All dogs wag their tails' (82). It is this lack of differential language that costs the dog its life. It wags its tail to both sides. It is both Hindustani and Pakistani because it is neither Hindustani nor Pakistani. The Manto story underlines the violence of species-humanism, the discordant communication or non-communication between the human and the nonhuman, and a sinister order where human categories of politics (and political identity) are imposed on the nonhuman.

In the charged political contexts of South Asian literature, posthumanism can become an effective heuristic device to unravel themes of the nonhuman that have a strong ethico-political implication. In Salman Rushdie's 1983 novel, *Shame*, on the artificial partition of India and Pakistan, we have the magical realist depiction of a character like Sufia Zinobia Shakil who holds within her body, a beastly Other that represents all that is wrong with the politics of partition. Set in Peccavistan (a play on the name 'Pakistan'), the novel tells the story of Sufiya Zinobia, daughter of General Raza and Bilquis. She is nicknamed 'shame' because her parents wanted a boy. As with the widening cracks on Saleem Sinai's body in *Midnight's Children* (1981), Rushdie uses Sufiya's corporeality as a site to project the traumatic wounds of partition. But in *Shame*, the portrayal of human embodiment is invested with an additional animality and a monster motif. Neil Badmington has drawn attention to the alien as a posthumanist figure in cinema. As he argues, though we claim to be welcoming aliens, we end up accepting them only as Others: 'They are desired only ever *as aliens*' (Badmington 151; emphases original). Likewise, within Sufia Zinobia rests an alien animality that takes to monstrous violence at the dead of night. The narrator Others the monster, hidden inside the human: 'On two occasions she fell grievously ill and almost died; and perhaps both illnesses, brain-fever and immunological collapse, were attempts by her ordinary self, by the Sufiya-Zinobia-ness of her, to defeat the Beast, even at the cost of her own life. But the Beast was not destroyed' (Rushdie 208).

The bloodthirsty creature that lurks within the partitioned female subject glimpses a posthuman horizon. Sufia's animality, driving her midnight acts of rape and crime, embody shame as the affective reality of partition. The creature is seen as a liminal figure, prohibited from the social mainstream of a humanist world: 'there is no place for monsters in civilized society. If such creatures roam the earth, they do so out on its uttermost rim, consigned to peripheries by conventions of disbelief...but once in a blue moon something goes wrong. A Beast is born, a 'wrong miracle', within the citadels of propriety and decorum' (210).

Civilisation is the domain of humanism. Monsters are forbidden to enter the gated communities of the civilised and yet it is in the ruses of this 'wrong miracle' (her father wanted a son) that the reality of the vivisected world persists. The 'barbarism' that grows within the 'cultured soil' (210) deconstructs the colonialist binary of the civilised and the savage. The narrator makes Sufia into an enigma by calling the beast an element of the 'unknown' and comparing her with a crystal that shatters if one tries to comprehend it (210).

Sufiya is married to the much older Omar whom she eventually beheads like most of her other headless murders. The beheading signifies castration. Sufiya's bottled up sexual urge overpowers her with its animal instinct and makes her a monster. This is a satirical comment on religious repression in society. The choice of a monster or a white panther to locate the problem of sexual violence and murder shows a tacit humanist species hierarchy operating through the novel:

> Sufia's corporeality is likened to an animal embodiment of violence and shame:
>
> the violence which had been born of shame, but which by now lived its own life beneath her skin; it fought the narcoleptic fluids, it took its time, spreading slowly through her body until it had occupied every cell, until she had become the violence, which no longer needed anything to set it off, because once a carnivore has tasted blood you can't fool it with vegetables any more. (257)

With yellow fire and veiled eyes, she is an incarnation of *Jahannam* (hell), a feminist monster of nemesis; a mythological white panther, killing men, dismembering their heads and eating their flesh. As in a fairy tale, Sufia is beauty combined with the beast. There is a debate whether Sufia's transformation is intentional. Had she chosen or created the beast? Her animalisation is situated as the dangerous freedom of an imagination that runs wild after being unshackled. The monster marks the paradox of liberty. The beast could mesmerise its victims and as a result, there is no trace of struggle on their bodies. The narrator writes: 'A cartoonist drew a picture of a giant cobra mesmerizing heavily-armed, but powerless, mongoose hordes' (276). Her killing spree plays a key role in creating a law-and-order problem and thus, in taking down her father's government. Let us note how the notion of female madness is conjoined with the animal motif. At one point, she is kept in the attic like a madwoman, in an anesthetised state by her husband Omar. Sufiya is characterised as psychotic and a grown woman with the maturity of a nine-year-old. She is a bizarre child, pulling out her hair and screaming for no reason. While growing up, she develops the odd habit of shifting the furniture around when nobody is watching. She fiddles around with material objects in a way that resembles how she fiddles around with male bodies later. The urge to change things remains constant in these acts. The narrator says that Sufiya is born from the corpse of a Pakistani, killed by her father in London for making love to a white boy. This postcolonial hybridity in her origin story adds to her teratological oddity. According to the narrator, Sufiya is a conglomerate of many ghosts, the last being a self-immolating boy. She is a messiah born to right the wrongs of the world. Sufiya is a freak of nature since her brain fever; she is able to absorb feelings that human beings struggle to internalise: 'preternaturally receptive to all sorts of things that float around in the ether enabled her to absorb, like a sponge, a host of unfelt feelings' (124). This intense affective dimension, as we have seen above, works well with a posthuman imagination. Sufiya is a post-gender cyborg body that surpasses the dualism of male and female.

After her nocturnal exploits resulting in a turkey massacre, Sufiya's body is covered by 'huge blotchy rashes, red and purple with small hard pimples in the middle; boils were forming between her toes and her back was bubbling up into extraordinary vermilion lumps' (145). Let me emphasise the posthuman nature of embodiment in the passage above. Be it her over-salivation or the bodily deformations, Sufiya's corporeality is in excess of the human. When she is taken to an immunologist in the hospital, it is diagnosed that her body's defence mechanisms have declared 'war' on her corporeal system (147). It is in this way that Sufiya's breaking body becomes symbolic of the broken polity of the nation-state. The doctor sees a tendency of self-damage in her. He calls her breakdown of immunity, the 'most terrible uprising' (148) he has ever seen, reinforcing the political analogy with revolutionary change.

After her marriage to Omar, when the beast reawakens in her after a hiatus, the trigger is corporeal. She loses sleep and that marks the rekindling of nocturnal animality. Omar tries to confine her but she gets away and transforms into a white panther, leading to Omar's beheading. Sufiya represents a posthumanist subjectivity of political resistance, standing for sexual liberation, freedom of desire, a rebellious non-binary, queer body, and a radical agent of social change contributing to the fall of Raza Hyder's Islamic government. Though the tropes of the monster, the animal, and the madwoman remain as traces of humanist Othering, Sufiya becomes posthuman by embracing these alterities and casting off her human body at the end. She is a great example of the posthumanist subject as a radical political agent.

To continue with the political implications of posthumanist subjectivity and maintain our critical focus on embodiment, Indra Sinha's 2007 novel, *Animal's People* will be our next sample. Rob Nixon has called this novel, an 'environmental picaresque' (51) that engages with ecological violence. I will use a posthumanist lens that deconstructs the human–animal binary to read the novel, but we will not address the environmental theme that Nixon has already analysed at some length. Set in the imaginary city of Khaufpur, meaning 'the land of horror', the novel traces the first-person story of a 19-year-old orphan boy, born just a few days before the 1984 toxic gas leak in Bhopal that killed thousands of mostly poor people who lived in small towns and villages around the plant. The narrator is named 'animal' due to a twisted spine that makes him walk on all fours. Though the novel is not actually set in Bhopal, Sinha himself has talked in detail about how closely he modelled Khaufpur on Bhopal in a 2007 piece in *The Guardian*. The novel has a technologically filtered form that can itself lay claim to the posthuman. The chapters, called 'tapes', are translations of Animal's

Hindi tape recordings. The journalist working on his story records his narration on tape and translates them. This technological mediation draws attention to the nonhuman dynamic.

Animal's People shows the dehumanising register of the animal metaphor in an explicitly political context. It is the aftermath of the leakage of toxic gas that leads to the animality of the narrator. He gets routinely jeered at and name-called by society at large for walking like an animal. Animality is addressed at the level of physiology as the body image of the human tilts toward an animal corporeality. The narrator accepts this animality and this is where Sinha's treatment of the animal motif could be called posthumanist. As the opening words of Tape One clarify, the human self is a blurred memory for the narrator: 'I used to be human once. So I'm told. I don't remember it myself, but people who knew me when I was small say I walked on two feet just like a human being' (Sinha 9). Animal tells Ma Franci, the French nun and his quasi-mother at the orphanage: 'I no longer want to be human' (10). He affirms a whole new world of seeing things below the waist as he gets closer to the ground. He may initially feel jealous about the humans who can stand on their feet, but as he grows, he starts hating the social world that hates him in their turn. For Animal, words like 'rights, law, justice' are shifty as they keep changing their meanings: 'such words are like shadows the moon makes in the [gas] Kampani's factory, always changing shape' (11). The novel takes up this question of social justice in the wake of the gas tragedy by looking into the life of a physically affected orphan boy's social marginalisation.

On the night of the gas leak, the newborn is found wrapped in a shawl, lying in a doorway. His parents have died of the poison unleashed that night. Animal is indifferent to his religious identity: 'I'm not a Muslim, I'm not a Hindu, I'm not an Isayi, I'm an animal, I'd be lying if I said religion meant a damn thing to me. Where was god the cunt when we needed him?' (22–23). At six, the pains start as his spine begins to twist, limiting his movement to a veritable crawl. When he bites a boy in the leg while playing kabaddi in the orphanage, they start calling him 'Jaanvar, jungli jaanvar [wild animal]' (24). Everyone starts calling him that, laughs at his inability to sit properly, and speculatively compares his sexual activities with the canine species on the street. Animal meets a female stray dog,

Jara, who becomes his close friend. The two start off as rivals for food on the street but the animal continuum soon flowers into what can be called a posthuman companionship and cohabitation. The human, having lost his privilege, is at one with the dog. Together they create an inter-species assemblage. They beg together. Jara often plays dead when Animal whines about their starvation. Hunger and sexuality become basic instinctual markers for the theme of animality as Animal is sucked into these corporeal drives. He does not differentiate between the love he gets from the two women, Jara and Ma Franci, because he is able to think beyond the species hierarchy. Animal often resembles the dog in his gestures as they become a unit: 'I roll over like a big dog, like Jara does to have her belly tickled' (93).

Protests erupt at the gas factory and the ominous American 'kampani' is dragged to court for the industrial disaster. Animal's activist friend Zafar plays a crucial role, conducting hunger strikes. After many violent protests, the factory is set ablaze and the chief minister is forced to cancel his deal with the authorities. In the end Animal gets an offer from his doctor friend Elli to go to America and straighten his spine through surgery, but he decides not to normalise or humanise himself. Animal sticks to his animalist resilience and shuts down the human. Like the nonhuman machine that he talks to, he has a range of voices in his head – a psychic tape with sonic entities, as it were. When he decides not to sign the paper for his operation in America, this ending is inflected by the tape-recorded story: 'It's then I've remembered the tape mashin in the wall. I will tell this story, I thought, and that way I'll find out what the end should be' (405). It is the nonhuman tape and its machinic mode of storytelling that influences his decision to remain nonhuman. Animal finds narrative and affective company in the nonhuman.

The rejection of human identity is a significant posthuman streak in the novel as animality and machinic tropes of technology come together. He chooses his twisted, crawling life of freedom over the life of a cripple on a wheelchair or someone walking with the help of a stick. In his animality lies his unique individuality: 'If I'm an upright human, I would be one of millions, not even a healthy one at that. Stay four-foot, I'm the one and only Animal' (405). His final rhymed couplet is an ode to this animalist singularity: 'I am Animal fierce and free/in all the world is none like me' (406). Animal's posthumanism is an ethico-political choice in the final words of the book that preserve the collective conviction of resistance: 'All things pass, but the poor remain. We are the people of the Apokalis. Tomorrow there will be more of us' (406). Sinha's novel thus shows how posthumanism, both contextually and textually, can become a committed political tool to treat a specific historical situation.

To conclude, this chapter established that posthumanism is neither asocial nor apolitical. We charted the move from the *bios*-driven politics of the human to a *zoe*-driven politics of all life-forms – animals, plants and objects – by going through different varieties of posthumanist thought, from ANT to OOO, and literary and social sites of posthumanist philosophy in practice. The chapter expanded the scope of post-humanities as a movement beyond single disciplines and sought to inflect posthumanism with the anti-caste discourse of Dalit studies. The Dalit minor science of posthumanism gave a geopolitical Indian slant to the larger question of posthumanist ethics and politics.

Zooming in on the socio-political under- and overtones of posthumanism made us realise how this tradition thinks through the political subject as a more-than-human species assemblage. The political subject of posthumanism cannot be solely human. It has the ethical commitment to continue becoming-Other in all its incarnations: becoming-plant, becoming-animal, becoming-corpse, becoming-casteless, becoming-nonbinary, becoming-woman, becoming-object, et cetera. Posthumanist thought redefines politics as a platform to practise species egalitarianism. It acknowledges the efficacy of material objects in socio-political processes, as a trans/multi/post-disciplinary formation. From here, I will move to the literary and cultural manifestations of the machine, the animal and the planetary object as three pivotal posthumanist sites of investigation.

NOTES

1. For an interesting dialogue between Irigaray and Marder on vegetal ontology, see the book *Through Vegetal Being* (2016).

2. For more on this, see Susan Harris' article 'The Posthumanist Cow'.
3. https://www.news18.com/news/buzz/bengal-bjp-chief-dilip-ghosh-wants-you-to-drink-cow-urine-to-fight-coronavirus-2722267.html
4. For instance, see Wendy Doniger's chapter 'Dogs as Dalits in Indian Literature' in her book *On Hinduism* (2015).
5. For a literary analysis of the animal trope in Dalit narratives, see Aniruddha Mukhopadhyay's 2021 article 'From Worse than Dogs to Heroic Tigers: Situating the Animal in Dalit Autobiographies'.
6. We can consider Nagraj Manjule's 2014 Marathi film *Fandry* (meaning pig) that tellingly shows this human–animal proximity for a Dalit family. Jabya, the Dalit boy is name-called as 'fandry' which equates the human with the pig.
7. For more on Haraway's ideas of the companion species, see the next chapter.

REFERENCES

Ambedkar, Babasaheb. *Writings and Speeches: Volume 1*. Compiled by Vasant Moon, Dr. Ambedkar Foundation, 2014, https://www.mea.gov.in/Images/attach/amb/Volume_01.pdf. Accessed 13 November 2021.

---. *Writings and Speeches: Volume 3*. Compiled by Vasant Moon, Dr. Ambedkar Foundation, 2014, https://www.mea.gov.in/Images/CPV/Volume3.pdf. Accessed 1 May 2022.

---. *Writings and Speeches: Volume 5*. Compiled by Vasant Moon, Dr. Ambedkar Foundation, 2014, https://www.mea.gov.in/Images/attach/amb/Volume_05.pdf. Accessed 13 November 2021.

---. *Writings and Speeches: Volume 7*. Compiled by Vasant Moon, Dr. Ambedkar Foundation, 2014, https://www.mea.gov.in/Images/CPV/Volume7.pdf. 1 May 2022.

Anonymous. "Bengal BJP Chief Dilip Ghosh Says Drink Cow Urine to Fight Coronavirus" *News 18*, July 18, 2020, https://www.news18.com/news/buzz/bengal-bjp-chief-dilip-ghosh-wants-you-to-drink-cow-urine-to-fight-coronavirus-2722267.html. Accessed 13 November 2021.

Bataille, Georges. *Erotism: Death and Sensuality*. Translated by Mary Dalwood, Walker and Company, 1962.

Bagul, Baburao. *When I Hid My Caste*. Translated by Jerry Pinto, E-book, Speaking Tiger, 2018.

Braidotti, Rosi. *Posthuman Knowledge*. E-book, Polity Press, 2019.

Byapari, Manoranjan. *Interrogating My Chandal Life: An Autobiography of a Dalit*. Translated by Sipra Mukherjee, Sage, 2018.

Chakraborty, Dipesh. "The Dalit Body: A Reading for the Anthropocene". *The Empire of Disgust: Prejudice, Discrimination, and Policy in India and the U.S.*, edited by Zoya Hasan, et al., Oxford UP, 2018, pp 1–20.

Colebrook, Claire. *Death of the PostHuman: Essays on Extinction, Vol. 1*. Open Humanities Press, 2014.

Cudworth, Erika, and Stephen Hobden. *The Emancipatory Project of Posthumanism*. Routledge, 2018.

Dabashi, Hamid. *Corpus Anarchicum: Political Protest, Suicidal Violence and the Making of the Posthuman Body*. Palgrave Macmillan, 2012.

Doniger, Wendy. *On Hinduism*. Oxford UP, 2015.

Edwards, Erin E. *The Modernist Corpse: Posthumanism and the Posthumous*. U of Minnesota P, 2018.

Hanafin, Patrick. "A Micropolitics of Posthuman Rights". *Posthuman Glossary*, edited by Rosi Braidotti and Maria Hlavajova, Bloomsbury, 2018, pp. 352–55.

Haris, Susan. "The Posthumanist Cow: Decolonizing the Ideological and the Radical". *Journal of Indian Posthumanism Network*, June 2021, https://posthumanism.in/articles/the-posthumanist-cow-decolonizing-the-ideological-and-the-radical-by-susan-haris/. Accessed 18 May 2022.

Harman, Graham. *Immaterialism*. Polity Press, 2016.

---. *Object-Oriented Ontology: A New Theory of Everything*. Pelican, 2018.

Irigaray, Luce, and Michael Marder. "Without clean air, we have nothing". *The Guardian*, 17 March 2014, https://www.theguardian.com/profile/luce-irigaray. Accessed 14 November 2021.

Jaaware, Aniket. *Practicing Caste: On Touching and Not Touching*. Fordham UP, 2019.

Latour, Bruno. *Politics of Nature: How to Bring the Sciences into Democracy*. Translated by Catherine Porter, Harvard UP, 2004.

---. *Reassembling the Social: An Introduction to Actor-Network Theory*. Oxford UP, 2005.

MacCormack, Patricia. *Posthuman Ethics: Embodiment and Cultural Theory*. Ashgate, 2012.

---. "Posthuman Ethics". *Posthuman Glossary*, edited by Rosi Braidotti and Maria Hlavajova, Bloomsbury, 2018, pp. 345–46.

Manto, Saadat Hasan. "The Dog of Tetwal". Translated by Ravikant and Tarun K. Saint, *Manoa*, vol. 19, no. 1, 2007, pp. 80–87, *Project MUSE*, https://doi.org/10.1353/man.2007.0042. Accessed 13 November 2021.

Marder, Michael. *Plant-Thinking: A Philosophy of Vegetal Life*. Columbia UP, 2013.

---, and Luce Irigaray. *Through Vegetal Being: Two Philosophical Perspectives*. Columbia UP, 2016.

Massumi, Brian. *What Animals Teach Us About Politics*. Duke UP, 2014.

Mukhopadhyay, Aniruddha. "From Worse than Dogs to Heroic Tigers: Situating the Animal in Dalit Autobiographies". *South Asia*, vol. 44, no. 4, 2021, pp. 756–71, *Taylor and Francis Online*, https://doi.org/10.1080/00856401.2021.1946642. Accessed 1 May 2022.

Nixon, Rob. *Slow Violence and the Environmentalism of the Poor*. Harvard UP, 2011.

Peterson, Christopher. *Monkey Trouble: The Scandal of Posthumanism*. Fordham UP, 2018.

Ray, Satyajit. "Septopuser Khide". *Golpo 101*, Ananda, 2001, pp. 29–39.

Roy, Sumana. *How I Became a Tree*. Aleph, 2017.

Rushdie, Salman. *Shame: A Novel*. Picador, 2000.

Sinha, Indra. *Animal's People*. Simon and Schuster, 2007.

---. "Bhopal: A Novel Quest for Justice". *The Guardian*, 10 October 2007, https://www.theguardian.com/world/2007/oct/10/india-bhopal. Accessed 13 November 2021.

Zolkos, Magdalena. "Life as a Political Problem: The Post-Human Turn in Political Theory". *Political Studies Review*, vol. 16, no. 3, 2018, pp. 192–204, *Sage Journals*, https://doi.org/10.1177/147892991772043. Accessed 13 November 2021.

Chapter Three

Posthumanist Tropes of Machines and Animals

HOW DO WE THINK TECHNOLOGY WITHOUT COLLAPSING INTO TRANSHUMANISM?

After wading through the history of the posthumanist idea's germination in philosophy and discussing it as an ethico-political framework, in this chapter we will look at two major posthumanist tropes of the machine and the animal. These manifestations of the nonhuman – be it in technology or in animality – are key to philosophical posthumanism. Let us begin with the theme of technology, and the machine as its pivotal trope, to see how it plays out in discussions of posthumanism by suggesting possibilities like the computer as an alternative to the human brain, Artificial and Emotional Intelligence, robotics, and structures like the Internet and DNA as life-making machines. At stake in technology is a transformation of the very notion of humanity. Is the technologically mediated body image we encounter in Skype and Zoom, human? How human is the virtual body produced by technology? Can the bot assume human consciousness and emotions? The technological question is tricky from a posthumanist perspective because it contains the risk of capitalist transhumanism that is subjectless and de-politicised. As we have seen, emancipatory posthumanism has the ethical task of depleting the technological determinism of transhuman culture. Robert Pepperell observes that 'the decaying category of "human" can be seen merely [as] a subset of an increasingly virulent "techno-biology" of which we might be but a transient phase' (Pepperell iv). In philosophical posthumanism, how do we think technology without lapsing into transhumanism? This question and its addressal will return us to the politics of posthumanism and the horizon of the resisting subject. As we shall see, to think of the co-constitutiveness of technology and humanity, to nonhumanise the human subject from inside and to combat the bio-power of the capitalist *becoming-machine* of the human, are the key actions that structure a posthumanist political subject.

Popular culture is fascinated by the humanity of the computer or the robot. The human–machine rapport is at the heart of global modernity. This is a complex love-hate relationship. In the Bengali-Indian filmmaker Ritwik Ghatak's movie *Ajantrik* ('Non-Mechanical', 1958), we have an anthropomorphic take on the taxi driver's relationship with his vehicle. As the title suggests, the car is humanised by Bimal, the owner who shares an emotional bond with the machine. But the film does not offer an unproblematic humanism of affect projected on the machine. The protagonist names the car 'Jagaddal', meaning a heavy and lifeless stone. When the vintage car stops working at the end, we notice the pathological dimension of Bimal's humanist projection. Getting frustrated with the car after his repeated failed attempts to mend it, he abuses it with the expression 'lohar bachcha' or 'metallic shit' (the cuss word in Bengali closely imitates the species-humanist slang, 'shuorer bachcha' or 'pig's offspring' in literal English translation) and breaks the windscreen with his fists. Ghatak underscores the machine as the nonhuman object that cannot reciprocate the human projection of affect. The machine resists human domestication and jettisons the transhumanist fantasy of human-becoming-machine. The human cannot become-machine because the machine recoils from humanity.

Another famous cinematic instance of the human–machine relation in technological modernity comes with Chaplin getting swallowed by a factory machine in *Modern Times* (1936). The scene is not without its sinister implications considering how it makes a comment on the dehumanising tendencies of capitalist modernity. If we follow the Chaplin scene carefully, he is processed and vomited out by the machine. When he comes back the same way he had gone into the machine, he uses the wrench to tighten the co-workers' noses and nipples, as if the machine has deranged him and made a machine out of his human self. We must also remember that Chaplin had accidentally gone into the machine because he couldn't keep pace with the speed of mechanised capitalist labour. Here we have another critique of transhumanism.

In a more contemporary digital context, we could think of Spike Jonze's futurist film *Her* (2013) that shows an amorous relation between a man and his gendered Operating System (OS). According to his sexual orientation, lonely Theodore chooses a female voice for the virtual assistant that comes with his OS upgrade. He gets so obsessed with this AI that it becomes a romantic relationship, triggering the typical question of whether machines have human emotions. How do we have a rapport between human emotions and the kind of feelings the AI is capable of? Samantha, the self-named AI, wants him to have relationships with actual women, but things do not work out and Theodore's verbal exchanges with her begin to assume an erotic tone. The human dimension lies in the sexualised AI voice. It hooks Theodore onto Samantha but soon the relationship reaches a stumbling block in the expectation of embodied sexuality. How can Theodore touch Samantha? How can he have sex with her? The two decide to have a sex surrogate who would simulate Samantha but the experience is discomforting. Complications creep in as Samantha discloses that she has been talking to many other human beings and has relationships with them as well. The machine loves the human but not exclusively, while the human wants exclusive and monogamous love. There are disjunctions like these between the human and machinic loves. They prevent the discourse from lapsing into transhumanism.

At the end with the disappearance of AIs, we are back to a world of human contact between Theodore and his best friend Amy who may have a romantic future together. When they sit beside one another in silence on the rooftop, as the dark sky is about to break into the first light of the day, we see a necessary return to the human. In *Her*, the AI is keen on maintaining Theodore's elemental humanity. Samantha makes a book from his letters to others. Theodore is a professional writer who writes personal letters for others who cannot express their emotions clearly. The film underscores the humanity of this epistolary exercise at the end as it resists the transhuman transformation of the human into the machine. We have seen in the previous chapters, with thinkers like Braidotti, that posthumanism does not and cannot abandon an essential and minimal humanity; what it foregoes is the anthropocentrism or the species-humanism of hierarchies. It comes as no coincidence that cinematic art becomes the platform to explode with representations of human–machine relations. Cinema is the most technological of art forms and its historical birth in the early-twentieth century goes hand-in-hand with the inception of high-technological modernity.

Let us proceed with the discussion of technology beyond cinema. In 1950, when British mathematician Alan Turing, having developed the first theoretical plan for what would become the computer, writes about the machine, his automatic analogy is with human mind and thinking. His famous question in the paper, 'Computing Machinery and Intelligence' is 'can machines think?'. Though he displaces this original question as he proceeds, he critiques the 'theological objection' to the thinking machine that would affirm thinking to be an exclusively human act. Turing remains critical of the humanist theology which suggests that 'God has given an immortal soul to every man and woman, but not to any other animal or to machines. Hence no animal or machine can think' (Turing 443). Glossing Turing's point, the cognitivist philosopher Daniel Dennett comments in a piece titled 'Can Machines Think?', 'His point was that we should not be species-chauvinistic, or anthropocentric, about the insides of an intelligent being, for there might be inhuman ways of being intelligent' (Dennett 132). Since machine is a human-made operative object, the inventors habitually compare and contrast it with the human system, be it the brain or intelligence. With advancements in technology, the power balance between the human and the machine tilts toward the latter. The human is not in control of technology, but technology starts taking hold of the human. As Pepperell reflects, 'The posthuman conception of technology is that of an *extension* to human existence, not of an external agent with a separate history and future' (Pepperell 152;

emphasis original). In this entangled understanding of the human and the technological, there is no grasp of the former without the latter. For him, what is posthuman about the contemporary culture of machines is their celebration of uncertainty à la Heisenberg (169). In Pepperell's posthuman idea of 'synthetic beings', we have complex thinking machines that work along with human beings in a complementary way instead of replacing them (153).

In *Signs and Machines* (2014), Maurizio Lazzarato conducts a Deleuzo-Guattarian analysis of the semiotic aspect of machines and subjectivities in late-capitalist society. Though the work is not explicitly posthumanist, it offers a critical insight into the way in which the posthuman continuum of the human–machine network functions. In what he calls 'machinic enslavement' (Lazzarato 26), Lazzarato finds a communication system, built from the human–machine assemblage, where the two entities become interchangeable. This carries a posthumanist slant. Following Deleuze and Guattari, capitalism makes the human into a desiring machine that is further manipulated by technology as we come to extended cognitive couplings between a human subject and a machine. We could ponder on our relations with gadgets like the smartphone, iPad, and laptop. They are not only our companion objects, but we also perform advanced cognitive tasks like reading a book, watching a film, and hearing a podcast with them. Our cognition gets extended onto them in such a way that we participate together as cognitive agents.[1] In this sense, we are desiring machines that become cognitively dependent on other machines. According to Lazzarato, the 'neoliberal economy' does not promise 'a new "humanization" of the alienated subject through industrial capitalism', but only ensures that 'subjectivity exists for the machine, that subjective components are functions of enslavement' (29). The machines produce our subjectivities in this system more than the other way round.

Technology in posthumanist thinking is neither an incorporation nor an externalisation vis-à-vis the human, but both. In addition, it is seen as an autonomous generative process. It internalises the human in its systematicity as much as it becomes an external manifestation or extension of the human. But this does not take away from its autonomy and generativity. While transhumanism will see this technological transformation of the human as a celebratory and progressive narrative of triumphalism, critical posthumanism must remain doubtful about technological fetishism in the capitalist world order. As scholars of technology such as R. L. Rutsky maintain, high *technē* has a tendency to reimagine spirituality and magic (Rutsky 144). For Rutsky, what modern, high technology reproduces is representation itself. There is no direct access to the human here as technology becomes a thing-in-itself – an autonomous entity. Technology is not simply a fetish object that is commoditised, but it also becomes invested with the religious affect of the sacred. This point runs counter to Walter Benjamin's famous theorisation of the artwork losing its aura with mechanical reproduction that deconstructs the idea of the original. Everything is a copy or everything is an original, and there is no aura in the work of art. As opposed to this de-sacralisation, we have an account of technology as spectrality in thinkers like Derrida. The simple and now-primitive technology of the telephone is an example. Through the mechanism of the voice the telephone makes us think that someone is there though no one is bodily present with us. As Derrida says in response to Bernard Stiegler, the camera does not need daylight to capture an image; it creates its own light and dark and once it captures us, we become televised spectral presences (Derrida and Stiegler 117). This spectral presence is generated by technology. We could radicalise this claim about technology as a haunting spectre of absent presence with platforms like Zoom, Messenger, WhatsApp, and other video/audio call and chat engines. Spectrality of technology contributes to its sacralisation. The problem with this discourse on spectral technology is that it may reduce the human to absence and give all the sovereignty to the technical. On the other hand, one may argue that the spectre itself is an intermediate posthuman entity.

Technology against the Transhuman: Literary Micro-Reading 1

In thinking technology, we encounter the risk of being co-opted into transhumanism and cognitive capitalism. The political task of critical posthumanism is to combat them by thinking a resistant use of technology that does not do away with what is essential (in a minimal sense) in the human. As Joseph Carvalko Jr writes, 'When we infuse the body and mind with technology, AI, or creative or intelligence genes, we become hybrids consisting of humans and technology' (230). Does this hybrid formation preserve the human? Let me take the trope of technology through a contemporary novel that brings in a political dimension of transhumanism and chooses to critically displace it with a residual humanism that defines the posthuman.

In the Canadian writer Iain Reid's novel, *Foe*, (2018) the calm of a country couple's (Henrietta and Junior) routine life gets disturbed by the arrival of Terrance, who declares that Junior has been longlisted by a Kafkaesque government organisation, OuterMore, for a mission ('Installation') that will make him visit another planet to see if humans can set up a colony ('Resettlement') there. Terrance glorifies the project's technology as post-VR. Junior had never enlisted for this but taking it up is made mandatory for him. Terrance sets up various monitoring machines on Junior's body after he gets shortlisted for the Installation. Junior does not want to leave Henrietta and becomes increasingly disgruntled with Terrance, who starts living with the couple to observe them. Eventually, much to Junior's resentment, Terrance proposes to make his 'biochemical duplicate' (Reid 101) for giving company to Henrietta while Junior is gone. He observes Junior, attaching a chip to his body so that a transhuman entity can be created to relieve Henrietta of her loneliness. As Terrance explains, this duplicate is not a robot; it is more like a 3D-printed copy of Junior: 'It's a new kind of self-determining life-form, an advanced automated computer program. A conflation of life and science' (102). The novel places the transhumanist narrative of technology on the side of statist control and governmental practices.

The finale reveals the reversal that the Junior who has narrated *Foe* all along is not the human-being Junior, but his biochemical duplicate created by OuterMore. With this disclosure, we realise that the novel has been narrated by a transhuman entity. Terrance tells the duplicate that it was brought in the day he visited the first time and the real Junior left to live on the Installation. It is part of the experiment to make the copy encounter the original. After the duplicate is removed, in the final few chapters the novel gets a human narrator, that is, the 'original' Junior. But where is the critical posthumanism to complicate the governmentalist discourse of transhuman planetary colonialism? When the original Junior returns, he cannot help suspecting Henrietta and her attachment to his copy. The question that plagues the 'original' Junior is whether she had sex with 'it' – his 'copy': 'Did you fuck it?' (246). The novel culminates in an awkward silence between Junior and Henrietta, symbolised by the blank letter she writes to him. After Junior's transhuman machinic copy is destroyed, we are left with this gulf between the husband and the wife that critiques the transhumanist narrative of the state. The state has destroyed the human relationship of the couple. But, can the human subject grow romantic or erotic feelings for a machine? Can the machine fall in love with the human? As Henrietta misses the transhuman Junior after the human Junior comes back from another planet, her regressive preference draws a line of inquiry that checks the victoriousness of transhumanist pseudo-progressivism. I would call this textual axis, posthuman. There is a vestigial humanism that brings into sharp relief, the capitalist–statist inhumanity of the transhuman paradigm.

The novel becomes critically posthuman by exposing the capitalist–governmentalist nexus of transhumanist machines. It humanises the machine as much as it underscores the humanist irony that the machine feels offended at the prospect of being replaced by a machine. As the replica of Junior unwittingly says, 'How can I accept being replaced?' (104). The 'copy' of Junior that narrates the book shows discernible traces of human emotion throughout the narration. It feels for Henrietta: 'No one understands me the way she does' (66) and she returns the compliment: 'We formed a bond' (237). According to her, 'it' did not care for her at the outset, but by the end, it developed feelings for her. It cannot remember anything long back in the past and its world entirely revolves around Henrietta whom it takes to be its soulmate. This affective humanisation of the machine sabotages the transhumanist project of the state by introducing a remainder of humanism without its species hubris. This humble humanism makes the readers feel bad for the destruction of the Junior machine at the end. It reads like a state-backed political murder.

Foe ends with another nonhuman image of horned rhinoceros beetles crawling in the sink. Junior hates them. As he crushes one against the sink, he says, 'They don't belong here. Nasty things' (260). Junior's species-humanist act contrasts the duplicate's silent observation of these creatures in the first half of the book. This is an ironic reversal of the humane and the inhumane in the human and the nonhuman. The machine becomes humbler and more accommodating than the human. The duplicate reflects how watching the beetle helps him get out of his 'narcissistic, self-obsessed neurosis' (85). That he could never understand anything about them, 'relaxes' him (85). There is an acceptance of the nonhuman in its opacities here. The machine that considers itself human accepts the nonhuman Other in co-belonging, whereas the human being kills the beetle and wants to kill them all. This inversion creates a posthuman space of contestation inside the novel. This is neither transhumanist nor humanist in a hierarchical sense. The beetles occupy this critical locus that unravels the violence of humanist hierarchy as much as it points to the failure of the transhumanist dream.

Stiegler and Critique of Technology

To continue with the technological trope, let me engage with the philosophy of Bernard Stiegler – the most significant contemporary thinker of 'technics'. For him, 'technics consists in the *organization of inorganic matter*, leading in return to the *organological reorganization of cerebral organic matter*' (Stiegler 2018, 42; emphases original). For him, technics involves an entanglement of inorganic and organic matter where the former's organisation mirrors the latter's reorganisation. This interweaving of mechanics and biology signals a posthuman turn where cerebral change is driven by changes in the object world. Stiegler offers a critique of technological capitalism anchored on cognitivist *episteme* (knowledge tradition). The cognitivist knowledge is a 'non-knowledge' and as Stiegler reflects, 'The cognitivist *anti-epistēmē* imposes *absolute non-knowledge* (the age of "post-truth"): it operates only through *the dissolution of all knowledge into and by calculation*, and, in so doing, it *accomplishes nihilism* – that is, the devaluation of all values' (140; emphases original). This is the IT turn from knowledge to information that is consistent with the cognitivist shift from thinking to mindfulness. Information is defined as a 'calculable signal' and a critique of information theory works in harmony with a critique of absolute non-knowledge.

Much like extended cognition/mind theorists Clark and Chalmers, who argue for an external coupling of the mind with machines, Stiegler talks about 'digital retention' in which the human capacity to retain things meets the storage of the digital systems. To remember things, we now check our Google Calendars or smartphone memos, or go online to search for what we cannot recall. Social media albums return us to the past. Particularly striking is the Facebook or Instagram memory function that brings back our old posts after one, two, three, and n+ years that we had shared on the same day. The question remains if we actually want to remember what Facebook or Instagram reminds us. Does technology not impose its own automatic memory on ours here? This is a transhumanisation of memory through digital technology. In his critique of cognitive capitalism, Stiegler takes on digital retention as part of the culture of anti-*episteme* or absolute non-knowledge. Digital retention produces a wealth of information without knowledge, not to mention the social inequality of digital access (147).

In the chapter 'Technology and Anthropology', part of *Technics and Time 1* (1998), Stiegler develops the idea of anthropology *as* technology following the works of Leroi-Gourhan and Simondon, not to mention Heidegger. To pick up on the posthuman underpinnings of his arguments, let me highlight how he draws attention to the paradox that 'the greater the humanity's power, the more "dehumanized" the world becomes' (Stiegler 1998, 90). The human intervenes into nature through technology, but the more technology dominates, the less humane this world becomes. There is a historical shift from old times when 'the human was a bearer of tools' to the modern techno-scientific world where 'machines are the tool bearers' while 'the human becomes either the machine's servant or its assembler' (23). This subversion of human power in relation to technology sabotages hierarchical humanism, but the technocracy it installs instead cannot be called posthumanist in a critical–affirmative sense. We are staring at the technocratic mastery of transhumanism here. For Stiegler, 'technocentrism' is homologous with anthropocentrism because both are charged by the same 'mastery and possession of nature' (93). As he explains, technocentrism sees technology as an end in itself and not as a means. In this orientation, technology is autonomised to form its own law which is tantamount to the hubris of the human as the technologically-empowered species par excellence.

Stiegler acknowledges how the human is an invention of the human science of anthropology. The discussion on the origin of the human in anthropology establishes the mythical nature of this origin, be it the birth of society or language. He agrees with Leroi-Gourhan and maintains that 'the human invents himself in the technical by inventing the tool—by becoming exteriorized techno-logically' (141). It is technology that invents the human and not vice versa. Stiegler adds that when we see technology as the externalisation of the human, we assume the human to be the interior. But this does not mean that the interior pre-exists the process of exteriorising. For him, 'interior and exterior are consequently constituted in a movement that invents each other respectively' (142). Technology invents the human as much as the human invents technology. We cannot distinguish between the two in the final run. This indiscernibility between the human and the technological interrogates the transhumanist fantasy of technocentrism. It contests both the taking over of the human by the machine and the human becoming a machine. This is a vision of the human being invented by the tool/machine and the machine being invented by the human in the same breath. We are talking about a co-constitutiveness of the human and the technological. In Stiegler, this co-constitutiveness is posthuman in its resistance to transhumanism.

Technology against the Transhuman: Literary Micro-Reading 2

Let me give one final literary instance of the technological trope resisting transhumanism, before moving on to the theme of animality. In the American writer Don DeLillo's novel *Zero K*, (2016) we stare at a dystopian future in which cryo-preservation is used to get past death. People diagnosed with terminal conditions are 'frozen' with the help of this technology before they die so that in future, when there is a technology to revive them, they could be brought back. If death makes us human, what will a technologically induced deathlessness signify for the human species? Once deprived of death in general and the uniquely singular dying experience for each human subject, are we still going to be human? The novel speculatively delves into a political dimension as we are introduced to the isolated institutional space, 'Convergence', where the freezing happens. The technology of cryo-preservation underlines the problem of identitarian continuity. What is the nature of the entity called 'dormant' that gets preserved in the pod? Is it human? After the process is over, once revived, will it be the same person? Will it still be a human identity? The transhumanist ideology provides a humanist promise: 'This is not a silicone-and-fiberglass replica. Real flesh, human tissue, human being. Body preserved for a limited time by cryoprotectants applied to the skin' (DeLillo 231).

Convergence is a sinister facility with screens that show wars and disasters from an apocalyptic future. The place reeks of violence with mannequin-like figures lying all around and a man, whom the protagonist Jeffry names 'the monk', wearing monk's robes. The monk has religious conversations with the folks on the verge of being frozen but seems disinvested in the project. For the apocalyptic monk, Convergence is the place they all come to die in. It has an absolute finality.

The family plot in *Zero K* revolves around a wealthy businessman, Ross, and his troubled relationship with his son Jeffry. Ross and his current wife Artis are about to get frozen. Artis is dying; Ross wants to accompany his partner and decides to go for the process though he does not have any terminal disease. As the novel progresses, we see a gradual dissolution of the familial structure. In the latter half, when Jeffry's adopted teenage son Stak goes mysteriously missing, Jeff goes back to Convergence to see his father undergoing the cryo-preservation process and the screen shows terrorists fighting in Ukraine. He sees a boy being shot by them. Jeff believes this boy to be Stak though there are no definitive answers.

Convergence is an incarnation of the state apparatus and its controlling ideology, charged with the philological dream of establishing a new language. Given that, in the humanist paradigm, it is language that differentiates the human from the nonhuman animal, this new language opens up a utopian progressivism of technological transhumanism: 'A language that will enable us to express things we can't express now, see things we can't see now, see ourselves and others in ways that unite us, broaden every possibility' (33). As Artis observes, the facility is a lab, working away at a futurist vision of humanity. This vision is that of a 'cyberhuman form' (67). It is 'ahistorical' or unaware of time. The novel asks speculative posthuman questions like 'how human are you without your sense of time' or 'Isn't death a blessing' (68, 69). The two questions are related as much as death is a signature of temporality. A consciousness of death has traditionally been the key differentiator between the human and the animal in species-humanism. The technological trope in *Zero K* delivers a blow to the humanity of death. But the consciousness of death is replaced by a meditation on deathlessness which retains the quasi-humanist hierarchy of rational thinking. Convergence dishes out a transhumanist fantasy, but posthumanism questions this dream by offering a point of unfixing, a point of contestation. DeLillo's novel is critically conscious of the illusionary nature of the Convergence project that situates science as the new religious dogma: 'Because we're human and we cling. In this case not to religious tradition but to the science of present and future' (74). We can see here how transhumanism is a techno-capitalist avatar of the old-style humanism. This transhumanism is betrayed by the humanist curiosity to know more. It is haunted by the posthumanist realisation about the impossibility of knowing everything: 'It's only human to want to know more, and then more, and then more' and 'there's no end to not knowing' (131).

For Stiegler, technology introduces temporality as much as it creates a rational presence of death in the human. The originary, pre-technical man '*does not have the feeling of death and does not anticipate*: he is not *in time*' (Stiegler 1998, 122; emphases original). In DeLillo's novel, contra Stiegler, the transhumanist project uses technology to remove temporality. Cryo-preservation is expected to give birth to a new generation of atemporal creatures. Posthumanism in

Zero K emerges as a dialectic that negates this technological fantasy of futurist transhumanism. After Ross and Artis are frozen, Jeffry gravitates away from Convergence, comes back to the work-a-day world and accepts a new job. The final chapter of the book returns us to nature with a geometric image of the setting sun aligning with the street's grid-like design. Jeffry is in a crosstown bus and keenly observes a differently-abled boy making excited noises at his mother as he watches '[t]he full solar disk, bleeding into the streets' (DeLillo 274). Jeffry tries to reassure himself by saying that 'the boy was not seeing the sky collapse upon us but was finding the purest astonishment in the intimate touch of earth and sun' (274). This apparent romantic return to nature in its transcendental effusion underscores a humanism that checks the transhumanist dream in a dialectical spirit of resistance. This iterability of humanism marks the posthuman space in the book. Jeff finds his solace in the 'boy's cries of wonder' and does not need 'heaven's light' (274). Much like what we saw in *Foe*, this residual humanist conclusion of *Zero K* is itself posthumanist, if we consider how it contests the transhumanist fable of technological mastery over human mortality. Our two literary micro-readings demonstrate the ethico-political commitment of the posthuman to produce a dialectical critique of transhumanist capitalism.

TRANSCENDING HUMAN LIFE THROUGH ANIMALS AND LACAN'S RESPONSE TO DERRIDA

Let us move onto animals and see what the posthumanist ethico-political task entails there. We start with Donna Haraway's *The Companion Species Manifesto* (2003) that frames an ethic and politics of Otherness humans learn from their interactions with dogs. By 'companion species' she means a life world where there is no hierarchy of culture over nature or human over nonhuman. She is interested in the co-evolution of the two. It is a 'kinship claim' with 'contingent foundations' (Haraway 9) that does not stay faithful to the foundationalist doctrine of species-humanism. In what she calls 'naturecultures' (21), signifier (language) and flesh (body) come together in the companionship of the human with the dog.

The dog is not a slave or a pet but a companion to the human. She uses the linguistic trope of 'metaplasm' (remodelling or change in the structure of a word) to ground the ever-changing, complexly indifferent, and fond relationship between the two. The companion species are cognitively coupled into a symbiotic–semiotic and corporeal unit. Haraway's imagination is posthumanist in the co-constitutive aspect of the human–nonhuman companionship. She critiques the humanist narrative that projects dogs as agents of unconditional love and emphasises the diverse relations that exist between humans and dogs: 'To regard a dog as a furry child, even metaphorically, demeans dogs and children—and sets up children to be bitten and dogs to be killed' (37). She raises the point about animal security and the risk of abandonment that lurks in petting dogs and discusses human–dog sport, detection, dog training, and models of pedagogy. Haraway prescribes a training that goes against anthropomorphism and respects the Otherness of the other species.

A posthuman animal ethic must preserve the nonhuman Otherness of animals within the gesture of embracing this Other. For example, J. M. Coetzee's ferocious guard dog in the story named after the animal ('The Dog', 2017) does not depict a harmonious human–animal rapport but a relation of extreme conflict, fear and sexual tension between the male dog and the unnamed female character who is terrorised by the dog's furious screams each time she passes the house where he lives. She projects a gendered hatred on the animal who is doing his job as a guard-dog – a particular kind of pet. One could argue that the dog's fury comes from the human assignment of the duty rested on him. He is frightening the passerby because he has been trained to frighten trespassers. It is not that the girl understands the dog and his fury with any degree of certitude but she speculates about the dog's psychology. It is in this ignorance that Coetzee preserves the Otherness of the animal, breaks the docile dog-stereotype and critiques the human impact on the pet who internalises the traits of fearfulness and hatred from his human masters to guard the house:

> The dog is a male, uncut as far as she can see. Whether he knows she is a female, whether in his eyes a human being must belong to one of two genders, corresponding to the two

genders of dogs, and therefore whether he feels two kinds of satisfaction at once—the satisfaction of one beast dominating another beast, the satisfaction of a male dominating a female— she has no idea. (Coetzee 246)

The girl's projection of gender (binary) on the dog structures the human–animal relation here and the uncertainty faced by her problematises the anthropocentric and anthropomorphic modes of thinking that fail to preserve the complex diversity of the animal world.

Gilbert Simondon in *Two Lessons on Animal and Man* (2004) charts the history of western philosophy from Greek antiquity to the twentieth century and argues how the contemporary thesis on human–animal relations in a certain way returns to antiquity. For him, antiquity has vouched for continuities between animal and human realities; though the two are severed in Cartesianism, the anti-Cartesian tenets of contemporary thought re-establish a continuity between the two realities. Simondon's thesis anticipates the posthuman as he maintains that the reversal of Cartesianism in contemporary philosophy is surprising and unexpected. Anti-Cartesianism suggests, 'the content of reality you put into the notion of animality' is the same that 'allows us to characterize man' or, 'it is by the universalization of the animal that human reality is dealt with' (Simondon 61). It is not the human that founds the animal as its Other across the reason/instinct hierarchy. Instead, the animal is the basis of the human insofar as the universalisation of the former's reality leads us to the latter's world. Simondon reflects, 'what we discover at the level of instinctive life, maturation, behavioral development in animal reality, allows us also to think in terms of human reality, up to and including social reality' (62). This posthuman (though Simondon does not use the term) foregrounding of the animal, as he notes, is different from the Renaissance mythologisation of the animal as nature and imparters of knowledge to the human. For him, there is no major ontological distinction between human and animal 'beings'. He traces a continuity between the animal and the plant worlds by comparing the 'anatomical organization in a plant' to the 'instinctive' 'behavior' of animals (79). This non-privileging of the human *qua* the animal and the plant points to a posthumanist horizon of thinking in Simondon. As we have seen in the previous chapter, there is a felt need to go beyond human life (*bios*) and approach life (*zoe*) in its multi-species form. This is the ethical task of critical posthumanism. Animal studies must further this action.

Let me come back here to the Derrida–Lacan debate on the presence and absence of the animal unconscious that we mentioned in the first chapter. In what follows, I will re-open this thread along a posthumanist axis to offer a Lacanian response to Derrida's deconstruction of psychoanalytic anthropocentrism. The discussion will signal a way of situating animal life within *zoe* and a becoming-animal of the human.

Derrida alleges Lacan of reducing animals to the Imaginary order of the psyche. He posits that Lacan cancels the possibility of an animal unconscious because he doesn't give Symbolic (linguistic) access to the nonhuman animal. According to him, the Lacanian animal only possesses a flat signalling system that does not have metaphor or metonymy. The nonhuman animal is deprived of human speech, and since the Lacanian unconscious is an effect of speech, there can be no animal unconscious. Though Cary Wolfe refers to this debate in *What is Posthumanism?* and *Before the Law* (2013), he only skims its surface and suggests that there could be an egotistical rivalry between Lacan and Derrida (see 2013, 64–66). Wolfe never questions the simplifications involved in Derrida's reading. After highlighting Derrida's active misreading, I will go on to nuance the question if animals have an unconscious. This is not the only question for me. The more pressing question is this: can the same speech that humanises the subject in early-Lacan be an event that nonhumanises (not dehumanises) the human in his later teachings? The nonhumanisation of the human from inside, as we have marked above, is a posthuman mode of thinking.

The third chapter of Derrida's *The Animal that Therefore I am* (2008),[2] 'Say The Animal Responded?', offers a complex reading of Lacan's treatment of the animal and the speculation about the animal unconscious. It is a critical reading that shows how for Lacan,

1. The animal can only react; it cannot respond. It can deceive but cannot deceive to deceive.
2. Animals don't have an unconscious because they don't have language. What they have is at best a code.
3. Animals can lie but cannot tell the truth by way of a lie. They can lay false traces but cannot lay falsely false traces.

Derrida appreciates Lacan's ethological work in his essay on the mirror stage that frequently refers to animals, especially Lacan's referencing of Harrisson's famous 1939 experiment that shows how the gaze acts in a sexual way for the hen pigeon: 'the ovulation of the hen pigeon is produced by the simple sight of a form evoking another member of the species, of a visual reflection, in short, even in the absence of an actual male' (Derrida 2008, 121). While this is an advancement, Derrida considers Lacan to be a species-humanist as he denies the animal unconscious:

> [Lacan] insists on dissociating the anthropological from the zoological: man is an animal but a speaking one, and he is less a beast of prey than a beast that is prey to language. There is no desire, and thus no unconscious, except for the human; it in no way exists for the animal, unless that be as an effect of the human unconscious, as if the domestic or tamed animal translated within itself the unconscious of man by some contagious transference or mute interiorization. (120–21)

If we follow this passage, there could at best be an animal unconscious in pets, as far as Lacan (in Derrida's version) is concerned. This unconscious is mediated by the human. The pet imbibes it as an infection from the human that makes Lacan anthropocentric. Derrida's apparently convincing critique develops the impossibility of distinguishing between pretence and pretence of pretence. All pretence can potentially lead to a doubling. All pretence of pretence essentially begins with a pretence. This is Derrida's crucial point: the line between pretence and pretence of pretence is blurry because each pretence can be iterated as a pretence of pretence. For Derrida, every trace contains its erasure within itself: 'It is inherent to a trace that it is always being erased and always capable of being erased' (136). According to Derrida, Lacan denies the animal the power of erasing a trace, but this cannot be the case as the animal can make traces. If the animal makes traces, it must know how to erase them: 'How can it be denied that the simple substitution of one trace for another, the marking of their diacritical difference in the most elementary inscription, which Lacan concedes to the animal, involves erasure as much as the imprint?' (135). As we shall see, Derrida simplifies Lacan here. Though he is correct in saying that Lacan denies animals the pretence of pretence, he never denies them the ability to erase traces.

Derrida acknowledges that Lacan's later-teaching, which increasingly abandons the dichotomy between the Imaginary and the Symbolic, may go on to problematise his deconstructive reading:

> I shall have to leave in suspense the question of whether, in later texts or in certain seminars (published or unpublished, accessible or inaccessible), the armature of this logic came to be explicitly re-examined. Especially since Lacan seems progressively to abandon, if not to repudiate, the oppositional distinction between imaginary and symbolic that forms the very axiomatics of this discourse on the animal. (Derrida 132)[3]

Derrida is right and this is the path we will take to show that Lacan's later theorisation of the Real unconscious is ethological. It takes life not as *bios* but *zoe*. This gives his thought a posthuman character. We must add to this a progressive nonhumanisation of the human subject, as Lacan's teaching switches from the logic of the signifier to the logic of *jouissance* in animal enjoyment.

Though Derrida is correct to assert that Lacan is sceptical about animals having an unconscious, the human unconscious reveals an animal dimension in Lacanian psychoanalysis. The so-called human unconscious is animal-like. The unconscious is not fully humanised. Let me first show how Lacan doesn't negate the speculative possibility of there being an unconscious in animals. For example, in *Seminar X* on anxiety, he says that animals have anxiety especially when they move out of their secure territories (Lacan 2014, 116, 297). In *Seminar VI*, he goes as far as to say that the dog has a superego, if not an unconscious (Lacan 2019, 89). In *Seminar VI* and *Seminar X*, Lacan discusses animals, erasing traces and this puts Derrida's critique under erasure. In *Seminar X*, we read, 'Effacing traces, operating with traces, isn't just one of mankind's properties. We see animals effacing their traces. We even see complex behaviour that consists in burying a certain number of traces, dejecta for example–this is well-known in cats' (63). Lacan qualifies that pretence of pretence is not reserved for the human at the cost of excluding the animal: 'Laying falsely false traces is a behaviour that is, I won't say quintessentially human, but quintessentially signifying' (63). Let me underscore the linguistic repair in Lacan's speech: 'I won't say quintessentially human, but quintessentially signifying'. Pretence of pretence is not exclusively human but a signifying semiotic practice. Does this mean that the animal world has no meaning? Certainly not.

In *Seminars VI* and *X*, Lacan focuses on the hippopotamus and discusses how it uses its waste to make traces. The hippo attributes a complex semiotic function to its faeces and 'marks its territory:

> he maps his territory, as it is called, by delimiting it with a series of relays or points designed to adequately indicate to all those whom this concerns—namely, his fellow creatures—that this is his turf. As you see, we find a first sketch of symbolic activity in animals. In mammals, it is a specifically excremental symbolism' (Lacan 2019, 106)

> The hippo gets anxious whenever it moves out of its excrementally marked zone. Lacan generalises this as a common mammalian trait: 'the hippopotamus, certainly, or even, because this extends beyond the mammals, the robin redbreast, feel invincible within the limits of their territory, but once outside it there is a sudden about-turn and they become curiously timid' (Lacan 2014, 305).

Contrary to Derrida's simplification, Lacan doesn't say that the nonhuman animal is incapable of erasing traces. Derrida's critique about the trace involving an erasure of trace within itself is not a true critique of Lacan, as the latter would agree with him. Lacan's insistence on human language and its ability for pretence of pretence is not as absolute as Derrida would have us believe. To re-emphasise, Lacan doesn't say that this pretence of pretence is human. He wants to highlight a complication of meaning in human language that doesn't exist in animal language.

Having underlined Derrida's simplified reading of Lacan, let me now shift the question from animals having an unconscious to the human unconscious being animalistic. How is the human unconscious nonhuman? Does speech nonhumanise the human? If we look for Lacanians who have responded to the Lacan–Derrida debate, there exists little. Todd McGowern's chapter from *Lacan and the Nonhuman* (2018) concentrates on the use and abuse of animal similes and extends the discussion to racism, but doesn't develop the idea of the animal subject. Alessandra Capperdoni's chapter on animal desire from *Lacan and the Environment* (2021) goes in a direction similar to mine by inquiring if enjoying and speaking subjects are the same. Is there a split between the speaking subject and the subject of *jouissance*? Is the latter more nonhuman than human?

In Lacan's 1974 talk 'La Troisième' ('The Third'), which Derrida does not mention, we have a mapping of the ethological unconscious. This mapping is consistent with the way later-Lacan eclipses the logic of the signifier (where the human–animal thesis is located) with the logic of *jouissance*. *Jouissance* refers to an enjoyment, irreducible to pleasure. It is a mixture of pain and pleasure – a mode through which the unconscious enjoys the body. This is the final frontier of Lacan's teaching in which language dissolves into lallation or what he calls 'lalangue' (the material sonic surface of language without meaning). Here we move toward a thesis on the Real unconscious. The Real unconscious is a switch from the classical Lacanian definition of the unconscious, structured like a language. As the linguistic unconscious is pushed into the meaningless, extra-linguistic Real, language gets displaced by a form of lallation that is not only like a baby crying, but also similar to the sounds made by nonhuman animals. These animal sounds may not have semantic meaning in the strict sense, but they are semiotic codes nevertheless. These sounds are like the cries of a child who is hungry or alone and wants to express themselves through the sound. The unconscious becomes an animal code in this confrontation with the Real.

'La Troisième' mentions the hedgehog as a thinking subject. Thought is corporeal. When the hedgehog feels threatened by something, it lowers its visor with a movement in its forehead. Lacan likens this 'wrinkling' movement with human thought:

> You imagine that thought resides in the brain. [...] it resides in the skin of the forehead, as much for the speaking being as for the hedgehog. [...] I love to see him wrinkling his forehead. After this, just like us, he rolls himself up into a ball. Good, anyway, if you can think with the skin of your forehead, you can also think with your feet. (Lacan 1974, 59)

In a joking style, Lacan gestures toward the animal unconscious. Like the hedgehog thinking with its forehead, human beings can think with their feet, head or any other part of the body. If there is a thinking brain, it is not in the head but distributed across the body.

After reintroducing the animal excitation of the body by the mirror image in the same talk, Lacan reflects, 'if there's something that gives us the idea of enjoying itself it's the animal. There's no proof, but anyway it seems to be implied by what is called the animal body' (59). To be a subject of *jouissance*, both the human and the nonhuman must have an animal body. Language unsettles this animal body of enjoyment. The ensuing discordance between language and body produces the unconscious. Radically put, language fails to humanise the animal body of the human. Unlike a species-humanist who will deny animals a complete 'world-making' experience, Lacan observes, 'the world is the world, the same for all animals' (59). Animals can form their own complete worlds just like humans do with their imagination. The nonhumanisation of language into lallation is indicated by the metaphor of the plant Lacan uses: '*lalangue*, where *jouissance* creates a deposit [...] corroborates at any rate that life, whose language grows shoots, gives us the impression that there is something plant-like about it' (43). There is something plant-like about language and human life. Language is not the humanising element in the human that it once was in Lacan's Symbolic-heavy early teaching. When the Real takes over, we stare at a gradual nonhumanisation of language into a plant-like and enjoyment-laden lallation. Lacan wonders if plants can enjoy (43). The field of *jouissance* stretches itself much beyond the human into the animal and vegetal worlds. In this we glimpse the posthuman in Lacanian psychoanalysis.

In Lacan's ethological obsession, there is a consistent attempt to put the human unconscious in comparison with animal behaviour.

We may remember the famous example of the praying mantis from *Seminar VI*. The mantis can devour its sexual partner while mating (Lacan 2019, 6, 22). This instance is brought up in relation to sexual fantasies of devouring, but human bodies cannot devour one another, unlike the mantis. In *Seminar XXI*, Lacan refers to bacterial sexuality and speculates about the kind of sexual relations they may have. This is to cross-match with the human domain of the sexual in which Lacan is establishing the idea that sexuality constitutes an asymmetrical non-relation more than a harmonious rapport. Citing Francois Jacob and Ellie Wollman's *Sexuality and the Genetics of Bacteria* (1961), Lacan develops the idea of sexuality as infection. This is not unlike the contagion that ends up transferring the human unconscious into the pet. The relation between the bacteria and the bacteriophage that sits on the former's wall like an infection is sexual. They have cellular exchanges analogous to human sexual intercourse. For Lacan, the bacteria enjoys the infection caused by the bacteriophage (*Seminar XXI*, session of 23. 4. 1974). We are back to *jouissance* as a nonhuman phenomenon here.

The phenomenon of *jouissance* in later-Lacan widens its scope to include the nonhuman in a significant way. In *Seminar XXI*, delivered the same year as 'La Troisième', Lacan speculates if the tree of life can enjoy itself as a tree (*Seminar XXI*, session of 23. 4. 1974). This is connected to the larger question if all life-forms enjoy. If they do, can enjoyment be considered a defining trait of *zoe*? Much like 'La Troisième', going back to *Seminar XVII*, we find Lacan asking the same question about the plant: 'the lily in the fields as a body entirely given over to *jouissance*— each stage of its growth identical to a formless sensation. The plant's *jouissance*' (Lacan 2007, 77). *Jouissance*, animal or plant, remains tied to the body. In the same breath, Lacan mentions animals in the field of *jouissance*. But unlike the plants who may not know a pleasure principle, animals do have an 'economy' of *jouissance* geared toward the idea of pleasure (77). The register of this thinking in later-Lacan remains speculative. He never says, all life is defined by *jouissance*. He only wonders. He also appeals to the lack of proof when it comes to these fields of knowledge. This impossibility of knowing must be read as a slant toward the Real. For example, he says in *Seminar XVII* that we will never know 'what the oyster or the beaver enjoys' (177). Lacan remains unsure about the human knowledge of *jouissance* in animals, but he never denies that there is *jouissance* in them. On the contrary, owing to the absence of the signifier, the oyster and the beaver, for Lacan, have a purer form of enjoyment as 'there is no distance between *jouissance* and the body' in them (177).

Let me return to 'La Troisième' to analyse why Lacan writes the word *vie* ('life') within the Real, that doesn't intersect with the Symbolic and the Imaginary. In his final teachings where these three orders of the unconscious are held together by the mathematical form of a Borromean chain, there would be some part of the Real that has nothing to do with the Symbolic and the Imaginary. But, why does Lacan write 'life' in that part? What is this Real of life? I would argue, the so-called human unconscious is not human but ethological and as we shall see in the final chapter, also ecological. This *vie* is not human life alone. This is life as *zoe* and not *bios*, to pick up on Rosi Braidotti's aforementioned posthumanist coda. In a text like 'La Troisième' that names animals and plants, not to mention the equivocation between 'life' (*animer*) and 'animal' (*animaux*) (6), Lacan associates this knot of life with the DNA that has a knot-like structure (double-helix). He says the following on the life in the Real that goes beyond the human:

> How is it that I have written at the level of the circle of the real, the word "life"? What's undeniable about life, apropos this vague term which involves announcing "the enjoyment of life", is that we know nothing else. And all that science leads us to is to see that there is nothing more real, meaning nothing more impossible, than to imagine how this chemical construction could [...] all of a sudden begin to construct a molecule of DNA. [...] it's indeed here we already see the first image of a knot, [...] *something in the real and not just anything, but life itself is structured like a knot.* (65; emphasis mine)

In this passage, we return to the moot question if all life can be defined by *jouissance*. DNA is not exclusive to the human life-form, and Lacan's point that science cannot account for the moment when the chemical concoction forms a DNA speaks to the Real of science as a figure of the unknown. This knot of life located in the DNA is a life in the Real shared by the human and the nonhuman, the animal and the vegetal. This is a posthuman conception of life as *zoe*. To round off, the human unconscious is not human because speech fails to humanise the so-called human body. What stages a return as a result of this failure is the animal *jouissance* of the body. The Symbolic unconscious deemed as human gets reoriented by the nonhuman in Lacan's final figuration of the unconscious as Real. To put this in non-Lacanian language, our unconscious mind that we mistakenly consider human, is not exclusively human. It shares a multi-species assemblage of life. Psychoanalysis as a clinical practice has to nonhumanise the human and push it away from any exceptionalist humanist discourse. It is this ethic that must mark posthuman practice.

Let us stay with the animal trope a bit further but without psychoanalysis. Kári Driscoll and Eva Hoffmann follow Derrida's idea that all poetic thinking (as opposed to philosophical thinking) is essentially animal thinking. It is aware of the animal gazing at the human as the human watches the animal. Driscoll and Hoffmann's idea of 'zoopoetics' – a word Derrida had used in the context of Kafka's writing – is a posthuman variety of thinking that sees the human as an object of animal gaze and not the other way. As they observe, a zoopoetic text does not need to be about animals, but it uses an animal way of thinking about everything it thematises (Driscoll and Hoffmann 4).

Nicole Shukin's work on animals as commodity in the context of biopolitical capitalism resonates with posthumanist implications. She takes up the term 'zoopolitics' to situate the non-criminal killing of animals that drives global market capital. For her, this violence is a 'zoopolitical supplement' to the Agambenian model of 'bare life' of the human in the concentration camp (Shukin 10). Taking the cue from Derrida's reading of Marx, Shukin highlights how Derrida '*animalizes* the spectral ontology of the commodity' (35). In the Marxist logic of commodity fetishism, animal and capital continuously mutate into one another and Shukin identifies three spectral modes for the circulation of animal capital: 'automobility' (animal capital in cars, films et cetera), 'telemobility' (animal metaphors and tropes in the telecommunication industry); and 'biomobility' (animal capital in family and kinship). Her work exposes the dimension of bio-power that underlines capitalism and contributes to the political attributes of posthumanism I have been analysing in this book.

Animal Philosophy and Three Literary Micro-Readings

A posthuman philosophy of the animal must begin from a humble acknowledgment of our inability to understand animals in their diversity and complexity. As George Bataille says, the animal world is totally closed in from the human in spite of the latter's descendance from the former. For him, the animal world is one of immediacy and 'we must confine ourselves to regarding animality, from the outside, in the light of an absence of transcendence' (Bataille 36). Even if we consider the animal as an Other species, the point is not to alienate them in a species-humanist way but to 'meet the other and to welcome them in their difference, to be reborn thus in a fidelity to ourselves and to this other', as Luce Irigaray says in a piece on human–animal relations (Irigaray 201).

Let us consider three world-literary instances of human–animal relations to chart a trajectory from the human to the posthuman. Though anthropocentrism is avoidable, it is difficult to avoid anthropomorphism in literary depictions of animals. To make them speak, they have to be humanised to a certain extent, insofar as speech itself is human. Does this mean, animal literature can never be truly posthuman? We could think about this problematic in a logic of scales. Bestial allegories in which animals are reduced to being nothing more than human metaphors cannot be called posthuman. But literary texts that do not resort to anthropocentrism in their treatment of animals can certainly be seen through the lens of posthumanism.

In American writer Paul Auster's novel *Timbuktu* (1999), we have a man–dog companionship that centres around the dog, Mr Bones, who is minimally anthropomorphised in the text. The dog remains the narrative mainstay after his soulmate and first master Willy, a homeless poet, dies halfway through the book. Most of the novel is written from the dog's point of view. There is a compassionate account of the 'companion species', as Haraway would have it, but the novel triggers the classical Hegelian question of death awareness as a differentiator between the human and the animal. In *The Philosophy of Right*, Hegel famously writes, 'It is man alone who can let go everything, even life. He can commit suicide, an act impossible for the animal' (31). According to Hegel, animals are devoid of self-consciousness to the extent that they are not in a position to understand death or have an ontological fear about it. On the other hand, human existence is almost always gripped by this presentiment of death. This difference creates a humanist hierarchy that Auster's novel undermines in the mythology of the utopian place of death named Timbuktu where 'dogs would be able to speak man's language and converse with him as an equal' (Auster 50). This invented signifier, 'Timbuktu' houses a posthuman land of death as inter-species equality. It is only in and through death (we have discussed its posthumanist implications in the previous chapter) that species-equality is conceived. Death is not the human privilege of reason and imagination. The animal too can craft its own death. At the end of the novel, an old, companionless, and exhausted Mr Bones practically kills himself by playing his dodge-a-car game on a six-lane super-highway. The dog's self-killing is indicated by the novel's last sentence which goes against Hegel's aforementioned claim that animals cannot commit suicide: 'With any luck, he would be with Willy before the day was out' (186). This is Mr Bones's subjective creation of dying as a unique individual process. The journey to the post-mortal neverland of Timbuktu is what unites the human and the animal in a shared imagination of mortality.

Contra Heidegger, for whom the animal at best has a half-formed world, Auster does not depict the dog as having a poorer subjective world than that of the human. Willy deeply appreciates Mr Bones's gift of smell, for example. There is a dynamic 'symphony of smells' (44) that forms the canine 'world' – a world that remains unreachable to Willy. Mr Bones foretells Willy's death in a dream that comes true almost entirely. The only difference is that in the dream, the dog sees a part of him becoming another nonhuman insect form – a fly that follows the ambulance taking the dying Willy to the hospital. This does not happen in reality and Mr Bones is left alone on the street when Willy is taken away by the paramedics. From the beginning of the book, Willy is dying and for Mr Bones, the fear of his master's death is tinged with existential anxieties like being trapped and slaughtered for food in Chinese restaurants: 'It was pure ontological terror. Subtract Willy from the world, and the odds were that the world itself would cease to exist' (4). It is not that Mr Bones does not or cannot form a world. In his fondness for his human companion, Willy *is* Mr Bones's world. Contra Hegel, the dog in Auster's world is intensely aware of death via the death of the Other. This relational consciousness speaks the posthuman language of multi-species entanglement.

Human society is portrayed as violent for the vulnerable Mr Bones: 'They'll kill you just for breathing' (122). After Willy's death, he has to rekindle his animal instincts of hunting for survival. But he fails miserably to catch even one pigeon, being out of the habit of foraging. Auster shows the difficulty of becoming a self-dependent animal again after being petted by a human. Mr Bones has young boys throwing stones at him; another boy hiding him in a box until his dog-hating father finds out and he has to leave. He is adopted by a family but they never care for him. He finally escapes and chooses his game of death on the highway. In Mr Bones's self-consciousness of death, attempt at suicide, and the promise of a posthumous world of human–animal equality, *Timbuktu* signals a turn toward the posthuman in its critique of anthropocentrism.

In the previous chapter's analysis of Sufiya Zinobiya in Rushdie's *Shame*, we have seen how the animality of the human body could become an important political trope for posthumanism. As Manuela Rossini comments, '[w]ithin a posthumanist frame, the human body or subject is seen as just another knot in the web of interspecies or intersubjective dependencies' (165). Pramod K. Nayar notes in his book *Posthumanism* (2013), '[p]osthumanist thought [...] often focuses on the body as a site for the new interpretations of the human' (80). Posthumanism collapses the hierarchical distinction between human and animal bodies. A novel like the French writer Marie Darrieussecq's *Pig Tales* (1996) bears testimony to this collapse in a feminist context. For example, Christine Daigle in her book *Posthumanist Vulnerability*, (2023) draws on this connection between posthumanism and material feminism. Darrieussecq's first-person female narrator, a masseuse and perfume seller in a boutique, slowly transforms into a pig as her body starts glowing with pink radiance. New rolls of fat and six teats pop up on her skin. The process is complete when she grows a tail and a snout. Her period stops and, while she thinks she is pregnant, her body exhibits a metamorphic animality that highlights how the patriarchal social system views her body as a fetishistic commodity. In her job, she is normatively subjected to the sexualised and objectifying male gaze of her customers who keep asking her for sexual favours. Unlike Kafka's Gregor, Darrieussecq's nameless woman does not turn into an animal overnight. The novel records this slow process of change in a corporeal mode that makes the animal trope transcend a mere metaphorical status. The animal body in *Pig Tales* resonates with a capitalist transhumanisation that becomes an object of critique for posthumanism.

As her body becomes pig-like, it increases her sexual appetite, but most men, especially her husband Honoré, lose sexual interest in her. The changed body upsets him. When Honoré tries to revive their relationship one last time, a pork meal comes in the way. The narrator-protagonist turning into a pig cannot have pork anymore. As her body reveals its animality, she does not fit into a saleable regime of beauty and her physical presence becomes socially and sexually unacceptable. Her doctor attempts to check her physical transformation by injecting serum into her system. While it works temporarily and her husband accompanies her to Aqualand, as the serum's effect wears out there unfolds a cruel scene in the water entertainment park where she becomes an object of ridicule for all the men present there. This is the irony of the transhuman in the figure of the animal. The becoming-animal body might be intriguing for its grotesquery, but the sanitised order of patriarchal erotics finds it unpalatable. For Pramod K. Nayar, 'in the case of animal studies, this is a posthumanist view: that the human can emerge only with the expulsion of the improper or the animal within' (89). In *Pig Tales*, it is not the expulsion, but the explosion of the improper animal from the human body that marks the knot of bio-capitalism. It is the animal that emerges from the human body to take stock of its fetishisation.

To make matters more complex, Darrieussecq's heroine does not turn into a pig entirely. She has a magical and somewhat arbitrary control over her body as it goes back and forth between human and animal. When she becomes feral and spends time underground in the sewer, the French political establishment changes and Darrieussecq's dark, fairytale narrative makes its heroine cosy up to the newly elected dictator, Edgar. The novel in this way connects the transhuman animal body not only with patriarchy, but also with a fascist polity. The protagonist's Arab lover is snatched away by the racist dispensation, books get banned and human rights activists are put behind bars. The text indicates that the corporeal transformation of the protagonist could have something to do with Edgar's nuclear power plant and the new diseases that may have come in its wake. A second speculation links her bodily change with her profession and dealing with diverse perfumes. All these connections make patent the socio-political dimension of transhumanism. The novel holds on to a critical posthumanism to combat this capitalist and dystopian corporeality.

In the middle of all this, we have a new romance between the pig-woman and a wolf-man, Yvan, brutally cut short by Edgar's state violence. As the protagonist goes back to her mother only to be betrayed by her, the question of her embodiment reaches a posthumanist crescendo: 'that odour was like the whole planet entering my body, conjuring up in me seasons, flights of wild geese, snow-drops, fruits, the south wind' (Darrieussecq 126) or again '[w]ith my entire body I felt once again the spinning of the planet' (127). This is a signature posthumanist body that is neither human nor animal. It is a planetary assemblage that combines the human, the nonhuman, and the ecological in a non-hierarchical fashion. In the end, the protagonist takes shelter in the forest and enjoys the young wild boars. She steals a notebook and writes her life story. This is the narrative we read in the form of *Pig Tales*. The protagonist maintains her intermediate corporeal subjectivity between the human and the animal. Writing as an activity preserves a trace of humanity in a wild life of pigs and boars in the jungle. As the final image of the novel indicates, the human and the animal are indistinguishable in her body's being: 'when I crane my neck towards the Moon, it's to show, once again, a human face' (135). *Pig Tales* underlines the biopolitics of the animal with an accent on corporeality as well as planetary ecology. It mounts a critique of biopolitical transhumanism.

Shifting from dogs and pigs to goats, let me first mention the political context behind the novel *Poonachi or The Story of a Black Goat* (2016) by the Tamil-Indian writer Perumal Murugan. Murugan's earlier novel, *One Part Woman*, (2010) had courted tremendous controversy for its depiction of a Hindu temple, invoking the ire of various religious groups especially on the far right. There were court cases, demands for an unconditional apology and eventually, a withdrawal of the novel from the market. The situation prompted an angry and exasperated Murugan to declare on his Facebook account that he was quitting writing. After this declaration in 2015, he came back to write *Poonachi* the following year. This context of censorship and right-wing political interference is important to remember as we read these words from Murugan's preface to the novel: 'I am fearful of writing about humans; even more fearful of writing about gods. [...] Yes, let me write about animals' (Murugan v). He goes on to say that of the animals he is familiar with, it is 'forbidden to write about cows or pigs' while dogs and cats are 'meant for poetry', and this leaves us with the 'problem-free, harmless' and 'energetic' goats (v). The author's decision to write about animals is triggered by religious bigotry and a humanist politics of deification. This gives *Poonachi*, an animal fable, a distinct ethico-political edge to start with.

Beginning like a perfect fairytale with 'once, in a village, there was a goat' (1), we have a mythical giant-like figure (Bakasuran), who one fine evening when the rains are awaited, comes to an old farmer and leaves him with a little, worm-like baby goat. This miraculous little creature is supposed to come from a golden line of descent in which her mother birthed seven kids in a litter and the last was Poonachi. As the mysterious man leaves without a trace, the old goatherd and his wife are tasked with taking care of the black goat.

The novel shows human greed in the goatherd's high expectations that it would birth many kids and bring in great money for the family. We are staring at the aforementioned animal capital argument. Moreover, the book shows how animals can be cruel to their own breed when the nanny goat feeds milk to her kids but refuses to feed the extra – Poonachi – and makes her teats go dry at the opportune moment. In addition, we have the governmental control mechanism whereby all domestic animals have to get themselves registered with name, age, address, and have their ears pierced. The fairs sell only pierced goat kids, but Poonachi being a foundling has no piercing. This is the important moment of entry for biopolitics in the life of the animal when it gets treated as capital in the market: 'When a new life was born anywhere in the territory controlled by the government, the authorities had to be informed immediately' (28).

The government, called 'regime' with a sinister anonymity, has wiped out all the black goats because they cannot be recognised in the dark while engaging in criminal activity. As a result, Poonachi's life is at risk. In the long queue at the ear-piercing office, the people gathered there speculate if the regime fears the goats' horns: 'Suppose they get a little angry and point them at the regime?' (36). In this serio-comic mode of satire, the novel marks the biopolitics of governmental control. The process of ear-piercing exhibits a statist cruelty toward animals. If anyone speaks out of turn, the officials are said to take revenge by piercing a vein in the goat's ear, which leads to serious injuries and even death on occasions. Poonachi gets a bad wound too but somehow survives. The state machinery has a number hoop hanging from the pierced ear of the animals. Number is utilised as an instrumentalist, bio-political tool to gain absolute control over the animal body. Each body is marked by a number, but the numbers often get blurred with all the wear and tear. It is one such blurred number that gets Poonachi into the system. The office scene establishes the fascist undercurrent of this biopolitical society.

The statist cruelty toward animals is juxtaposed with another kind of cruelty whereby Kaduvayan, a male goat with insatiable sexual urges, has to be castrated after all attempts to curb his sexual attacks fail. Though not directly a product of the controlling state ideology, this population control is another micro-political face of bio-power. There is a relation between macro- and micro-politics because the goatherds' attempt at population control is prompted by the linear numbering system of the state where it becomes difficult to register or justify non-linear mating across family and clan lines. The goatherds would have to keep a track of who the father is and declare the paternal number to have the child numbered accordingly.

As the book depicts the instinctive life of animals, it also brings up the question of consent in animal sex. There is a moment when Poonachi decisively declines Kaduvayan's wild attacks to mount her. However, as a fellow goat, she does feel bad to see the docile Kaduvayan after his body has been 'disciplined' and he loses all zest for life. While on a family pilgrimage with the old couple and their daughter who is visiting, Poonachi gets lost in the forest and has a brief moment of dilemma about whether she should start living an independent life in the forest or go back. She eventually resists the temptation and gets frightened by the possibility of being eaten up by wild boars. The goatherd's wife finds her and the episode re-establishes their bond and her maternal positioning of herself vis-à-vis the black she-goat.

The novel highlights the status of the animal as capital when one of Poonachi's playmates, Uzhumban, dies, thanks to a farmer throwing a stray stone, and the old couple agree to have his meat sold for cash compensation. Poonachi has no agency in this human market. She wants to mate with Poovan but is forced to have sex with an old ram. The litter, as per Bakasuran's promise, produces seven kids indeed. The miracle surprises the people around as well as the government that conducts a suspicious investigation to figure out how a little goat could breed seven kids. The miracle has a curse attached to it as 'even if you fart, you have to register with the government' and 'we might have a law which says you can only fart twice in a day' (117). After some initial trouble, the government settles the matter of seven kids.

In the middle of this satire on the fascist government whose officials keep calling people 'dogs', there unfolds the tale of animal helplessness. It is not easy to foster six goat kids and the old couple sell them off. Poonachi has no say in this. When one fine morning all her children disappear, she is left with great angst and despair. She gets an opportunity to mate with her lover Poovan when they visit the daughter's place and after a night of passionate lovemaking between the two, Poovan is suddenly taken away to be sacrificed, beheaded and skinned. In all these episodes, what emerges is the lack of agency on the animal's part as they are caught up in the spectral machine of bio-capitalism.

The irony of the miracle as curse continues when Poonachi delivers seven kids a second time, leading to another sale of the children in due course. As she prepares for a third litter amid drought and famine, there is nothing to eat either for her or for the old couple. Poonachi grows weak and finally dies on the brink of delivery. Her death puts an end to the old couple's troublesome thoughts about how to foster another set of seven kids in an era when nobody has money to buy animals. The text uses a telling metaphor of the object, that is, the stone, to talk about Poonachi's death in a corporeal sense: 'Her body turned hard as a stone and sank into the dirt'; and again, '[w]hat lay there was not Poonachi, but a stone idol' (170). While the stone body imagery focalises the object in a posthuman way, the word 'idol' takes us back to the fact that Poonachi's last thoughts were about her lack of memory about Bakasuran who had given her off to the old goatherd. Poonachi could never remember spending time with him but, from the old couple's talks, she had formed her own image of Bakasuran.

Poonachi uses anthropomorphism and, on occasion, allegorises the figure of the animal. But there is enough of the goats in flesh, blood and instinct for it to qualify as an anti-anthropocentric text, especially in its trenchant critique of governmental biopolitics and the reduction of the animal to market capital. The novel chastises the human life world for its insensitivity to the desires, choices and emotions of animals. Murugan uses the 'problem-free', 'harmless' goat as an animal trope to launch his indictment of species-humanism in collusion with a fascist governmental regime. Much like *Pig Tales*, *Poonachi* activates the animal motif against governmental fascism and hierarchical (trans-)humanism as two sides of the same coin.

To conclude, this chapter studied technology and animality as two central posthumanist sites in philosophical texts and literary works. The theoretical and literary engagements underlined the political ethics of posthumanism in critiquing capitalist transhumanism, biopolitics, and governmental control of the citizen subject. We arrived at a posthuman ethic of not-becoming-machine and becoming-animal. Nonhumanising the human, not reducing the human to technology, and situating life beyond the human constitute some of its pivotal axioms. As we saw in all three novels, the posthuman political subject critiques technocentrism and exposes it as a capitalist commodity fetishism. It challenges the governmental control of biopolitics and thinks the rights of the nonhuman. This subject is relationally aware of its own intrinsic animality and takes its humanity as incomplete without the larger life world of *zoe*. Posthumanism as a dynamic rubric becomes useful as a praxis of interpretation to approach and close-read themes like technology and animality, and as we shall see in the next chapter, the world of objects. Instead of seeing the machine and the animal as negations of the human that help us in defining it, posthumanism makes the border between the human and nonhuman permeable. It offers a vision of human–nonhuman entanglement in which the nonhuman stands in autonomy vis-à-vis the human.

It is interesting to think through the relation between machine and animal as two posthuman figures. Are these figures standalone or interrelated? Where does the object come in? In the body of a toy object for example, the animal and the machine could come together. The techno-capitalism of machines and animal capital have a different kind of consonance. Like human beings, animals have their own technology too, if we allow the word 'technology' to have a wider meaning as a technique to get work done.

In the following chapter, I will analyse another important posthuman theme of the object that is not coterminous with the machine. There are things in the world around us that are not technologically transformed into machines and yet they are significant for a posthumanist worldview.

NOTES

1. For more on this, see the book *The Extended Mind*, edited by Richard Menary.
2. I will restrict myself to this text though Derrida reiterates his arguments on Lacan across the two volumes of *The Beast and the Sovereign* seminar, because his essential critical point against Lacan remains the same. The new angle in *The Beast and the Sovereign I* is legality and crime as Derrida deconstructs Lacan's comment that human cruelty toward another species could very well target a fellow human (05–109). Without going into a detailed response, let me simply say that Derrida generalises Lacan's point. Lacan never says that *all* human cruelty toward animals is disguised cruelty toward another human being, as Derrida would essentialise. Lacan's comment is purported to underscore the way humans project themselves on animals, and their relation with animals often mirror inter-human relations. The fact that Lacan highlights this process doesn't make him an anthropocentrist, contra Derrida.
3. In *The Beast and the Sovereign II*, when Derrida returns to his critique of Lacan on the animal question, he himself, as in the passage above, wonders if there is an odd moment in Lacan where he ends up slipping in some half-formed Symbolic access to animals (247). In *The Beast and the Sovereign II* he adds the dimension of power (power of the Symbolic and Lacan's approaching humans and animals as 'powers').

REFERENCES

Auster, Paul. *Timbuktu*. Faber, 1999.

Bataille, George. "Animality". *Animal Philosophy: Essential Readings in Continental Thought*, edited by Matthew Calarco and Peter Atterton, Continuum, 2004, pp. 31–36.

Capperdoni, Alessandra. "Does the Animal Desire?". *Lacan and the Environment*, edited by Clint Burnham and Paul Kingsbury, Springer, 2021, pp. 155–76.

Carvalko, Joseph. *Conserving Humanity at the Dawn of Posthuman Technology*. Palgrave Macmillan, 2020.

Chaplin, Charlie, director. *Modern Times*. United Artists, 1936.

Coetzee, J. M. "The Dog". *The Pole and Other Stories*, Harvill Secker, 2023, pp. 245–50.

Darrieussecq, Marie. *Pig Tales: A Novel of Lust and Transformation*. Translated by Linda Coverdale, Faber, 1996.

Daigle, Christine. *Posthumanist Vulnerability: An Affirmative Ethics*. Bloomsbury, 2023.

DeLillo, Don. *Zero K*. Picador, 2016.

Dennett, Daniel. "Can Machines Think?". *Alan Turing: Life and Legacy of a Great Thinker*, edited by Christof Teuscher, Springer, 2004, pp. 295–316.

Derrida, Jacques. *The Animal that Therefore I am*. Translated by David Wills edited by Marie-Luise Mallet. Fordham UP, 2008.

---. *The Beast and the Sovereign I*. Translated by Geoffrey Bennington, edited by Michel Lisse and Marie-Louise Mallet, U of Chicago P, 2009.

---. *The Beast and the Sovereign II*. Translated by Geoffrey Bennington, edited by Michel Lisse, Marie-Louise Mallet and Ginette Michaud, U of Chicago P, 2011.

---, and Bernard Stiegler. *Echographies of Television: Filmed Interviews*. Translated by Jennifer Bajorek, Polity Press, 2002.

Driscoll, Kári, and Eva Hoffmann, editors. *What is Zoopoetics?: Texts, Bodies, Entanglement*. Palgrave Macmillan, 2018.

Ghatak, Ritwik, director. *Ajantrik*. L. B. Films International, 1958.

Haraway, Donna. *The Companion Species Manifesto: Dogs, People, and Significant Otherness*. Prickly Paradigm Press, 2003.

Hegel, G. W. F. *Elements of the Philosophy of Right*. Translated by H. B. Nisbet, edited by Allen W. Wood, Cambridge UP, 1991.

Irigaray, Luce. "Animal Compassion". *Animal Philosophy: Essential Readings in Continental Thought*, edited by Matthew Calarco and Peter Atterton, Continuum, 2004, pp.193–202.

Jacob, Francois, and Ellie Wollman. *Sexuality and the Genetics of Bacteria*. Academic Press, 1961.

Jonze, Spike, director. *Her*. Warner Bros. Pictures, 2013.

Lacan, Jacques. "'La Troisième/The Third". 1 November 1974. Translated by Ellie Ragland and Yolande Szczech, https://freud2lacan.b-cdn.net/LA_TROISIEME-bilingual-5cols-new.pdf. Accessed on 12 November 2021.

---. *The Seminar of Jacques Lacan Book VI: Desire and Its Interpretation*. Translated by Bruce Fink, edited by Jacques-Alain Miller, Polity, Press 2019.

---. *The Seminar of Jacques Lacan Book X: Anxiety*. Translated by A. R. Price, edited by Jacques-Alain Miller, Polity Press, 2014.

---. *The Seminar of Jacques Lacan Book XVII: The Other Side of Psychoanalysis*. Translated by Russell Grigg, Norton, 2007.

---. *The Seminar of Jacques Lacan Book XXI: Les Non-Dupes Errent: 1973-74*. Translated by Cormac Gallagher, http://www.lacaninireland.com/web/wp-content/uploads/2010/06/Book-21-Les-Non-Dupes-Errent-Part-1.pdf

http://www.lacaninireland.com/web/wp-content/uploads/2010/06/Book-21-Les-Non-Dupes-Errent-Part-2.pdf

http://www.lacaninireland.com/web/wp-content/uploads/2010/06/Book-21-Les-Non-Dupes-Errent-Part-3.pdf. Accessed on 12 November 2021.

Lazzarato, Maurizio. *Signs and Machines: Capitalism and the Production of Subjectivity*. Translated by Joshua David Jordan, Semiotext(e), 2014.

McGowern, Todd. "Like an Animal: A Simile Instead of a subject". *Lacan and the Nonhuman*, edited by Gautam Basu Thakur and Jonathan Michael Dickstein. Palgrave Macmillan, 2018, pp. 177–98.

Menary, Richard, editor. *The Extended Mind*. MIT P, 2010.

Murugan, Perumal. *Poonachi or The Story of a Black Goat*. Translated by N. Kalyan Raman, Context, 2016.

Nayar, Pramod K. *Posthumanism*. Polity Press, 2013.

Pepperell, Robert. *The Posthuman Condition: Consciousness Beyond the Brain*. Intellect, 2003.

Reid, Iain. *Foe: A Novel*. Scout Press, 2018.

Rossini, Manuela. "Bodies". *Cambridge Companion to Literature and The Posthuman*, edited by Bruce Clark and Manuela Rossini, Cambridge UP, 2017, pp. 153–69.

Rutsky, R. L. *High Techne: Art and Technology from the Machine Aesthetic to the Posthuman.* U of Minnesota P, 1999.

Simondon, Gilbert. *Two Lessons on Animal and Man.* Translated by Drew S. Burk, Univocal Publishing, 2004.

Shukin, Nicole. *Animal Capital: Rendering Life in Biopolitical Times.* U of Minnesota P, 2009.

Stiegler, Bernard. *Technics and Time 1: The Fault of Epimetheus.* Translated by Richard Beardsworth and George Collins, Stanford UP, 1998.

---. *The Neganthropocene.* Translated and edited by Daniel Ross, Open Humanities Press, 2018.

Turing, Alan. "Computing Machinery and Intelligence". *Mind*, vol. LIX, no. 236, 1950, pp. 433–60, https://doi.org/10.1093/mind/LIX.236.433. Accessed 13 November 2021.

Wolfe, Cary. *Before the Law: Humans and Animals in a Biopolitical Frame.* U of Chicago P, 2013.

Chapter Four

The Human in the Object
LITERATURE AND POSTHUMAN OBJECT INDEPENDENCE

THE INDEPENDENCE OF OBJECTS BEYOND THE HUMAN

After technology and animals, this chapter will examine the theories of object as a posthumanist avenue of thought not only in philosophy, but also as a development of literary thinking that gains traction in the twentieth century with the discourses of scientific and cultural modernity. The modern notion of 'objectivity' is certainly not synonymous with object-thinking but the former often paves way for the latter. Traditionally speaking, subject and object have been paired together in a dualistic structure. But, can we uncouple the object from the subject? This would be a key posthuman step: to think the object without a subjective dependency. But as we shall see, it is not easy to think this independence even when we reverse the traditional hierarchy and give prevalence to objects over subjects. In what follows, we will negotiate with diverse philosophical theses on the subject–object relation to arrive at a tentative independence of objects through OOO and modernist theorisations of the object in literature, but without letting go of subjectivity. Instead, there will be a reorientation of human subjectivity as an object in posthumanism. This posthuman objectal subjectivity is not patently political but it has historico-political undertones. The posthuman subject considering themselves 'under' the objects has an ethic that we will come to underline. In readings of E. L. Doctorow's novel, we will encounter the menacing nature of accumulating objects in the subjective obsession of hoarding, but not without a strong historico-political inflection. In John Banville's novels, we will locate a spectral affect in objects that withdraw from the meaning the human subject wants to impose on them. There is an element of resistance in this withdrawal that speaks to the larger political agency of posthuman objects.

Let me begin by talking about a famous thesis of subject–object dualism in Indian philosophy. The Samkhya school asserts that the world comes into being through an interaction of *prakriti* (usually translated as matter) and *purusha* (usually translated as spirit). In a finer sense, *prakriti* refers to the cognitive, psychological and moral dimensions of reality as perceived by the mind, and *purusha* is a witnessing consciousness that works upon *prakriti* to give birth to the world as such. While Richard Garbe sees this as a thesis of subject–object dualism, for Paul Oltramere, Samkhya presents a dualism of being and becoming, and not that of the subject and the object (Larson 24). *Prakriti* is initially unmanifest but in contact with *purusha*, it is transformed and becomes manifest with consciousness. Going into the details of this becoming (from the three qualities of *prakriti* to the twenty-three *tattva*s or principles that emerge from the interaction of the two) is beyond our scope. But let me highlight the point that Samkhya dualism differentiates being from becoming, or subject from object. Objects depend on subjects just as becoming depends on being. This dualistic thinking is symptomatic of hierarchical humanism as it makes the material world of objects dependent on a subjective consciousness of witnessing.

As we have noticed with Francesca Ferrando in the first chapter, philosophical posthumanism must be post-dualistic. For the posthumanist, objects are independent of any subjectivity, or better still, they are subjects in their own right. For posthumanism, being *is* becoming. But in dualistic philosophy, there falls a shadow between the two. Dualism encounters its own difficulty when Samkhya struggles to explain the relation between the subject and the object in terms of *purusha* and *prakriti*. This is a major critique Sankara mounts on Samkhya philosophy (Larson 229). Samkhya admits that there is 'something' that doesn't appear and yet allows everything to appear in the *prakriti–purusha* becoming. This 'witnessing something', Samkhya acknowledges, is neither 'subjectivity' (*buddhi/*

intellect, *manas*/mind, *ahamika*/ego) nor 'objectivity': 'whatever this "something" is, it is not adjectival to *prakriti* but, rather, a contentless medium or transparency apart from *prakriti* through which and for which *prakriti* shows itself' (Larson 230). This is an auto-deconstructive point within philosophical dualism that falls into the conundrum of subject and object. The posthuman task is to liberate the material world of objects from this conundrum and give them agency without lapsing into an anthropomorphism of nature.

We have seen in the first two chapters that the object as matter is an incarnation of the nonhuman and an important motif in posthumanism. To think ontology from the perspective of objects is a form of anti-anthropocentrism because the object is not dependent on the subject in this orientation of thinking. The object is not the dialectical opposite of the subject. It is not there to complete or complement the subject. Objects stand on their own. They are material things, not reducible to human meaning. In *Theory of the Object* (2021), Thomas Nail argues that objects pre-exist the human. Beyond science and technology, the object exists as 'an eddy in cosmic energy' (Nail 4). Nail's example is the river as a 'process-object', made without human intervention (24). As he says, constructivists reduce objects to human invention and not discovery, but it doesn't explain how objects emerge and change (9). In posthumanism, we must think the object beyond its human relationality and dependency. In Nail's language, '[m]atter is self-observing; it does not need a human to observe it to be known or exist' (59). Thomas Nail's book studies nonhuman objects in their own agency to create and reproduce themselves in the history of science.

In *The Allure of Things* (2014), there is an attempt to bridge object-oriented philosophy with process-oriented philosophy—both of which have posthuman slants. Objects, in a materialist process-ontology of matter as becoming or flow, represent a lure and an allure to surpass the anchorage on the subject that exists in anthropocentric thinking. The editors define the titular allure of objects as

> something like an affirmation of the desire to think outside of the framework of representation that has been so important to

much epistemology- or subject-centered philosophy. Another might see the inaccessible noumenon of Kant as a prototypical withdrawn object of the kind theorized by speculative realism. (Faber and Goffey 4)

Be it the beyond of subject-centric philosophy or the lack of direct access to the object, this philosophical project does not abolish the subject as much as it rethinks it qua both object and process as nonhuman realities of the world. Transcending the 'correlationism' of subject-object duality, this philosophical approach positions the subject as an *effect* of object and process and not their cause. For example, Levi Bryant in his chapter from *The Allure of Things* mentions Alain Badiou's positioning of the subject as an index of the event and not a subjectivity that pre-exists the evental process (Bryant 2014, 74).

We cannot expand here on Badiou's complex theory of the event as an aleatory encounter with that which exists minimally in the world but it suffices to highlight that his subject is a result of the event and in this subordination lies its resistance to the humanist subject. Let me briefly note that for the Badiou of *Logics of Worlds* (2009), the 'human animal' cannot become a subject without the event. The event that unsettles 'the logic of object' (object for Badiou is a form of being-qua-appearing or the generic form in which a being appears in the world) creates subjectivity as a discipline. The subject is not the 'human animal' but a process that comes into being through 'the evental modifications of objectivity' (Badiou 222). The object as an appearing of being in the world gets modified by the event and the subject is born in the process. Badiou's subject is not only an aftereffect of the event but also an aftereffect of the change in the existing configuration of objects. The posthuman implication of this philosophy lies in separating the subject from the human and treating it as an ontological effect of evental processes that are based on a change in the objectal arrangement of the world. This evental transformation of the objectal configuration is a revolutionary change for Badiou. The subject is not a human agent but the functional embodiment of this socio-political change in the order of objects.

To look at the socio-political dimension of objects, in a discussion of market capitalism, Arjun Appadurai mentions an 'anthropology of objects' (Appadurai 55) that revolves around Marx, Marcel Mauss, and the idea of object as commodity. Money is used to create exchange value for objects, but money itself is a human-made object. Commodity is a classic example of human meaning, redefining the thing as a saleable object in the market. The anthropology of objects is almost always part of a humanist style of thinking. In *Provincializing Europe* (2000), Dipesh Chakrabarty refers to historian D. D. Kosambi's fascination with the ancient saddle-quern as a kitchen object in the modern Bengali household: 'It intrigued Kosambi that such an ancient-looking object should exist in the same space that was also occupied by the electric stove, a veritable symbol of modernization in India of the 1950s' (Chakrabarty 242). As Chakrabarty argues, the stone object represents a temporal knot in which multiple historical periods (Stone Age implements and electric or kerosene stove) can exist together. This is another instance of cultural and anthropological value as human signification inscribed in the object. What dominates this discourse is the object's human meaning over its own existence as an object. OOO tries to upturn this hierarchy and think the object as an ontological entity, independent of its human meanings.

Graham Harman, the object-oriented-ontologist in *Tool-Being* (2002), establishes an autonomy of the object, singular in its being. We consider what elements make up the object, but these constituents are not the object. One object gets into complex relations with other objects. But we often consider these inter-objective relations to be human. As an unnamed female character in the Mahesh Elkunchwar play 'The Reflection' (1987), reflects, 'One thing proves the existence of another. Or else an object has no meaning. Now look at this inkpot. It gets its meaning from this pen. This pack of cigarettes. It has a meaning because of this box of matches' (209). What is noteworthy in this quote is the human and signifying nature of one object's relation with another. The inkpot's existence becomes humanly meaningful due to the existence of the pen. The cigarettes and the match box do not have an unmediated relation. Their relation is filtered by the human agent who gives meaning to these objects by using them. This human meaning projected on an object's being creates a roadblock for any posthumanist thinking on objects.

In Harman's *Guerrilla Metaphysics* (2005), the object is irreducible to this inter-objective relation. The object is neither its components nor its relations, but the difference between the two. OOO is posthuman in thinking objects as pre-human, independent, and related with other objects without the necessity of a linking human subject. The sensorial world is no absolute privilege of human beings. Sensoriality exists in the world of plants and objects. For OOO, humans themselves are object-oriented. Humans have no primacy in this network. They are often made to acknowledge their role as objects rather than subjects. Human beings, according to OOO, have no direct relation with the world. They must mingle and permeate with objects to establish such relations. The objects have always already-established such relations among themselves: 'humans do not shatter a monotonous rumble of being into districts for the first time, since this has happened long before we arrive on the scene' (Harman 2005, 254). This is the posthumanist implication of OOO.

In *Form and Object* (2014), Tristan Garcia places the thing as the difference between intrinsic and extrinsic relations of meaning. For him, meaning and signification are different (120). The former could be intrinsic to a thing, but the latter lies in one object relating to another in a network. To be in the world is the ultimate meaning of objects. They 'accumulate' and make 'significations' when they associate with other objects in various relations and capacities. For Garcia, if they do not accumulate, they have meaning but no signification. In such an inert world, their only meaning is their existence. In Garcia's philosophy, human beings are interstitial – between animals and machines: 'Humans no longer think they are the centre of the world, but they remain a milieu. Humanity only makes sense *between*' (239). This idea of the human as milieu resonates with our posthuman subjectivity as an environmental multi-species entanglement. A human being is a thing, not because of its oneness as unity but because of its oneness as solitude (54). This solitude is the primary condition of things. Things can come together only because they are elementally solitary. Levi Bryant in *The Democracy of Objects* (2011) builds a 'flat ontology' or 'onticology' on two claims:

> First, humans are not at the center of being, but are *among* beings. Second, objects are not a pole opposing a subject, but exist in their own right, regardless of whether any other object or human relates to them. Humans, far from constituting a category called "subject" that is opposed to "object", are themselves one *type* of object among many. (249; emphases original)

This idea of human as a *type* of object is our horizon to rethink posthuman subjectivity in an object-oriented way. The posthuman coordinates of OOO become evident here.

If Bryant sees a consonance between psychoanalysis and the flat ontology of OOO (drawing on Lacan's ideas of sexuality to arrive at an object-oriented-ontology of immanence), for another philosopher, Alenka Zupančič, Lacanian psychoanalysis, unlike OOO, will not reduce the subject to the object. This does not make psychoanalysis humanist in a speciesist sense. There is nothing special or superior about this subject and it does not have to be human. As Zupančič reflects, 'the subject is not simply an object among many objects, it is also the form of existence of the contradiction, antagonism, at work in the very existence of objects as objects' (122). Let us underline that in Zupančič's formulation the subject is not necessarily human. It is an existential form that puts objects in relations like contradiction and antagonism. For her, subjectivity is presented as an ontological principle of objects. This ontological principle is political for Zupančič. To have her critique on board is thus to preserve the politics of posthumanist subjectivity as the possibility of antagonism, contradiction, and resistance. If we combine Bryant with Zupančič on this point, we see that OOO does not have to be subjectless. This returns us to the aforementioned debate about whether posthumanist ontology is without subject(s). As I have already said, we must fight to preserve the posthumanist subject for political reasons.

Posthumanist ontology is not subjectless, though subjectivity is not coterminous with the human in this ontology. Subjectivity is an overarching principle of objects in a relational (including contradiction as political relationality) ontology. For Bryant, there is no 'world' or 'super-object' to contain all the objects in the form of a totality. Objects have the same type of relation with each other that human beings have with objects. The idea of flat ontology does not deny inequality in the world of objects. But Bryant agrees with Ian Bogost, another object-oriented-ontologist, who maintains that 'all objects equally exist, but not all objects exist equally' (Bryant 290). If there is existential equality to start with, human interference and rearrangement produces existential inequality in the world of objects. Bryant formulates it with a slight difference: 'Flat ontology is not the thesis that all objects contribute equally, but that all objects equally exist' (290). For him, objectal existence is equal but the way they contribute or operate is not equal. The idea of contribution brings in human filters. Objects often contribute according to the way the human world allows them to contribute. OOO is therefore, as Bryant puts it, an attempt to think the 'being of objects unshackled from the gaze of humans in their being for-themselves' (19). This is the ethical, egalitarian axiom of object independence in posthumanism.

The posthumanist thesis on objects is more realist than idealist. It believes in the existence of objects independent of the mind. It is one thing to uncouple the object from the subject in a bid to give it autonomy. It is another to say that there is no subject. The object of posthumanism is subject-independent, but not subjectless. The thesis is that a subject itself is an object because the self-consciousness of the human subject makes it into its object.[1] In other words, the human consciousness can think its own subjectivity as an object of its thinking. To acknowledge that a change of perspective is enough to shift the subject into an object has posthumanist implications. Similarly, if we understand subjectivity as an extension of the very condition of objects (Zupančič), it debunks a humanist and hierarchical notion of the subject that must be superior to objects. If we turn to Lacanian psychoanalysis, the theory of the object bypasses anthropocentrism when the object becomes the driving force – the object causes the subject of human desire. In interpersonal relationships, especially love, human beings translate each other into objects of their desires. Psychoanalysis allows us to think of the human subjects in parallel, as objects of inter-human desire. As we have seen, situating the human subject as object could itself be called a posthuman disposition.

For Jacques Lacan, the object that triggers human desire is a Symbolic (linguistic) object in lack. As he says in *Seminar IV*, dedicated to the theme of object-relations, 'in the human world the structure, the point of departure for objectal organisation, is the lack of the object' (Lacan 2020, 48). We want something only insofar as we don't have it. It follows from the Lacanian thesis that to think the object within the human paradigm is to treat it as a lack in language. To go beyond the human view would be to undo the desiring network with the object and see it, not in its Symbolic lack, but in its independent being outside human language. In the psychoanalytic clinic, the object constitutes the desiring subject of language and not the other way round. This is a reversal of humanist subjectivism. The Lacanian 'object a' that finally emerges from the analysis is radically external to the subject's orientation. It doesn't pre-exist therapy but gets formed during the analytic process. Analysis arrives at its end on the slope of this new object of desire. As Jacques-Alain Miller has noted in the essay 'Another Lacan', the end of analysis for Lacan does not occur on the subjective plane but on the plane of the object (Miller 2016). This new object stands outside the subject and changes the pre-existing subject in the profoundest way by becoming its radically exterior anchor point. This sway of the object over the human subject and its extreme exteriority to the subject are markedly posthuman. The subject, recast from the dialectical throw of this new object, is not humanist. It is an object-driven subject that knows how to acknowledge the agency of the radical exterior, be it the nonhuman animal, the machine, or the environment at large.

Literary Thinking on the Object

Having looked at the move from subject–object dualism to axioms of object independence and an object-oriented recasting of subjectivity, let us now come to literature's own ways of thinking about the object. In the 1924 *Manifesto of Surrealism*, André Breton complains about extended descriptions of setting in Fyodor Dostoevsky's novel *Crime and Punishment* (1866). Dostoevsky's passage describes the character in a small room and the narrator mentions details like yellow wallpaper, geraniums, windows, curtains, and so on:

> There was nothing special about the room. The furniture, of yellow wood, was all very old. A sofa with a tall back turned down, an oval table opposite the sofa, a dressing table and a mirror set against the pierglass, some chairs along the walls, two or three etchings of no value portraying some German girls with birds in their hands – such were the furnishings. (Dostoevsky, qtd. in Breton, 7)

Breton attacks this object description, calling it as vacuous as a stock catalogue (7). For a surrealist, the realist detailing of unnecessary objects is equally unnecessary. Breton's tirade suggests how objects that form a realistic narration are burdensome for the experimental surrealist. In contrast to this, we shall see that in Alain Robbe-Grillet's conception of the French *Nouveau Roman* ('New Novel'), object description becomes experimental and anti-realist. We will focus on narrative objects and their role in a fictional world in the theoretical context of posthumanist materialism.

To take a step back, let me note that a novel conjures up its world in the act of narrativisation. When we read it, the narrative world unfurls itself. The world brought into being could be like or unlike, or be both like and unlike the world outside the text. As we move into this textual world, we see, hear, and feel the beings that people it. It is not only human beings who populate the textual world. Narrative worlds go beyond the human in depicting nonhuman animals, other living beings and inanimate matter. We often neglect the objects that solidify a narrative world. We will soon see how literary modernism's narrative worlds rethink the traditional neglect of objects in literature. In the avant-garde literary tradition, inanimate objects are a lot more than 'things' that pile up alongside metonymic details, constructing a narrative world of reality. The narrative experiments in European modernist traditions often put pressure on the functionality of the object by emphasising their intrinsic being. This entails a shift of emphasis from the meaning of the object to its being. The experimental worlds of modernist novels move away from reducing objects to their purpose and function in the narrative. They help us think through the being of objects. This being cannot be reduced to any number of meanings that the object may have in a given narrative world.

I will signal this switch from object function to object ontology through a variety of anti-realist, avant-garde literary discourses, culminating in Robbe-Grillet's theory of objects in the French New Novel in the 1960s. We will get into this discourse on the object in European modernisms through the philosophical lens of OOO to claim its pre-figuration in Robbe-Grillet and Roland Barthes' reading of the literary object. Moving forward in time, I will trace this modernist legacy in two contemporary writers of experimental world literature – the Irish writer John Banville whose novels dramatise the inert and yet enlivening spectrality of objects, and the American writer E. L. Doctorow. We will read Doctorow's late novel *Homer and Langley* (2009) that goes back to two twentieth century real-life characters whose famous 'hoarding' of things underpins a symptomatic relation between the human subject and the objects around them. Banville's novels, *Eclipse* and *Shroud,* on the other hand develop a spectrality around objects that recoil from human signification.

There is philosophical literature exploring the presence–absence problematic of 'fictional objects'. We could consider Robert Howell and Jay Bachrach who are interested in non-actual and possible objects in fictional worlds that may or may not exist. The philosophical category of the 'non-existent object' has been mobilised to theorise literary objects that do not actually exist in the real world. This body of critical literature has approached the category through the linguistic representation of and reference to real objects. They have foregrounded the logical property of language, primarily in the Anglo-American or 'analytic' philosophical tradition. We will see how the contemporary 'continental' philosophy adds to this ontological discourse on objects. In an important philosophical study of 'fictional objects', Charles Crittenden comes up with various object functions like contradiction, incompleteness, existence and non-existence. His critical register remains metaphysical and his literary references are limited to the popular realism of the Sherlock Holmes narratives (1991).

Bill Brown, a prominent voice in the field of material culture and literature, engages with modernist and postmodernist contributions toward the thinking of objects. In *Other Things* (2016), he covers a diverse set of theories from the Kantian thing-in-itself, to the psychoanalytic theory of the 'lost object' in Freud and Lacan, and Latour's theory of actor-networks. There are resonances of OOO in Brown but Graham Harman or Tristan Garcia, its chief proponents, do not get a serious mention. He limits Robbe-Grillet and Barthes' thoughts on objects in fiction to a footnote. I will extend Brown's work by bringing back some of these neglected threads like Robbe-Grillet and Barthes, and in the spirit of his move, proceed to talk about contemporary writers (he does not discuss Banville and Doctorow) who carry this legacy. While Brown self-admittedly works with the 'ontical' function of objects, I will operate on their 'ontological' (being of being) layers with a posthuman intent.

In the chapter devoted to objects in the *Cambridge Companion to Literature and The Posthuman* (2017), Ridvan Askin argues that literature has a special approach to the thing-in-itself because it can sidestep conceptual thought. While conceptual thinking creates a mediated access to objects (what I have called object function above), the literary discourse, for him, is all about non-conceptual sensation. Literature has a more direct approach to objects. Evoking the Russian formalist Viktor Shklovsky, Askin posits 'literature as the very human means of going beyond the human' (172). He mobilises Gilles Deleuze and discusses the literary as a zone of 'affects' and 'percepts' (perceptual entities differing from 'concepts'). Surprisingly, what is missing in this discussion of posthumanist objects in literature is literature's depiction of things and matter at large. Askin's readings of Margaret Fuller and Charles Olson bypass the literary portrayal of the world of things. He ends by making a broad point about the great exterior of materiality entering the inward reality of literature, but we do not encounter any tracing of this movement. In what follows, I will read the object as a representational content in the narrative world and the complex dynamic of meaning and being in the literary depiction of objects. In analysing this, we will speculate if literature can truly become object-oriented and posthumanist in a new materialist sense.

Literary Objects: The Meaning–Being Complex

To uncouple the object from the human subject, we must stop reducing the object to its function and think its being away from the human ascription of meaning. Discussing Dutch landscape paintings and images of still life, Roland Barthes draws our attention to the rift between the 'form' and the 'attribute' of an object. He reflects that in reducing an object to its use, we are limiting it to its attributes and losing out on the fundamental form of the object: '[a]n object's *use* can only help dissipate its essential form and emphasize instead its attributes' (Barthes 5; emphasis original). Use turns an object into a tool, if not a commodity. Therein lies its function as an ontical means to other ends. This is how an object is humanised, but the ontical functions of an object do not deepen object ontology and independence. In an essay published in *New Materialisms* (2010), Sara Ahmed complicates the Marxian discourse of use value and exchange value of objects as commodities to argue how the wood that forms a table is 'formed matter' in itself (Ahmed, "Orientations" 242). She diagnoses an irreducibility of objects vis-à-vis commodities and discusses 'a history of changing hands', inscribed in objects: 'This table was made by somebody, and there is a history to its arrival, a history of transportation' (243). Insofar as an object is the product of labour, it carries this human history in its body. This discourse may offer a critique of Marxist materialism in its new avatar of 'mattering', but it is dominated by the human, nevertheless.

How could this discourse become posthuman? Let us look at a moment from Paul Auster's novel *Sunset Park* (2008). In this novel, written in the wake of the global economic meltdown, we encounter Miles Heller, working toward 'home preservation' for a corporate company. He gets obsessed with taking pictures of scraps, left behind by families in houses emptied during the recession:

> He has no idea why he feels compelled to take these pictures. He understands that it is an empty pursuit, of no possible benefit to anyone, and yet each time he walks into a house, he senses that the things are calling out to him, speaking to him in the voices of the people who are no longer there, asking him to be looked at one last time before they are carted away. (5)

Auster's narrator suggests an anthropomorphic function of useless objects in empty houses that call out to Heller as a sad reminder of bygone lives. These objects have life because they were once used by human subjects. As scraps, they still hold onto a spectral remainder of human lives, once lived around their presence. They carry a Sara Ahmed-like human history of use in their hearts. Though with the passage of time these things have become useless, they cannot be seen independently of the human. And yet Heller's camera captures a world of objects without human beings in the present photographic moment. These objects were once commodities but now they are back to being objects, pristine in their uselessness. As scraps, they are in a space away from the human, but Heller brings them back to the field of human gaze by clicking their pictures. He makes the useless useful only to problematise the gap between object and commodity. The passage exposes this difficulty of thinking literary objects in a narrative world beyond humanity, surpassing the human meaning imputed to them. I will continue to trace this paradox in what follows.

To contrast the codification of objects into human meaning in Auster, let me refer to a theatrical moment from Harold Pinter's play *Ashes to Ashes* (1996) in which Rebecca and Devlin debate whether things can possess human meaning, and the answer is in the negative. Rebecca tells Devlin that she had put her pen on the coffee table but it rolled off. How could the pen roll off by itself? This makes them take up the point about object agency and they speculate if the pen could be 'innocent'. For Rebecca, the pen is innocent but Devlin disagrees and reasons: 'Because you don't know where it had been. You don't know how many other hands have held it, how many other hands have written with it, what other people have been doing with it. You know nothing of its history. You know nothing of its parent's history' (Pinter 410).

This is the theme of the object's human meaning, or what Ahmed calls 'a history of changing hands', written on the object body. The pen is not considered innocent because it has been used by human beings. Each object used by the human subject has a human history of meanings that takes it away from its material being. Importantly though, Rebecca punctuates and clinches this conversation by responding to Devlin's human theory of object history with, 'A pen has no parents' (410). This aphoristic climax closes off the dialogue on the pen. Devlin anthropomorphises the pen to give it human meaning but Rebecca contradicts him. She resists the humanisation of the pen. The pen rolls back into the penumbra of being from the clarity of meaning after her punctuating final statement that it is without parents. It turns out that we must cut away from object function and meaning to concentrate on its independent being.

Literature almost always makes us aware of the difficulty of delinking meaning from the object's being. Sometimes, the very being of an object contains emotive meaning for the human. Consider the first vignette 'On the Sidewalk' from Jhumpa Lahiri's *Whereabouts* (2021) that depicts the narrator's encounter with a memorial marble plaque on her everyday walks. Though she doesn't know the dead man, the plaque as a mnemonic object facilitates a strange relation she develops with the dead man and his mother who leaves a handwritten thank-you note at the plaque. The plaque, the candle, and the note attached to the wall just above the plaque make her speculate about how the man may have died by accident at that very spot. The narrator has never seen the man or his mother but reading his name and her note makes her feel 'slightly less alive' (Lahiri 4) as she walks on. What we notice here is the affective impact of the object's very being on the human subject. The deadness of the object that makes the human affectively less alive is testimony to its sway over the human. If this is a posthuman breakthrough, what complicates the scenario is that the ontology of such an object is itself impossible to uncouple from the field of human meaning. How do we imagine the memorial plaque without the human meaning invested in its materiality? The meaning–being complex and its underlying subject–object relation remains obstinate.

Toward a Literary Posthumanism of Objects

Within the posthumanist discourse of the nonhuman, animals overshadow inanimate objects. We want to turn the table and ask if situating ontology by way of objects, rather than through human subjects, is posthumanist in an intrinsic sense. Can objects be theorised in a nonhuman way? If imputing a personal affective meaning to things is necessarily humanist, how can we have an actual posthumanism of objects? When we connect these philosophical questions with literary texts that express objects in their own ontologies, the task of arriving at a posthumanism of philosophical and literary objects becomes problematic. How are objects localised in literary narratives? If they are plotted and imbued with textual meanings that are unmistakably human in the final assessment, how can we have a true 'post' to the human interaction with objects?

As seen above, for Breton, Dostoevsky is guilty of taxing his readers with needless descriptions of things. If this makes us think that description is orthodox for the experimentalist, let us think again. We have a counter-move in Alain Robbe-Grillet's conception of what Barthes calls 'objective literature' in the French New Novel. Opposing the psychological novel of high modernism, Robbe-Grillet etches out a geometric theory of surface objects. In Robbe-Grillet, the description of objects exposed in their bare being without narrative meaning, becomes a literary experiment: 'Around us, defying the noisy pack of our animistic or protective adjectives, things are there. Their surfaces are distinct and smooth, intact, neither suspiciously brilliant nor transparent. All our literature has not yet succeeded in eroding their smallest corner, in flattening their slightest curve' (Robbe-Grillet 1965, 19)

To reiterate Barthes' aforementioned argument, uncoupling the object from use (including realistic descriptive use) highlights its form. Robbe-Grillet is foregrounding the need to engage with the geometric surface of objects around us. This is a structural engagement with the body of the object as form. He is not interested in the attributes or meanings that the object may have in a narrative flow. This formalisation can happen when we step away from the mania of psychologising objects with deep human meaning. Robbe-Grillet continues his critique of the cultural and psychological attribution of human meaning onto objects: 'At every moment, a continuous fringe of culture (psychology, ethics, metaphysics, etc.) is added to things, giving them a less alien aspect, one that is more comprehensible, more reassuring' (18). He sees the human subject 'drowned in the depth of things' only being able to experience 'in their name, totally humanized impressions and desires' (68).

Robbe-Grillet invests in the experimental possibilities of object-description and makes the human subject, an external entity to the field of objects:

> To describe things, as a matter of fact, is deliberately to place oneself outside them, confronting them. It is no longer a matter of appropriating them to oneself, of projecting anything onto them. Posited, from the start, as not being man, they remain constantly out of reach and are, ultimately, neither comprehended in a natural alliance nor recovered by suffering. (70)

It is here that we glimpse a posthumanist approach to objects. This is a view of object description that ousts the human subject from what is described. The human is no more a part of the world of objects. The human gaze stops projecting anything onto them. Barthes reflects that Robbe-Grillet attempts 'to withdraw man from the fabrication or the becoming of things' (22). The mathematically contoured body of the object underlines its being-there while it subjugates its narrative meaning. In Robbe-Grillet's cinematic snapshot of objects, what seems like a silent human gaze looking at the objects, often reveals itself to be a gaze coming from the objects themselves. But this discourse does not lapse into anthropomorphism. We will see an example soon.

Tristan Garcia in *Form and Object* observes that the geometric form of an object is part of its matter. It is what constitutes an object. He makes a distinction between form in general and geometric form in particular. In his view, form has no relation to objects while geometric form and matter co-constitute an object:

> "geometric" form, a body's figure, is not its form but rather a part of its matter. Its form is something else. Considered in this way, the geometric figure of the cube is not the form of the cube insofar as it is a thing. The geometric figure of the cube is something that constitutes it in the same way as the wood. The cube's wood and geometric figure are equally components of the matter of this object, the wooden cube: they both enter into the wooden cube. (137)

If mathematical form is built into the object just like its component, it becomes part of its material being. Garcia's point throws new light on Robbe-Grillet's mathematical objects as matter. We see here how an emphasis on the mathematical structure of an object resonates with new materialism. In Robbe-Grillet's mini-story 'The Dressmaker's Dummy' from *Snapshots* (1962), there is no human presence. A descriptive narrative voice creates a scene in which nothing happens. Complex visual frames develop from the simple opening image of a coffee pot on a table when the pot's surface reflects a window with three sections: 'In the spherical surface of the coffeepot is a shiny, distorted reflection of the window, a sort of four-sided figure whose sides form the arcs of a circle. The line of the wooden uprights between the two window sections widens abruptly at the bottom into a vague spot. This is, no doubt, the shadow of the dressmaker's dummy' (Robbe-Grillet 1986, 5).

There is a mathematical emphasis on the play of square and circle in the coffeepot's surface reflection of the window. There are narrative promises in these premises but Robbe-Grillet is not interested in forming a plot from these descriptions. The dressmaker's dummy is the objectified trace of something like a human subject in this inert world in which inertia stands for the mattering of matter. The subject has become an object here. The posthuman subject is material in its embeddedness to objects.

From Accumulation to Hoarding: E. L. Doctorow

To become posthuman, literary objects need to exist independently, separated out from the human meaning of plot. They need to be there without being reduced to narrative tools. They must have their own being-there. This object ontology can oust the human and even kill it. To illustrate this danger, let me come to the psychic phenomenon of hoarding where a human subject symptomatically accumulates objects and cannot let go of anything they possess. As we shall see, this symptom becomes murderous in E. L. Doctorow's *Homer and Langley* (2009). The novel reconstructs the lives of two famous twentieth-century hoarders from America: Homer and Langley Collyer who made their ancestral house into a museum. In 1947, the Collyer brothers died under the debris of the things they had themselves accumulated. Hoarding, as a symptom that has to do with objects, differs from Garcia's aforementioned idea of 'accumulation' by giving primacy to the human subject as a hoarder. And yet the paradox is that this is a specific kind of accumulation in which there are no inter-objective networks of meaning. More than object semantics, hoarding is about object syntax. Homer and Langley do not hoard things because these things establish new meaning when heaped together with other things. They hoard objects for their material being-there rather than meanings they may develop in a relational matrix.

Homer, who is losing his eyesight, finds comfort in the being-there of the hoarded objects around him: 'it was all very eclectic, being a record of sorts of our parents' travels, and cluttered it might have seemed to outsiders, but it seemed normal and right to us and it was our legacy, Langley's and mine, this sense of living with things assertively inanimate, and having to walk around them' (Doctorow 6–7). What is the 'assertion' of inanimate objects mentioned above? The nostalgic objects reminding the brothers of their parental lineage assert their being around them. These objects have had historical meaning of human use in the past. But now they are exhausted into insignificance. For the blind Homer, there is no ontological distinction between inside and outside. This indistinction translates into a hoarding of objects from the outside world to the inside world of the house. They inject their fantasies into this world of objects. As they hoard newspapers, Langley imagines the project of making a world newspaper that would have every news item and not need any addition whatsoever. This absolute archive is a phantasmatic meaning imputed to the objects by the human gaze. It takes away from their being-there by suffusing them with subjective meaning. Having said that, the fantasy of the absolute archive of newspapers is dropped like a generic semantic bomb on the newspapers. It fails to create any inter-objective network of meanings between one newspaper-object and another.

In post-War America, the Collyer house becomes a veritable war museum: 'It was as if the times blew through our house like a wind, and these were the things deposited here by the winds of war' (102). The context of the wars adds another cultural and historical meaning to the hoarded objects. As the place becomes full, the brothers build passageways to move through the objects. These tunnels create the image of the trench in wars. As the brothers become recluses and the threat of intrusion increases, Langley designs all the hoarded objects into an 'infernal machine' that would collapse on any intruder: 'rubber tires, an iron pressure cooker, dressmaker's dummies, empty bureau drawers, beer kegs, flowerpots' (206). This labyrinth of objects becomes a menacing assemblage; 'each room has a punishing design of our things' (206). As Homer suggests at an earlier point, with all the stuffed objects around him he cannot think about nothingness (151). Hoarding could have the psychic economy of a defence mechanism: a strategy to stall the void. Objects, for a blind man, solidify the concrete world around him. It allows him to divert his thoughts away from nothingness. This is how the material and inert being of objects reasserts itself away from the plethora of meanings and fantasies invested in them. In the final moments when Homer, the sightless narrator, feels for the hoarded things, we sense the material being-there of objects as company for the human: 'I feel my typewriters, my table, my chair to have that assurance of a solid world, where things take up space, where there is not the endless emptiness of insubstantial thought that leads to nowhere but itself' (207).

Let me highlight the repeated use of the possessive pronoun ('my') for all the objects mentioned above. These objects do not relate to one another and construct meaning in Garcia's sense of accumulation. Their very being-there is an affective meaning, felt by the human subject seeking assurance of solidity from them. They rescue Homer from lapsing into the thought of nothingness, the 'endless emptiness of insubstantial thought'. Homer can distinguish between 'the images of things' and 'the things in themselves' (207) and he is not happy to have the former replace the latter. For a blind man, this is being-becoming-meaning. In our meaning–being complex in which one subtracts the other, this is a new turn. It is a fresh insight in which being-there itself becomes affective meaning for the human subject.

Hoarding as a human symptom anchors the treatment of objects in *Homer and Langley*. The novel cannot think objects without the human. It converts the independent existence of objects into emotional meaning for the human subjects. But does this mean it fails to imply anything beyond the humanist depiction? I do not think so. As we have seen above, when we search for a posthumanist treatment of objects in literature, it does not necessarily mean that there is no human presence. Robbe-Grillet wants to exclude the human but the question remains if it is possible to do that in a literary life world where the narrative voice almost unfailingly retains a vestigial humanity. The posthumanist object ontology is about decentring the human *qua* object rather than an absolute exclusion of the human. *Homer and Langley* opens up a new horizon of literary posthumanism by turning the humanist object relation on its head and suggesting the objects' hierarchical sway over the human. The hoarded objects are the masters here. The humans need them and not the other way around. The objects pile up and eventually kill the Collyer brothers. There is an element of reversal in this death. The objects that the two brothers set up to kill the interloper end up killing them instead. The objects lord over the human subjects by becoming the ultimate master of death. Do they kill the hoarders as revenge for hoarding? To consider objectal vengeance is to anthropomorphise the objects. Doctorow's text gives this lethal and sardonic agency to objects without anthropomorphising them. It exposes the human being's pathological dependency on the objects and subverts the anthropocentric discourse in the process.

Spectrality and Objects: John Banville

The literary quest for a posthumanist approach to objects yields more paradoxes than affirmations. We started with a distinction between objectal being and subjective meaning but found that these two categories are not watertight. Objectal being itself can become human meaning, as in Doctorow. When objects hold their sway over the human and the human is reduced to an object, the human is not out of the picture. The inversion of the human and the object's hierarchy is itself an effect of human disposition. In the spirit of this paradox, let me evoke Irish writer John Banville whose work is replete with a dialectical tension between the affective human meanings of objects and their actual nonhuman presence as matter in the world. In *Eclipse* (2000), Banville spells out the human signification of objects as a complex spectral feeling. What makes him relevant for our posthuman lens is that his work delineates a withdrawal of human meaning from the object and brings it back to its material inertia. The objects themselves recoil from human meaning, and yet they are not anthropomorphised. Be it the phantom chair that doubles itself before disappearing in *Eclipse* or the vase that cleaves into two discrete halves in *Shroud*, Banville is attentive to the bifidity of the object between anthropomorphic meaning and nonhuman presence. In his world, there is an acknowledgment of the independent life of things that decentres the human subject. Objects are in perpetual waiting as they bide their time.

In *Eclipse*, Alexander Cleave, an actor, returns to his childhood home and experiences a haunting that happens through inanimate objects. A full reading is beyond our scope but let me concentrate on an important moment from the novel that portrays this objectal haunting and establishes spectrality as an affect written into things. As we have mentioned in the previous chapter, the spectre is itself of the order of nonhuman. In Banville we have one nonhuman converging on another when objects produce spectres. Cleave reflects on the creaking objects in his childhood home that spook him out of his wits. Talking about ghostly forms that he keeps spotting around the house, he observes, 'They have their own furniture, in their own world. It looks like the solid stuff among which I move, but it is not the same, or is the same at another stage of existence. Both sets of things, the phantom and the real, strike up a resonance together, a chiming' (Banville 2000, 48)

Objects double up in another reality where each thing has its spectral counterpart. It is notable that there is no conflict between the two worlds. They have a 'chiming'. Let me quote again:

> If the ghostly scene has a chair in it, say, that the woman is sitting on, and that occupies the same space as a real chair in the real kitchen, and is superimposed on it, however ill the fit, the result will be that when the scene vanishes the real chair will retain a sort of aura, will blush, almost, in the surprise of being singled out and fixed upon, of being lighted upon, in this fashion. (48)

The spectral double objects leave an aura on the real object after the uncanny world vanishes. But this aura does not last: 'The effect soon fades, however, and then the chair, the real chair, will step back, as it were, out of the spotlight, and take its accustomed place in dim anonymity, and I will cease to notice it, try as I might to go on paying deference to this plain thing that has known its numinous moment' (48). The real object and its spectral double are considered to be the same thing, in two different stages of existence. We must make a distinction between 'being' and 'existence' here. While the former (being) is being as being, the latter (existence) is being as it appears in the world. The chair is the same in its being but is 'at another stage of existence' when it appears as a phantom chair. These two different stages of existence for the same being create a divided affect of spectral doubling. The object alienates itself from the human grasp of understanding through this real–phantom doubling. The solid, volumetric presence of the object in space dissipates into a ghostly double. This is an ontological shift at the level of existence though the kernel of being remains the same.

The same furniture doubles up in two worlds but after the phantom object disappears with the whole scene around it, the object in the real world is bathed in an 'aura' as a result of this interplay. Banville anthropomorphises this movement by using the word 'blush' for the object that returns to real existence from its phantom existential order. But why does the object blush? It blushes because this spectral doubling breaks what Garcia calls structural equality (Levi Bryant's 'democracy') of things. It makes this particular thing feel special and more equal than others, to speak in Orwellian language. The object blushes 'in the surprise of being singled out and fixed upon, of being lighted upon, in this fashion' (48). Banville demonstrates the process by which human beings project spectrality as an affect on the world of things when they cannot process the bare materiality of inanimate matter.

If his narrator had stopped here, Banville would not have become that engrossing a writer for a posthumanist portrayal of objects. But he doesn't. In addition, he depicts the return of structural equality among things when the human imputation of subjective meaning evaporates and the object loses its noticeable presence. The narrator calls it a 'numinousness' from which the object returns to its 'dim anonymity' – the order of bare materiality. This is the a-signifying materiality of the inanimate world. The human subject will now 'cease to notice it'. As the narrator pontificates over the vanished 'aura' of the phantom object that was just a creation of his mind, he fails to notice the 'plain thing'. It is the portrayal of this withdrawal of human meaning from the object that makes Banville an important case study for posthumanist depiction of literary objects.

At another point in *Eclipse*, the narrator says, 'I have come to distrust even the solidest objects, uncertain if they are not merely representations of themselves that might in a moment flicker and fade. The actual has taken on a tense, trembling quality. Everything is poised for dissolution' (48–49). This anxiety about the solidity of objects is human, but objects slip away from solidity as they turn spectral. This is how they recoil from the human. Banville's objects elude human understanding by being on the cusp of 'dissolution'. These objects lay bare the human pathology of layering things with meanings as the objectal world in its inherent meaninglessness is unbearable for the human. There is a posthuman accent in this critical exposure of human weakness that fails to deal with material existence of objects without sedimenting them with infinite semantic layers of their own fantasies.

In *Shroud* (2002), part of a trilogy that includes *Eclipse* and *Ancient Light* (2012), Banville responds to the point about the object's anthropomorphic symbolic value, coming from the human meaning imputed on it. Let me draw attention to the reflection on a vase. It is the last gift the narrator-husband buys for his wife, Magda. The vase marks the fortieth anniversary of their marriage. Once it is installed, Axel Vander, the narrator, starts to hate it. He finds it menacing. But Magda falls in love with it. She sits still and observes it for hours. The day after Magda's death, the vase breaks into two equal halves. Let us look at this event of the object:

> On the day after Magda's death I was reclining on the sofa in the dimness of the lounge […] with a bag of ice on my brow and a steadily diminishing bottle on the floor beside me, when a loud report, sharp and incontrovertible as a gunshot, brought me rearing up in fright […]. I scrambled upright and

swayed at a drunken list into the living room to investigate [...] (Banville 2002, 109)

Let us mark how the object produces a sound-event to address its existential autonomy, as it were. It cleaves and announces its being-there:

> The vase had shattered, not into fragments in the way that glass should, but into two almost equal halves, vertically, and remarkably cleanly [...] As I may already have remarked, I am not of a superstitious nature – or was not, since this was before Magda's ghost had begun haunting me – and I knew that it was simply that there must have been a fault in the glass, a crack so fine as to be invisible, that had succumbed at last to an infinitesimal shift in air temperature or change of atmospheric pressure. (109–10)

Here we spot the human inclination to explain away what happened to the object. The explanation is laced with affective human meaning:

> I thought, with a pang almost of remorse, of the once-hated thing standing there, day after day, suffering my baleful glances and the hours of Magda's fond but perhaps no less assailing gaze, locked motionless in agonised struggle with the irresistible forces of the world working on it, straining to hold itself together for another hour, another minute, another few seconds, the last few, of wholeness and poise. I am thinking, of course, of Cass Cleave. For that is how it was with her, too, she was another tall, tense, fissile vessel waiting to be cloven in two. (109–10)

These passages describe an object event of deconstruction, showing the movement from the happening to its human explication. When the vase breaks, we feel the tremor in the world of objects as if 'everything is poised for dissolution' (48–49) to quote the narrator of *Eclipse* again. The description of the event makes us aware of an independent life and agency in the world of things. Vander wonders how the vase does not break into shreds but gets divided vertically into two equal halves. He speculates that there must have been something in the composition of the object (a 'fault' or 'crack') leading to its decomposition. He sees this decomposition as an internal possibility of the object in conjunction with its environment ('infinitesimal shift in air temperature or change of atmospheric pressure'). This is no anthropomorphism but a physicist's acknowledgment of object agency. If this is the acknowledgment of bare materiality, the passage, on the other hand, indicates the human projection of personal affect onto the event of the object. Vander internalises the cleaving of the vase as a metaphorical reminder of Magda's death. She was very fond of this object. He makes the vase a symbolic representative of their cracked and about-to-break marital relation. The equally halved vase becomes a subjective token of cloven relationships and divided subjectivities, not to mention mortality and the associated notion of discontinuity or death as a break. Vander associates the 'cleaving' of the vase with Cass Cleave, Alex Cleave's daughter (from *Eclipse*), with whom he has been having an affair and who is about to die. The signifier for the object event of de-construction – 'cleaving' – by subjective association, leads Vander to the human name 'Cleave'. This movement from the word 'cleave' written into the object event, to the name 'Cass Cleave' is another attestation of humans imposing their own meanings on the object. The vase is saturated with human meaning – Magda, Cass Cleave, death, failed relationships, adultery, et cetera. Does it break itself due to this semantic saturation, as a matter of protest?

The narrator goes into the associative human meanings imparted onto the object, but the object in Banville also has a self-dissolving agency. He contrasts these subjective associations with the aforementioned physicist's explication of how the vase breaks. The narrator reflexively characterises his web of subjective (even pathological) associations around the object as 'superstition'. He speculates that the vase cannot tolerate his hateful gaze and Magda's excessive affection for itself. It may appear to be anthropomorphic, but this is the object's self-deconstructing resistance in Banville's world. The object responds to the subjective ascription of meaning by dividing itself. This is its way of resisting subjective projection. It protests against the human inclination to impose meaning on it by breaking itself into two pieces. This breakage tantalises the human imagination to read more meaning into the object event. The object mocks the human mania to interpret everything that happens from their own anthropocentric vantage of understanding.

On the one hand, Banville's objects have a secret life of their own. Their relative autonomy lies in their opacity to human cognition. The objects are alienated from the human gaze that fails to understand them. They often appear spectral because of their ontological enigma vis-à-vis the human interpretation of their being-there in the world. If their spectrality is a result of their opacity and autonomy, it is also a human affect inscribed onto the thing. Banville's fiction does not have these autonomous objects alone; it is full of human beings projecting fellow human beings and emotions onto objects. As Sara Ahmed argues in *The Cultural Politics of Emotion* (2004), '[I]f emotions are shaped by contact with objects, rather than being caused by objects, then emotions are not simply "in" the subject or the object' (6). She observes that emotions are neither in the human subject nor in the thing; they lie somewhere in between. Human beings can nevertheless 'read' an emotion as being 'resident' in the object (6). For Ahmed, 'affective economy' doesn't originate or conclude with the human subject but the subject is 'simply one nodal point' (46) in the network of emotions that involves objects as well.

Without going into the political aspects of Ahmed's argument that has to do with object value and fetishism, let me highlight her displacement of the human subject from the centre of affective economy. In *The Promise of Happiness* (2010), she formulates, '[w]e are moved by things. In being moved, we make things' (25). As we project our own emotions onto objects, we make them in our own image. This act may involve narcissistic violence. The object ceases to be itself and becomes humanised. But as we have seen, the things lying around us may resist this humanised 'making' or re-making. The objects in Banville are imbued with the human emotion of spectrality. Spectre, notwithstanding its nonhuman character, is tamed into becoming a human feeling. This is the paradoxical conundrum of the object. Banvillean objects are both human and posthuman. They are human as indices of the human psyche's complex projections, and they are posthuman in their uncanny autonomy and clandestine texture. They are also posthuman in their ability to alienate human understanding. Their opacity decentres the human subject who fails to build a bridge with them. Objects subject the human to their own order in Banville's world.

To conclude, this chapter concentrated on inanimate objects as a posthumanist theme in philosophy and literature to argue how we can relativise and undercut the anthropocentric worldview by rethinking ontology through objects. The shift of emphasis away from subjectivist ontology does not mean that we get rid of the subject. We need the subject in posthumanism for the political cause of emancipation and change. Instead of advocating a subjectless posthumanism, I have evoked a non-anthropocentric version of the subject that takes the object into consideration, not just as a correlate but as something that may cause the birth of the subject in a particular context. We can surmount the impossibility of thinking for the object by resisting its humanisation, or by showing how the object itself resists the human ascription of meaning. To be peripheral to the object, not to pump it with excessive meaning, to allow the objects to exist independently, and to acknowledge oneself as an object are key ethical considerations in the exercise of posthumanist subjectivity.

We looked into European modernist and contemporary literary iterations to track the ontology of inanimate matter as representational content in the narrative formation of a world. We zoomed in on the intrication of meaning and being in objects. Reducing meaning and dwelling on the being of objects was our posthuman materialist trajectory. We realised how intimately related being and meaning are. Literature may still become posthumanist by marking a departure toward the meaningless being of the object world. With examples from Auster and Pinter, we saw how difficult it is for literary discourse to shed all human meaning and concentrate on the being of the thing. Utilising Tristan Garcia's OOO, we made inroads into the object body as mathematical form in Alain Robbe-Grillet who proposed an object-oriented ontology in literature from the 1960s, before the point was raised in contemporary continental philosophy.

With E. L. Doctorow, we extended Garcia's notion of accumulating objects by focusing on hoarding as a subjective symptom and noticed how being itself could become emotive meaning for the solitary Collyer brothers. It is no coincidence that they die under these hoarded objects that fall over one and crush him to death, while the other dies alone in the packed house. This death is the thing's way of hitting back at subjectivist hoarding and yet the text does not anthropomorphise the death-by-object. In John Banville, we spotted a paradox of hyper-subjective objects that create a dense web of human meanings, symbolisms, pathologies and associations. But these objects also resist human interpretations, hoarded on them. They become opaque to human understanding. They break and dissolve, taking away from the human assurance of an inert and solid object world. The objects decentre the human subject by alienating themselves from their grasps.

In considering the Banvillean ontology of objects, we could make a distinction between being (being as being) and existence (being as appearing). Banville's fiction shows this dialectical process where meaning is attributed to the object and demonstrates how the object withdraws itself from this spell of human meaning and stands aside in its a-signifying materiality. The human cannot grip this a-signifying nature of matter and mattering as process (the breaking of the vase as mattering and flow). In exposing this weakness of the human, the work becomes posthuman. This is posthumanism as process and intersectionality rather than product. There is a new posthuman materiality we extrapolated from modernist and contemporary literary discourses. It is a dialectical materiality that continues to uncouple being from meaning, situate being as meaning, and internally split being into being-for-being and being-for-appearing as existence (the domain of meaning). Though this dialectic may not be synthetic in its contradictions and blind spots, it offers an idea of matter as dialectical process that subsumes the human in its radical becoming. In the next and final chapter, I will extend matter into the larger environmental space and discuss how ecology emerges as a posthumanist field of reflection.

NOTE

1. For more on this topic, see Arindam Chakrabarti's book *Realisms Interlinked*.

REFERENCES

Ahmed, Sara. *The Cultural Politics of Emotion*. Edinburgh UP, 2004.

---. "Orientations Matter". *New Materialisms: Ontology, Agency and Politics*, edited by Diana Coole and Samantha Frost, Duke UP, 2010, pp. 234–57.

---. *The Promise of Happiness*. Duke UP, 2010.

Askin, Ridvan. "Objects". *Cambridge Companion to Literature and The Posthuman*, edited by Bruce Clark and Manuela Rossini, Cambridge UP, 2017, pp. 170–81.

Auster, Paul. *Sunset Park*. Faber, 2010.

Appadurai, Arjun. *Banking on Words: The Failure of Language in the Age of Derivative Finance*. U of Chicago P, 2016.

Bachrach, Jay. "Fictional Objects in Literature and Mental Representations". *The British Journal of Aesthetics*, vol. 31, no. 2, April 1991, pp. 134–39.

Badiou, Alain. *Logics of Worlds*. Translated by Alberto Toscano. Continuum, 2009.

Banville, John. *Eclipse*. Picador, 2000.

---. *Shroud*. Vintage, 2004.

Barthes, Roland. *Critical Essays*. Translated by Richard Howard, Northwestern UP, 1972.

Breton, Andre. *Manifestoes of Surrealism*. Translated by Richard Seaver and Helen R. Lane, U of Michigan P, 1969.

Brown, Bill. *Other Things*. U of Chicago P, 2015.

Bryant, Levi R. *The Democracy of Objects*. Open UP, 2011.

---. "The Time of the Object: Derrida, Luhmann and the Processual Nature of Substances". *The Allure of Things: Process and Object in Contemporary Philosophy*, edited by Roland Faber and Andrew Goffey, Bloomsbury, 2014, pp.71–91.

Chakraborty, Dipesh. *Provincializing Europe*. Princeton UP, 2000.

Chakrabarti, Arindam. *Realisms Interlinked: Objects, Subjects and Other Subjects*. Bloomsbury, 2020.

Crittenden, Charles. *Unreality: The Metaphysics of Fictional Objects*. Cornell UP, 1991.

Doctorow, E. L. *Homer and Langley*. Little, Brown, 2009.

Elkunchwar, Mahesh. *Collected Plays*. Oxford UP, 2009.

Faber, Roland, and Andrew Goffey, editors. *The Allure of Things: Process and Object in Contemporary Philosophy*. Bloomsbury, 2014.

Garcia, Tristan. *Form and Object: A Treatise on Things*. Translated by Mark Allan Ohm and Jon Cogburn, Edinburgh UP, 2014.

Harman, Graham. *Guerrilla Metaphysics: Phenomenology and the Carpentry of Things*. Open Court, 2005.

---. *Tool-Being: Heidegger and the Metaphysics of Objects*. Open Court, 2002.

Howell, Robert. "Fictional Objects: How they Are and How they Aren't". *Poetics*, vol. 8, 1979, pp. 129–77.

Lacan, Jacques. *The Seminar of Jacques Lacan Book IV: The Object Relation*. Translated by A. R. Price, edited by Jacques-Alain Miller, Polity Press, 2020.

Lahiri, Jhumpa. *Whereabouts*. Bloomsbury, 2021.

Larson, Gerald James. *Classical Samkhya: An Interpretation of its History and Meaning*. Motilal Banarsidass, 1969.

Miller, Jacques-Alain. "Another Lacan". Translated by Ralph Chipman, *The Symptom 10*, 21 April 2016, https://www.lacan.com/symptom10a/another-lacan.html. Accessed 12 November 2021.

Nail, Thomas. *Theory of the Object*. Edinburgh UP, 2021.

Pinter, Harold. *Plays 4*. Faber, 1993.

Robbe-Grillet, Alain. *For a New Novel: Essays on Fiction*. Translated by Richard Howard, Grove Press, 1965.

---. *Snapshots*. Translated by Bruce Morrissette, Northwestern UP, 1986.

Zupančič, Alenka. *What is Sex?*. MIT P, 2017.

Chapter Five

Posthuman Ecologies

HOW DO WE THINK ABOUT THE ENVIRONMENT IN A POSTHUMAN WAY?

This final chapter will discuss ecology in relation to posthumanism and show how the theory and practice of environmentalism can open up critical directions against species-humanism. As Cary Wolfe reminds us in his 2020 book on ecopoetics, it is not enough to decentre the human; we also need to show how this decentring is performed. According to him, a large part of contemporary environmental discourse is not posthumanist. Instead, it falls back upon what Wolfe calls 'humanist posthumanism' that reduces ecological thought to a discussion on 'questions of *use*, management, distribution of goods, and extension of rights with the discourse of "sustainability" as perhaps the most familiar example' (xix). If sustainability is a human-centric way of talking about environment, what could be the horizons of posthumanist ecological thought? Posthumanism would see the human subject as an embedded ecological phenomenon. As we have seen with technology and the machine, the nonhuman and the object, there is nothing exclusively human about the 'human' subject. What we call 'human' is intrinsically entangled with the nonhuman that includes, among other things, ecology. In contemporary understandings of cognition, the human being is not the sole cogniser. Ecology cognises on its own. The discourse of embedded cognition theorises the human mind as nothing but an 'environmental vehicle' (Menary 21). Neither is the human subject completely human, nor is ecology a passive envelope for the human. As we shall see, the experience of the world (or 'worlding' as a process) that ecology opens up is posthuman. We will start by working our way through the posthuman implications of ecological thought and develop the notion of an ecological unconscious that goes beyond the human. We will then run this idea through two novels to highlight the relation between the psychic and the environmental in a way that would return us to posthuman subjectivity.

Before we come to the posthuman, let us ask how ecology becomes political. The section on Dipesh Chakrabarty's work on the Anthropocene later in this chapter will give us a response, as will the two novels that interweave the ecological with the political by bringing in statecraft and capitalism. But for an initial figuration of the eco-political, we may turn to John Bellamy Foster who, in *Marx's Ecology* (2000), charts the relation between nature and political materialism and returns to ecological materialism in *The Return of Nature* (2020). We cannot go into details here but Foster's reconstruction of Marx's 'naturalism' is in sync with humanism. He quotes Marx: 'fully developed naturalism, equals humanism, and as fully developed humanism, equals naturalism' (qtd. in Foster 2000, 79). Though Foster makes ecology inclusive beyond the human, there is no radical decentring of the human in this socialist ecology that remains primarily focused on the human relation with the environment. As another eco-Marxist thinker Kohei Saito argues, 'capitalism is fundamentally characterized by alienation of nature and a distorted relationship between humans and nature. Accordingly, he envisions the emancipatory idea of "humanism=naturalism" as a project of re-establishing the unity between humanity and nature against capitalist alienation' (Saito 2017, 14).

The equation of humanism with naturalism prevents this ecology from becoming posthuman. For example, Saito in his more recent book, *Marx in the Anthropocene*, (2022) goes on to agree with Kate Soper's denunciation of posthumanism on grounds that it is itself anthropocentric (124). More than the anthropocentric nature of posthumanism, Saito's critique of it is centred on the point that 'only humans can consciously act to repair the [metabolic] rift' (124). The energy of eco-Marxists is invested in addressing the 'metabolic rift'[1] that marks the human relation with nature, wherein the human's capitalist productivity alienates nature. Though not posthumanist, what eco-Marxist theory facilitates is a socio-political understanding of ecology which is important for our purposes. The idea of a dialectical ecology based on Engels that engages with labour in human evolution informs Foster's *The Return of Nature*: '[e]cology transcends the boundaries between society and extra-human nature. Looked at from this standpoint, human social systems are both inescapably part of the natural world' (177–78). Though this is a human-centric understanding of ecology, it helps us think through the political relations in the ecological domain. As Saito reflects, ecology must deal with 'the fundamental nature of a society of generalized commodity production' and 'the problem of the "separation" of humans from the earth' (258). If ecology (otherwise considered a politically neutral science) is political, how do we see the posthuman political subject there? If the ecological space is an object, we have to rethink the posthuman subject as an object-oriented, relational entity, inhabiting the said space.

Timothy Morton: From 'Hyperobject' to 'Ecology without Nature'

To continue with political ecology and its posthuman possibilities, and picking up from the last chapter's discussion on objects, Timothy Morton terms global warming a 'hyperobject' that 'cannot be directly seen, but it can be thought and computed' (Morton 2013, 3). 'Hyperobjects' are things, 'massively distributed in time and space relative to humans' (1). We see here the link between the environment as a concept and the idea of posthumanism. In considering the problem of global warming, we must approach a deep macro-time of massive proportions that goes beyond any human scale. The ecological world cannot be measured by human degree. Timothy Morton is aware of the posthumanist implications of this argument. He evokes it at the end of *Hyperobjects* (2013):

> Nonhuman beings are responsible for the next moment of human history and thinking. It is not simply that humans became aware of nonhumans, or that they decided to ennoble some of them by granting them a higher status—or cut themselves down by taking away the status of the human.

> These so-called posthuman games are *nowhere near posthuman enough* to cope with the time of hyperobjects. (201; emphasis original)

Morton critiques the posthuman as a patronising human appellation. It echoes Wolfe's aforementioned posthuman humanism, Saito's critique, and Colebrook's position about a certain kind of posthumanism as ultrahumanism that we will soon encounter. As Morton suggests, it is not for us humans to usher in a posthuman era of hyperobjects. The hyperobjects were already there: '[t]hey contacted us' (201) and not vice versa. This is a simple but important critique. As I have mentioned in the first chapter, the Anthropocene signifies that humans are geological agents, but by no means does it cement a discourse of human exceptionalism. Humans are responsible for the climate crisis and we need to exit species-humanism to remedy the situation. To quote Morton, 'we are no longer able to think history as exclusively human, for the very reason that we are in the Anthropocene' (5). Let us go deeper into Morton's work beyond the identification of global warming as hyperobject.

For Morton, 'ecological awareness' always-already contains a critique of anthropocentrism: 'It means that humans are not totally in charge of assigning significance and value to events that can be statistically measured' (16). In his argument, the end of the world is not forthcoming but it has already happened. With James Watt's 1784 discovery of the steam engine, the history of carbon deposition in the Earth's crust started. For Morton, that was when the world died because it marked 'the inception of humanity as a geophysical force on a planetary scale' (7). Discussing the thirty-thousand-year-old paintings in France's Chauvet cave, he calls these gigantic timescales, 'the *horrifying*, the *terrifying* and the *petrifying*' (59; emphases original). He speculates how '7 percent of global warming effects will still be occurring one hundred thousand years from now as igneous rocks slowly absorb the last of the greenhouse gases' (59), leading to the extinction of humanity.

To consider hyperobjects, we must situate space and time as autonomous entities and go beyond the human–world correlation. We need to think of not just the inter-subjective but also the inter-objective that floats between one object and another. The working of the human mind is a mirror of hyperobjects and not vice versa: 'an account of hyperobjects was among other things an account of the fabric of the human mind. My thinking is thus a mental translation of the hyperobject—of climate, biosphere, evolution—not just figuratively, but literally' (85). The human mind is environmentally embedded. It has no agential primacy. This point initiates an environmentalist critique of anthropocentrism and marks a posthuman entangled subject. This posthuman subject is a mental translation of ecology.

Hyperobjects are not relational entities *qua* the human. They have their own independent histories. Morton calls it the *'time of hyperobjects'* (88; emphasis original). His example is La Niña, a Pacific weather system: 'they [raindrops in California] record how the Japanese tsunami scooped up some of La Niña and dumped it on trees and hills and other objects in the object called the United States. La Niña itself is the footprint of a hyperobject called *global warming*' (88; emphasis original). In Morton's view, the world is a construct composed of biosphere, climate, evolution, capitalism and so on. He treats it like a hyperobject. While the world as such evaporates in global warming, causing complex shifts in the weather, human beings realise that they never had a 'world' (101). As he reflects, 'Global warming is a big problem, because along with melting glaciers it has melted our ideas of *world* and *worlding*' (103; emphases original).

Morton considers the apocalyptic narratives that keep pushing the end into the future, as part of the problem of climate crisis. Ethically speaking, it is better to declare that the world has already ended. In this endnote to the world, Morton depicts the image of the human as 'a shadow of the conversion of matter to energy' (195). His example is a picture of the human atomic shadow in Hiroshima. All that is left of the human is a spooky shadow. This is how he paints the human in an endangered ecology of global warming.

The cognitive paradox is that as a hyperobject, global warming is 'nonlocal'. The notion of the local is just a 'false immediacy' (48). The 'nonlocal' is more real than the local. We can both see and not see global warming. To use Morton's example, when we see the sun, shining on the solar panels on the roof, we are looking at global warming and yet we cannot see it directly (38). Morton goes further into a study of 'geotrauma' (53) as an ecological incarnation of anxiety. Anthropogenic climate change causes trauma to the planet and stopping this becomes part of the posthuman ethic of action. Morton engages with art, music and literature that comes in the wake of climate crisis as attempts to tune into the reality of worldlessness. He goes through the Romantic literary construction of nature to argue for an ecology without nature. This ecology is about a massively layered co-existence: 'the notion of coexistence— that is after all what ecology profoundly means. We coexist with human lifeforms, nonhuman lifeforms, and non-lifeforms, on the insides of a series of gigantic entities with whom we also coexist: the ecosystem, biosphere, climate, planet, Solar System' (127–28). Morton ends *Hyperobjects* with a recasting of the human as a category of ecological co-existence when he examines the ways in which the human beings attune themselves to the hyperobject. Ecological co-existence is the defining dimension of posthuman subjectivity.

In *The Ecological Thought*, (2010), a prequel to *Ecology without Nature* (2009), Morton clarifies that ecological thought is not only about climate crisis but also about grief, depression, anxiety, politics, society, sexuality, subjectivity, ideology, critique, and so on. In his Levinasian conviction, being is always *being-with* and ecology revolves around this fundamental co-existence. In *The Ecological Thought*, Morton works with ideas like 'mesh' (interconnectedness) and 'strange strangers' (encounter with the Other species) as aspects of ecological thinking and develops his theses on ecological scale, ecological art, and ecological politics. He not only advocates ecology without nature but also speaks for an ecology without environmentalism. For Morton, environmentalism itself is reduced to a capitalist policy ideology and true ecological thinking must critique this formation. His navigation through John Milton's *Paradise Lost* bespeaks the need to visualise the planet on a cosmic scale as a prerequisite for ecological thought. Humans are embedded in galactic space. They are dethroned from any optics of authority. The planetarity of Milton is carefully contrasted with Google Earth, Google Map and YouTube that create digital fantasies of complete visibility (Morton 2010, 25). He gives examples of Indigenous communities in America and uses the Tibetan imagination of space to take the argument outside Western societies. Ecology cannot be limited to the earth but has to consider the space of the sky, the cosmic and the galactic.

As Morton argues, there is no world anymore because there is no background or foreground, but only an interconnected 'mesh' with infinite differences. The loss of the world may produce a serious psychological setback for the modern ecological subject. Worldlessness could even induce madness. We will come back to this point later and consider an ecological idea of the unconscious through Lacanian psychoanalysis. The interconnectedness of everything is not just comforting but it can also be disconcerting. It can well become a disturbing mesh that produces a paranoia of endless meanings. Working through Romantic poetry (Wordsworth and Coleridge), Morton comes up with instances of ecological thought that are not only about joy and harmony but also about fissure and disturbance. This thinking involves an ethic of co-existing with the Other species, admitting their opacity and strangeness. Morton brings the Freudian discourse of the uncanny into conversation with ecology and dwells on the psychic ramifications of our entangled ecological crisis. He reads Freud's famous metaphor of being lost in the forest in a literal sense where the idea of uncanniness meets the ecology of the forest. Morton holds, 'The more ecological awareness we have, the more we experience the uncanny [...] This psychological dimension includes weird phenomena that warp our psychic space' (54). As he unfurls the affective landscape of ecology in processes of grief, loss, mourning and melancholia, Morton critiques a clichéd posthumanism that wants to get rid of humanness, whereas ecological thinking must preserve the subject as a category and make humanism more humane than what it is (113). For the politics of emancipation, we need the ecological subject: 'Thinking that personhood is the enemy of ecology is a big mistake' (120). We want a human subject but without hierarchical humanism.

In *Ecology without Nature*, Morton sees the narrative of nature as an impediment to true ecological thinking. By deconstructing the Romantic literature of nature writing, he formulates an 'ecocritique' to rethink environmental art. He goes into the linguistic and stylistic aspects of environmental literature to problematise the position of nature: 'Whether we think of nature as an environment, or as other beings (animals, plants, and so on), it keeps collapsing either into subjectivity or into objectivity. It is very hard, perhaps impossible, to keep nature just where it appears—somewhere in between' (Morton 2009, 41)

Morton argues that nature writing shows nature as a fantasy of the writer's own self. Following Lacan, he calls it a 'sinthomatic' ('sinthome' as a symptom that binds the psyche) fantasy. This means nature has never been there. It is a consumerist fantasy that generates enjoyment for both the writer and the readers. It holds human psyches together. Morton evokes Hegel's idea of the beautiful soul as a romantic, nature-loving personage and utilises it against the grain to go beyond the discourse of nature and resituate the ecological subject.

The notion of ecology without nature results from a de-romanticisation of ecology where it is made to lose its aura of transcendence. To have ecology without nature is to nullify the transcendental status of nature. Morton agrees with Latour on this point (168). Nature creates a false unity in ecology whereas ecology without nature is a project in division, disunity and otherness as diverse difference: 'If ecology without nature has taught us anything, it is that there is a need to acknowledge irreducible otherness, whether in poetics, ethics, or politics' (151). The crucial point for us is Morton's insistence on preserving the subject in ecology. Nature works like an 'automation' that makes the subject redundant: 'The ultimate fantasy of ambience is that we could actually achieve ecology without a subject. Ecological awareness would just happen to us, as immersively and convincingly as a shower of rain' (181). Ecology without nature is ecology with a subject who makes critical choices instead of being swayed by the chimera of nature. Ecology divides the subject and creates multiple cracks in it at the level of desire, anxiety, melancholia, grief, and so on. However, as Morton suggests, this is a Lacanian subject in its divided form (198). We will come back to this division in situating posthuman subjectivity in ecology.

From Colebrook to Chakraborty: The Political Ethics of Posthuman Ecologies

To move to other thinkers of critical climate change who invoke the posthuman, Claire Colebrook reminds us that the study of climate is an interdisciplinary combination of hard sciences (climate science, earth sciences) and humanities that forms a 'human science' (Colebrook 46). It is a trans/post-disciplinary formation that considers ideas like sustainability and species extinction, co-belonging of the human and nonhuman, anthropogenic climate change, deep ecology and James Lovelock's Gaia hypothesis (the earth as a living being), among others. Colebrook reflects on the inflection of globalism as a worldview on ecology. Globalisation has created an image of the planet that has put social justice under pressure by making equality increasingly unsustainable. The unequal division of environmental resources raises a point. The globalist unsustainability of equality is a wicked problem, climate justice and any egalitarian discourse of posthumanism must deal with. Rob Nixon calls climate injustice, a form of 'slow violence': 'a violence that occurs gradually and out of sight, a violence of delayed destruction that is dispersed across time and space, an attritional violence that is typically not viewed as violence at all' (Nixon 2). Nixon contends that environmentalism is not the same for the rich and the poor as the balance between the global north and the global south is perilously skewed: 'The environmentalism of the poor is frequently catalyzed by resource imperialism inflicted on the global South to maintain the unsustainable consumer appetites of rich-country citizens and, increasingly, of the urban middle classes in the global South itself' (22).

To come back to Colebrook, in *Essays on Extinction* (2014), she argues that posthumanism in its dominant iteration is a form of 'ultrahumanism': 'It is an ultrahumanism precisely because once man is abandoned as a distinct system or inflection he returns to characterize nature or life in general, just as the death of God left an implicit and widespread theologism that no longer had a distinct or explicit logic' (163). In a human-less world, everything else gets imbued with a human essence. This is what converts a particular variety of posthumanism into ultrahumanism. The context of her discussion is climate change which makes this argument relevant for our purposes. The Gaia hypothesis, that sees the planet as a life-form, could be taken as an example of this posthumanist ultrahumanism. Human solidarity facing climate change is welcome as long as this solidarity does not fuel a unification and solidification of the human species: 'posthuman has been a return of the human into one single life with one single inclination, that of ongoing self-maintenance' (177). Colebrook suggests that the 'posthuman celebrations of a single ecology would not be able to face a condition of climate change *in general*' (180; emphasis original). She agrees with Morton that there is no climate in the strict sense of the term. For her, this is what climate change teaches us: 'if the experience of climate change were to be experienced it would disclose that there is no climate, biosphere or environment. There is not 'a' world, existing in the manner of an organism, that maintains and sustains itself' (58).

If climate is that which environs us, the humans and the environment are themselves a product of humanist thought. Following Michel Serres, Colebrook declares that humanity is and must be 'parasitical'. It contaminates and gets contaminated by what surrounds it: 'To be a body is to be a consuming body, to be in a relation of destructive consumption with what is effected as other, as resource, through consumption. Climate change would be the condition of human organicism in general' (178). Anthropogenic pollution is a type of overeating and indigestion (echoing Foster and Saito's focus on the metabolic rift in Marx and capital as metabolism). But, 'pollution' may have a positive meaning as it takes us away from a single climate and leads to multiple ecologies, layered inside and outside one another. There is no one ecology but ecologies in the plural that must ethically interact, infuse and contaminate each other. Colebrook links 'climate' with 'inclination' and 'clinamen' (meaning 'swerve' in pre-Socratic atomic philosophy by which one atom encounters another to create the world) where the human and the nonhuman encounter each other by swerving (179).

Dipesh Chakrabarty is another thinker, largely responsible for the discussion of the Anthropocene in humanities. In *The Climate of History in a Planetary Age* (2021), he suggests that posthumanism cannot address the political by itself:

> Any theory of politics adequate to the planetary crisis humans face today would have to begin from the same old premise of securing human life but now ground itself in a new philosophical anthropology, that is, in a new understanding of the changing place of humans in the web of life and in the connected but different histories of the globe and the planet.
>
> (91)

Posthumanism needs to be reimagined in a political way. Throughout this book, I have insisted on the importance of politicising posthumanism both as a philosophy and as a heuristic framework, especially in the context of India and the global South. If we could go beyond the populist understanding of the posthuman as transhumanism, it opens up a politics and an ethic of emancipation. As we have seen, this politics lies in the critique of the transhuman and the humanities, not to mention the deconstruction of the human–nonhuman hierarchy. In this chapter, we are concerned with the eco-political dimensions of posthumanism.

We will come back to Chakrabarty's point about posthumanism failing to address the political, but before that, let me give an example of the eco-political intersection from recent public memory. In 2021, when the young Swedish climate activist Greta Thunberg tweeted in solidarity with the farmers' protest in India against the current government's new agricultural laws, it connected the ecological with the political though the farmers' protest did not have an express environmental dimension. Thunberg's solidarity tweet was considered a breach of India's political autonomy by pro-government players including numerous celebrities. The Indian climate activist Disha Ravi, connected with Thunberg, was arrested on charges of fomenting unrest on 13 February 2021 and was released later. State crackdowns on environmental activists is not a new phenomenon and not limited to India. The interesting point about this case is that ecology is, at best, a remote background to the farmers' protest. What constitutes its foreground is the Capitalocene – the farmers gathering against the corporate capitalist regime. And yet, an international solidarity network develops across ecological and political issues within the larger umbrella of resistance. The political and the ecological are thus intertwined even when they are apparently not. A detailed analysis of the farm laws is beyond our scope or purpose. But, apart from the eco-political intermeshing, the other lesson we draw from this example is the importance of the political subject. Thunberg and Ravi are proper names of non-anthropocentric human subjects of political action. These are human subjectivities formed by eco-political events. They are not anthropocentric.

To continue with Chakrabarty, in his aforementioned book he talks about the need to bring the postcolonial in contact with the posthuman. He agrees with Latour's idea of incomplete modernity and the destruction of the nature–culture divide, but points to Latour's non-engagement with anti-colonial thinking on modernity and its tribulations. Where are figures like Gandhi, Fanon and Nehru in Latour's story? (Chakrabarty 105). This is Chakrabarty's complaint. In response, he engages with Nehru's texts to discuss his complex negotiation with postcolonial nationhood and a fossil-fuel driven idea of modernisation (Chakrabarty 106–13). This rich reading shows Nehru's romanticising of nature, the deep spiritual aspects of positing modernisation as a secular religion, and yet his consistent wish to utilise the resources of the Himalayas to build the postcolonial Indian nation. From his discussion of Nehru, Chakrabarty concludes that we have to add to posthumanism and Capitalocene, the postcolonial narrative, to address the eco-political:

> While it could be argued that it is important to inaugurate a regime of politics that took the nonhuman seriously irrespective of whether or not humans could act as spokespersons for the nonhuman, the conversation will not proceed very far without negotiating the desire to be modern that anticolonial ideologies of the twentieth century expressed and that came to shape postcolonial and post-imperial formations of politics […]. (113)

Chakrabarty highlights the postcolonial tryst with modernisation that drives the history of anthropogenic climate change in certain parts of the world.

Chakrabarty's idea of the political, he clarifies, is informed by Hannah Arendt's notion of politics as a relation among human beings and not something intrinsically human (9). He adds a rejoinder from

Carl Schmitt who considers politics to be a 'pluriverse', beyond 'a single, rational consensus' (13). There is a politics in picking apart the globe from the planet in Chakrabarty, and not making them interchangeable entities as Schmitt does. Chakrabarty contends that the globe of globalisation is not the globe of global warming, and we need to differentiate between the global and the planetary. The globe is a human construction but the planet decentres the human. However, as he shows in the third chapter of *The Climate of History in a Planetary Age*, the planet too is a humanist category. The planet is neither the globe nor the world. It is not the same as the earth either, to invoke the Heideggerian categories, Chakrabarty uses. The planet emerges from the project of globalisation, not as its successful product but as a by-product of its failure (69). The planet does not talk to the human. It is indifferent to humanity. For Chakrabarty, the globe privileges the human-centric term 'sustainability' while the pivot of the planetary discourse is 'habitability', a term that works for all life in its complex multicellular forms. The humanist project aims to bring the planet progressively into the fold of the globe, but the planet resists with its alterity. Chakrabarty calls for a planetary politics because '[t]he institutions humans have used so far to secure human life have reached a point of expansion and development whereby that very fundamental premise of human politics—securing human life—is undermined' (91). This politics must go beyond the human as the security of the human species is overshadowed by their geophysical agency: 'Late capitalism, in this sense, destroys the human-political project the world over. In such circumstances, there is surely the danger, as Latour points out, of a rebarbarization of the world, a prospect that many authoritarian leaders and parties today implicitly or explicitly embody and hold out' (91). Chakrabarty sees a covert link here between the current right-wing authoritarianism across the world and the late-capitalist destruction of humanist politics. What we need is a posthuman understanding of the political.

Chakrabarty's reading of the Indian Dalit student, Rohit Vemula's 2016 suicide note exposes a gap in the understanding of posthuman politics. He argues that there is no political thought that can connect the two strands of the planetary and the political in Vemula's last letter. The poetical displaces the political: 'How do we bring both versions of the human—in Vemula's terms, "every human being treated as a mind" and the same person as "star dust"—together to constitute a new kind of political thought?' (130). For Chakrabarty, this is a poetic vision unsupported by a political thought. I will counter-argue that this poetic vision is, in itself, a species of political thinking. Chakrabarty surprisingly does not consider how the poetic has always been an important version of the political, be it old traditions of political poetry or poetic lyricism as a strategy in political speech. When the Dalit body seeks transcendence from social indignities and wants to be acknowledged as a mind by seeing itself as a planetary entity made of stardust, the planetary has already become political. Irrespective of whether it is supported by existing political theory, this transcendental romanticism, informed by Vemula's admiration for Carl Sagan's astrophysics, is deeply political.

Chakrabarty's deconstruction of Kant's idea of the animal and the moral lives of the human, works toward bringing back the animal in the human. Unlike what Kant thinks, the animal life of the human subject is not a given, 'to be provided by the planet' (146) or the biosphere. We need to go back to the human as an 'animal species' before we can approach the 'moral species' in the human. Chakrabarty reflects that human responsibility has now shifted to the ecological. Animal and moral lives are ecologically entangled. He signals a shift from the geological time of the Anthropocene to the political time of world history that must accommodate planetary history. He proposes a scale-shifting between the deep time of centuries and the everyday of the political. To reiterate the fundamental point, all this calls for a posthuman politics that takes into its scheme, the asymmetry of the human–planet relation: 'It is as if the Earth system, the planet, were saying to the conscious part of its constituents, humans—to borrow again from Lacan's language— "you never look at me from the place from which I see you."' (177). The planet maintains its alterity by not allowing the human to see it from where it sees them. This asymmetry is integral to posthuman subjectivity.

Toward an Ecological Unconscious in Lacan

Let me use Chakrabarty's tacit reference to Lacan and take it toward an ecological notion of the unconscious. I have previously commented on the posthuman possibilities of psychoanalysis. It has been an important source for posthumanists as well. As we saw in Chapter 3, the unconscious is ethological. The point now is to see the unconscious subject as an ecological entity where the ecological complements and extends its ethological dimension. If the Lacanian unconscious is inter-subjective in its approach to the Other, this Other is not only the species Other but also the climatic Other. The endangered ecology of our times presents one of the strongest incarnations of this Other function, churning out a series of unconscious affects and signifiers such as, anxiety, survival, resilience, and so on. In Lacan's final teachings, when we have a thesis of the Real unconscious as materiality, it goes beyond his earlier definition of the linguistic unconscious and encompasses the ecological. As he says in *The Triumph of Religion* (2013), 'the physical reality' is 'totally inhuman' (read nonhuman) (Lacan 36) and again: 'The real is the difference between what works and what doesn't work. What works is the world. The real is what doesn't work' (61). The Real does not form the world of ecology. It falls out and does not make it to the ecological world-building. What is excluded from 'worlding' finds its way into the unconscious subject. This waste of the world is at stake in what we would call the ecological unconscious. This is the anxious, divided subject of the Anthropocene that fails to form a complete world. The ecological unconscious presents posthuman subjectivity as a knot, caught up in the rejects of a human-centric figuration of ecology.

As Jacques-Alain Miller, the foremost Lacanian analyst, argues in his 2012 talk, 'A Real for the 21st Century', once upon a time, nature was the name of the Real when there was no disorder in the Real. With capitalist modernity reaching unprecedented heights in the twenty-first century, there is a breech between nature and the Real. It exposes a great disorder in the contemporary Real. Just as later-Lacan theorises the lawlessness of the Real, for Miller it shows a 'complete rupture between nature and real' (Miller 2012). Nature is no more the guarantee for the Symbolic order of language. It is no more a stable Other for the subject to fall back on. Miller observes that capitalism and science have made nature vanish. If we replace the word 'nature' with 'ecology' (unlike Morton, Miller uses them interchangeably), we have a gesture toward the Real ecological unconscious.

Another famous Lacanian, Colette Soler, in her 2013–2014 Paris lectures focuses on the 'inhuman' (read nonhuman) aspect of the Real unconscious by putting the term 'Humanisation?' with a question mark in her title. To quote Soler, the human animal is 'denatured by the effects of the unconscious on the real' (10). As she suggests, in later-Lacan when the paternal function of the Oedipus is abandoned, there is nothing left to 'humanize' the unconscious (31). It follows that the Real unconscious is nonhuman. In Miller we see how the human–nature relation is ruptured. In Soler we notice another kind of alienation of the human from nature or 'naturing'. Both these cuts happen through the Real unconscious. This cut founds the ecological unconscious in Lacan.

Lacan does not explicitly talk about climate change for historical reasons. The global climate discourse started mostly after his death in 1981. The ecological unconscious I am talking about is a critical construction derived from Lacan. I am mobilising Lacanian psychoanalysis for envisaging a posthuman ecology. In Lacan's late teachings, language is not simply the Symbolic order that works in tandem with the Imaginary and creates meaning. The Real is, strictly speaking, without meaning. In this final phase of his teaching, Lacan treats language in its material, syntactical, and sonic level as it borders on the meaninglessness of the Real. Language is an event of the body. It is something that makes the body resonate in its dissonance with ecology. What dominates in the Real of language is *jouissance* or a tormenting enjoyment that combines pleasure with pain. In *Seminar XVII*, Lacan hints at an ecological dimension of this signifying apparatus of *jouissance*: 'When the signifier is introduced as an apparatus of *jouissance*, we should thus not be surprised to see something related to entropy appear, since entropy is defined precisely once one has started to lay this apparatus of signifiers over the physical world' (Lacan 2017, 49; emphasis original).

Jouissance in its wasteful surplus form is entropic, and the discourse of entropy has a climatic aspect as the *jouissance* of the signifier spreads across the ecological system or the so-called physical world. The body of the signifier that carries *jouissance* spreads itself across the environment as an entropic surplus. This body has a dissonant relation with its ecological surrounds. It is indicative of anthropogenic climate change where the earth's entropy shifts rapidly due to global warming.[2] Lacan implies that there is a link between the earth's entropy and the entropy of the Real when the signifier becomes an apparatus of *jouissance*, spread out like a gigantic body of polluted air across the atmosphere. This gives the unconscious a specific ecological property that appeals to the reality of climate change.

In *Lacan and Environment*, (2021), we have a diverse set of approaches to the ecological theme in Lacanian psychoanalysis. Editors Clint Burnham and Paul Kingsbury start with a startling question about whether to see the environment as mother or child (1). They read climate-crisis denials and climate action via psychoanalytic symptomatology: 'How we think about the environment, about nature, in the age of climate crisis and the Anthropocene, has psychoanalytic resonances: we take an unconscious enjoyment in not acting, or we wonder why others (climate deniers, corporations, and governments) do not listen to science, do not act' (Burnham and Kingsbury 3). As they argue, the Real of environment concerns a topology of nature where the inside is outside and vice versa. Nature is both inside and outside. Though the book does not explicitly articulate an ecological unconscious, the idea is supported by the reading of ecological trash that recurs in the volume (for example see 5, 189). The growing industrial waste in an ecology of global pollution meets the unconscious as another kind of waste: the waste of the signifier in the Real. While Cindy Zeiher talks about environmental politics by locating it as an object-cause of desire, Alois Sieben studies anxiety as an ecological object of desire. Sasha J. Langford conceptualises a non-linear and recursive 'psychotopology' of climate change, as opposed to the line chart that is conventionally used to visualise the phenomenon.

Moving out of Lacan, but staying within psychoanalysis and psychotherapy in general, Theodore Roszak theorises 'ecopsychology' grounding it on an ecological ego. Ecopsychology aims at addressing the human subject's alienation from ecology. For Roszak in *The Voice of the Earth* (1993), if individual insanity has to do with family problems, the sickness of a society as a whole is related to the human inclination to destroy its own habitat. He calls this Freud's search for a 'transcultural standard of sanity' that attempts to 'integrate the mental and the physical' within an 'ecological framework' (Roszak 69). Here we have an echo of Morton's idea about the uncanny affect of climate change. The ecological endangerment is not just maddening for the human but also a product of human death-drive, as Roszak indicates. For his idea of the ecological unconscious, he takes the Jungian path of the collective unconscious, different from our Lacanian analysis above. The unconscious of archetypes that stores the pre-human animality of the human as well as a history of the very evolution of the human species has an ecological status. Using this to tie the mind with the cosmos, Roszak reflects, 'Mind, far from being a belated and aberrant development in a universe of dead matter, *connects* with that universe as the latest emergent stage on its unfolding frontier' (303; emphasis original). Endorsing the Gaia hypothesis, Roszak links it with the id and conceptualises an ecology that listens to the repressed voice of the earth. The ecological unconscious assumes a mystical character in his work. According to Roszak, the direction of cure is to un-repress the ecological unconscious (320). It seeks to develop a child-like enjoyment of ecology and create an ecological ego.

Having said that, we need to acknowledge 'ego' itself as a problem. Ranjan Ghosh uses the term 'anthropogenic ego' to mark this humanist idea in *The Plastic Turn* (2022). We need to 'challenge the ego's authority and dominance' over 'nature' (R. Ghosh 181). Ego is the phallic hubris of species-humanism. We don't want it. What we want instead is a humbler notion of the posthuman subject. Unlike the unitary ego, we need a divided subject. Ghosh echoes Morton in identifying the uncanny as the central affect of this new subject and the need to 'displace' the 'anthropogenic ego' that alienates the human from other species and the earth (181). What he calls 'plastic ego' is an attempt to think the subject vis-à-vis the nonhuman world. For Ghosh, the 'plastic ego' is 'embedded' in the 'nonhuman environment' and this environmental embeddedness 'contributes to its individuation' (183). For him, this new ego (I would rather use the term 'subject') is 'interrupted' by the nonhuman but it 'negotiates' this interruption to take the nonhuman on board. While the 'plastic ego' approximates our idea of the posthuman subject, I would go one step further to argue that the ecological unconscious is not interrupted by the nonhuman but co-constituted by it. The nonhuman is not a negotiated interruption for the posthuman subject but an element integral to its ontology.

Unlike Roszak, the Lacanian ecological unconscious is not collective but singular. Each subject may feel endangered by global warming but in Lacanian terms, each have their singular unconscious that acts upon the same problem differently. The Lacanian ecological unconscious is immanent and not transcendental. It is a material, embodied unconscious that connects with the world as ecology but fails to make a world out of the endangered ecological system of entropy. It derives a strange *jouissance* from the ecological Real of dissonance and creates a waste subject. We can connect this ecological *jouissance* with the disturbing mode of enjoyment Dipesh Chakrabarty observes in Theo, a child in his neighbourhood who walks around an earth-moving machine and plays with, what Chakrabarty insightfully calls, 'Anthropocene toys'. Theo moves sand in a sandpit with the help of a miniature version of the same machine. This profound psychoanalytic moment (though Chakrabarty does not engage with psychoanalysis) of observing a child's play leads to the telling comment: 'our capacity to act as a geophysical force is connected to many modern forms of enjoyment' (Chakrabarty 11).[3] This *jouissance* not only concerns the child's unproblematic joy in the company of the Anthropocene toy but also includes the onlooker's painful realisation after watching the game. It is a classic instance of inter-subjective *jouissance* that divides pleasure from pain as it combines them across the subject and the Other. This is a moment of the ecological unconscious.

Dona M. Orange, a New York-based psychoanalyst and philosopher, floats the idea of the 'environmental unconscious' and insists on an ethic of confronting climate change in the clinic to counter the logic of denial. In *Climate Crisis, Psychoanalysis and Radical Ethics* (2016), she critiques the psychoanalytic institutions' silence on the issue and urges the community to wake up to the environmental reality that has a strong purchase on the clinic and the symptoms offered by our era. More than climate denial, Orange talks about a 'double-mindedness' where we live in two realities. At one level, we are aware of climate emergency but at another, we wash our hands off it by saying that it is too big a problem to solve (Orange 63). She studies the possible sources for the subjective evasion of climate crisis in ideas of shame, fear of responsibility, fear of vulnerability, and so on. Orange advocates a clinical ethic where the practice of analysis would help generate a deep sense of ecological entanglement, active concern, and responsibility. From a dodgy double-mindedness, she insists on moving to ecological single-mindedness. She also offers some practical solutions like online analysis to reduce carbon footprints owing to excessive air travel to meet the analyst (a common enough practice especially in the 'first world').

To return to Lacan, when he coins the term 'alethosphere' (161) in the aforementioned *Seminar XVII* from 1969–70, by combining the Heideggerian word for truth or 'aletheia' (un-concealment) with the word 'atmosphere', he gestures toward what I am constructing as the Lacanian ecological unconscious. The truth that remains hidden is to be unravelled from the atmosphere. If we substitute 'atmosphere' with 'ecology', we get a discourse of ecological unconscious truth. Lacan talks about the microphones used by the astronauts going toward the moon. They stay within the alethosphere by being hooked onto the field of voice as an object-of-desire. The voice as an embodied, unconscious drive-object interacts with the environment that the rocket is cutting through. Lacan's example solidifies the ecological aspect of the inter-subjective unconscious. The alethosphere is neither nature nor culture. It is at the cusp of both. It breaks down the nature-culture binary. When the rocket cuts through planetary space, the astronauts are neither in nature nor in culture, but at their border. The microphone that embodies their voice is a trace of technological culture. So is the machine they are placed in. And yet, their bodies are suspended in space that manifests the Otherness of the planet. The traces, left by the rocket as it furrows through the atmosphere, form a writing in the air – an act of calligraphy on the cosmic canvas. It is an inscription of unconscious truth in the interstices of nature and culture.

Soon after this seminar, in a 1971 text on literature titled 'Lituraterre' when Lacan discusses the writing of the Real unconscious as a paradigm of inscription, it is notable that the inscription in question is geological (35). While flying back to Europe from Tokyo, Lacan had seen streams on an otherwise barren Siberian riverbed that looked like etchings on the earth. The writing of the Real becomes an ecological writing on the geological surface here. This writing culturalises what would have been called 'nature' otherwise. Though this geological etching is a human metaphor, these are nonhuman lines drawn on the earth surface. The streams on the Siberian riverbed are not human-made national borders. There is something nonhuman about these lines drawn on the earth's surface. This earth-writing is another indication that Lacan is moving toward an ecological understanding of the unconscious as Real in his later teachings.

Literature, Climate Change and the Ecological Unconscious

To segue into literature, let me begin by talking about the novelist Amitav Ghosh's *The Great Derangement* (2016) that brings the literary in conversation with climate emergency. He starts with a clarion call for literary writers to wake up to the Anthropocene. Taking the Indian mangrove forests of the Sundarbans as an example, he laments the lack of fictional texts that tackle the destruction of its ecology. Through his own practice as a novelist, Ghosh has tried to fill in that void but we will not talk about his much-discussed novels in what follows. To stay with his ideas on climate fiction, he urges fiction writers not to genre-pack the theme of climate change. The fiction of climate crisis need not be science fiction: utopian or dystopian. Climate crisis is a socio-political emergency and needs to be treated in narratives that go beyond genre-fiction (see A. Ghosh 117–62). He wonders if depicting climate catastrophe takes the novel as genre into realms of improbability. The Delhi tornado evokes the uncanny but at the same time Ghosh thinks that the freakish weather events that are results of anthropogenic climate change go beyond the Gothic genre. Romanticism of Nature is not enough to give voice to our endangered ecology. Ghosh would agree with Morton here. The central question regarding fiction's ethical stand in Ghosh is as follows: how do we make literary fiction amenable to climate crisis by developing it as just another novelistic theme, like love, family and society?

Anna Kavan's Ice: The Eco-Political meets the Psychic

To address Amitav Ghosh's point, let me read a literary fiction (not genre-fiction) from 1967 that focuses on global warming in a near-prophetic way. This is *Ice*, a novel written by the English writer Anna Kavan. Often read as an allegory of Kavan's own addiction and substance abuse problems, *Ice* forewarns us about ecological catastrophe. It conflates the ecological and the political, merging the psychic with the environmental in a way that grounds the ecological unconscious. The Kafkaesque plotline portrays a male narrator's search for a mysterious 'ice-maiden' in the middle of a nuclear war in an unnamed sunless world in the process of being engulfed by ice walls. The icy frozenness of the narrative world may have an association with the whiteness of heroin and Kavan's drug addiction, but it does not take away from the consistent ecological motif in the novel. As the psychic reality of the narrator collapses, the world itself seems to come to an end through environmental disaster. The Lacanian Real of the ice dominates this ecology as its dark, unsustainable waste. The inside–outside distinction does not work in the ecological unconscious as the psyche becomes at one with what is happening in the ecological world. The narrator says, 'In a peculiar way, the unreality of the outer world appeared to be an extension of my own disturbed state of mind' (Kavan 67). The reality in *Ice* is like loose stitch-work with nothing at its core, 'mist and nylon with nothing behind' (33) or again, 'scene made of nylon with nothing behind' (67). It is a hollow texture, or shall we say, an empty text of the signifier that converges on the Real as ecological anxiety and the uncanny. When the Atlantic ice caps melt, the world becomes white and the narrator's search for the white girl turns into a diagnosis of climate change: 'Indestructible ice-mass was moving around, implacably destroying all life' (112).

In *Ice*, the world is like a trap: 'The world had become an arctic prison from which no escape was possible, all its creatures trapped as securely as were the trees, already lifeless inside their deadly resplendent armour' (21). The eco-political dimension opens up as climate change leads to a global nuclear war among nations. The anonymous warden, a Hitler-like figure, rules the world as we are offered an insight into the link between climate emergency and political fascism. The striking image of an ice army coming in to terminate the world conveys this eco-political nuance: 'icy giant battalions' (103). Trees are compared to armies. When people start disappearing and the government does not disclose facts, whatever is left of an ecology is put on deathbed. Vast populations migrate from one country to another. Politicians ban foreign news but travel is not restricted. Food riots break out. The narrator has to fight with the Warden to win the girl in this political quest for control. The ice maiden, who represents ecology, is endangered by this masculinist project of control politics. Like the girl, who rarely gets a voice, ecology is not tamed by the warden and the narrator's biopolitical games. The eco-psychic reality of ice is compared to a dream, and the narrator's obsession with writing about lemurs and their strange language consolidates the novel's engagement with the nonhuman.

The novel records the impact of climate change on animals. They start behaving in bizarre ways. Kavan's intense imagery creates the ecological uncanny (*pace* Morton) as the world becomes increasingly alien: 'Dazzling ice stars bombarded the world with rays, which splintered and penetrated the earth, filling earth's core with their deadly coldness, reinforcing the cold of the advancing ice. And always, on the surface, the indestructible ice-mass was moving forward, implacably destroying all life' (112). This ecology is replete with a strange planetary alterity. To invoke Amitav Ghosh,

Ice is not science fiction and does not reduce climate emergency to a particular literary genre. The novel is a strange mix of the ecogothic, the psychological, and the political in a non-realist narrative form. At the end, ecology and the ice girl converge in a startling image of catastrophe:

> a wall of rainbow ice jutting up from the sea, cutting right across, pushing a ridge of water ahead of it as it moved, as if the flat pale surface of sea was a carpet being rolled up. It was a sinister, fascinating sight, which did not seem intended for human eyes. [...] The ice world spreading over our world. Mountainous walls of ice surrounding the girl. Her moon white skin, her hair sparkling with diamond prisms under the moon. The moon's dead eye watching the death of our world. (150–51)

This apocalyptic ecology is uncanny and almost entirely nonhuman, if not posthuman. The novel does not hesitate to blame this turn of events on the human species: 'The ultimate achievement of mankind would be, not just self-destruction, but the destruction of all life; the transformation of the living world into a dead planet' (164), or again, 'A frightful crime had been committed, against nature, against the universe, against life. By rejecting life, man had destroyed the immemorial order, destroyed the world, now everything was about to crash down in ruins' (165).

In the final moment, the narrator is alone with the ice girl in a car as nuclear winter sets in on the outside. He has a 'reassuring' gun in his pocket. Is it to protect her or to kill her? The ambiguity remains in this ironic conquest that coincides with the destruction of ecology. By making psychic decimation homologous with ecological destruction, Kavan's novel gives ground to the ecological unconscious. It points to a posthumanist ecological condition of uncanny worldlessness that we have seen in Morton's theorisation. The vulnerable posthuman subject is entangled in this apocalyptic ecology that vomits out the Real of its climatic waste. This is no unitary or egotistical human subject but a broken subjectivity enacting an extension of the frozen ecology.

Wyl Menmuir's The Many: *Ecological Unconscious and the Uncanny*

To pursue a more recent literary fiction that does not limit climate catastrophe to any particular novelistic genre, let me end this chapter by discussing English writer Wyl Menmuir's 2016 Booker-longlisted novel, *The Many*. It deals with the life of a fishing community in an undefined village on the north Cornwall coast. Though steeped in a melancholic residue of humanism, the novel engages with endangered ecology by portraying the environmental pollution that affects the business of fishing and the life of the community. The Department of Fisheries cordons off the fishing area with a ring of container ships that loom large in the distant waters. The fishermen are instructed not to overstep this sinister limit. With each passing year, the number of edible fish goes down with water pollution. The fishermen cannot sell the fish in the open market and become dependent on the mediators who come to the village to buy the fish. The novel revolves around the haunted house of a dead fisherman, Perran, who drowned in the sea a decade ago but still exerts a spectral influence on the village folk. Timothy Buchanan comes to buy Perran's old house, much to the surprise and suspicion of the gated community of fishermen. Timothy is an 'emmet' (outsider) for them. The novel is narrated by Perran's fisherman friend Ethan and Timothy alternately, with multiple flashbacks in italicised paragraphs, dreams and hallucinations that make the reality of the novel unstable and unreliable.

The humanist story is embedded in the larger ecosystem of the sea. Ethan tells us about his father, also a fisherman, who had warned him about fish running out. He had told Ethan the story of a man 'who is cursed to fish an empty ocean for as long as he lives, the shore just in sight but never any closer' (3). The human subject here is left at the mercy of an endangered ecology with resources drying up. In this nature–culture or human–nature conflict á la Ernest Hemingway's maritime classic *The Old Man and the Sea* (1952), Ethan's rejoinder to his father's apocalyptic story is telling: 'The seas were as full as ever; it was the number of edible things in it that had changed was all' (3). The comment implies climate change by hinting at water pollution due to chemical deposition, garbage in the sea, and so on. This is the Lacanian Real of waste, rejected by reality but heaped alongside it. This Real is that which doesn't work in the world. It sabotages the ecological world. Children do not play in the water like they did earlier. They know the polluted water can make them sick. The Department of Fisheries calls it 'a profusion of biological agents and contaminants' (23). They add this note on the notice board in the winch house. When Ethan and his fellow fishermen go into the sea on a boat, ironically called 'Great Hope', they only find jellyfish. The sentence that repeats itself exasperatedly is: 'No fish, no fish, no shrimp nor shark, just jellies' (25). Finally, when they catch something else, it is tainted by the disastrous effects of climate change: 'The dogfish look burned, as though with acid, their eye sockets elongated and deep, showing through to the bone at the ends and there are white lesions down the side of each body. Their rough black skin is dull and flaked away in patches, the fins thin and ragged where there should be muscle' (26). The famished corporeality of the fish is testimony to the ecological meshing of the human and the nonhuman. The mesh is not harmonious but disturbing. The human and the fish are both vulnerable in this catastrophic situation of climate change. The degrading ecological mutation that happens in the body of the fish is presented with a sense of indignity. These poisoned fish are comparable to the children of Hiroshima who are born with physical deformities, decades after the atomic explosion. It is like a trans-generational geotrauma. The ethic of trans-species care, implicit in the tone of the above passages, signals an ecological principle of co-existence. It indicates shared vulnerabilities. Ethan's dreams are haunted by a sea-creature that represents the monstrosity of the damaged ecology around him: 'a fading shadow merging itself with the darkness of the deeper water' (30).

When Timothy looks at the sea, the horizon does not offer a beautiful meeting point of water and sky. All he finds are the container ships, motionless in their ghostly vigilance. Ethan warns him not to swim, not just because of the tidal currents but also due to the unhealthy 'chems' (chemicals) in the water (43). We may remember here Kohei Saito's aforementioned point about how capitalism deforms 'the universal metabolism of nature' (Saito 2017, 15). The poisoning of sea water signals 'metabolic rift' as capitalist indigestion in the alienated world of nature. We will come back to this point.

To continue with the inter-subjective psychic aspect, be it Ethan or Timothy, their dreams are punctuated by ecological images. Timothy in his dream encounters the question about what lies on the other side of the container ships. His dreams are haunted by the oppressive space in which it becomes impossible to distinguish between the sky and the sea. Timothy dreams about a posthuman ecology: 'He dreams of the vents where life still clings on to the hydrothermal streams that escape the earth's core, of the shrimps, the crabs, the biosludge that survived the great oceanic apocalypse' (63). This imagination of life that outlives the human on the planetary scale appears in the dream – a Freudian formation of the unconscious. These are textual instances of the ecological unconscious that show how the psyche responds to the uncertain survival of *zoe*, and not *bios* (the life-forms in Timothy's dreams are not exclusively human) in the context of climate change.

Timothy, who replaces Perran as Ethan's friend, accompanies him on the 'Great Hope' when they transgress the limit of the container ships and approach the water beyond the legal line drawn by the ships. The ships are the statist–capitalist markers. They stand for the capitalist degradation of ecological metabolism that makes the fish inedible. As both John Bellamy Foster and Kohei Saito dwell on the famous example of the fish from Marx's *The German Ideology*, we cannot consider water as the 'essence' of the fish. If we think that freshwater is the fish's ontological essence, it makes a critique of water pollution impossible because the moment the river is made to serve the industry, water stops being the essence of the fish (see Foster 112 and Saito 2017, 59–60). The fish in *The Many* are alienated from nature by capitalist production. It fragments their being as they become food and increasingly inedible due to water pollution.

An italicised flashback tells us how the Department of Fisheries came one day and put up their notices in obscure technical language, declaring how the limit was set up for '"*the containment and management of harmful waterborne agents*"' (Menmuir 52; emphasis original). When Timothy and Ethan overhaul the limit, they are not stopped. They read illegible letters on the outer surface of the container ships and come back with a new variety of fish in large numbers, strangely white and translucent. They get a great price for this catch and the village is excited about their feat. Timothy is spooked by the milk-white scales of the dead fish. He gives them a strange burial under a distant tree. The mystery around the purpose of the container ships thickens, making us wonder about the difference between the fish inside and outside the frontier. The edge marked out by the ships is like an edge of knowledge. This edge raises questions in Ethan's psyche: *'whether the ships might always have been there, unnoticed and waiting for their chance to edge closer towards the shore, into sight'* (53; emphasis original). The unconscious topology of the edge threatens to enter consciousness. What lies beyond the limit is the unconscious in all its ambiguous ecological implications. Is the department deliberately restricting the fishermen to dogfish? Are the fish on the other side better or worse? Why are they white? These questions loom large in the inter-subjective ecological unconscious of the fisherfolk.

Timothy gets sick in Perran's house and suspects that his delirium is caused by swimming in the polluted waters of the sea. In his feverish dreams, the ecology of the place takes over as he sees water everywhere, as if the village itself was made of the sea. In a terrifying nightmare, he finds himself running through the water to a replica of Perran's house which seems to stand perilously on the verge of destruction by the tides. These dreams reinforce the ecological unconscious on the one hand, and on another, his failed quest to know Perran after many attempts to question Ethan and the villagers. Ethan only tells him how Perran was brought up by them after his mother died while giving birth to him. The dead Other is at one with ecology here. The villagers imply that Perran is like a quasi-divine gaze. He is everywhere and nowhere. Nobody wants to talk about him to an outsider.

The inside is the outside. What is happening within the psyche is happening in the world. They are not only co-dependent but also co-constitutive. This is why the topology of the Lacanian unconscious assumes an ecological facet. One night as he comes back to his house that was once Perran's, Timothy can smell chemicals in the air and in the house. He has the uncanniest dream that night. He watches a multitude of Perrans coming out of the sea to surround him and the place from all directions. The figures, emerging from the sea as the 'many' (a nod to the book's title), are 'faceless and featureless' (112). But Timothy knows they are 'Perran upon Perran upon Perran' (112). These Perrans present a spectacle of the human-becoming-fish and fish-becoming-human. The sea vomits them out like the undigested Real of bad metabolism. This moment of subjective division produces multiplication. The posthuman ecological subject is a subject of divided uncanny. The dream speaks to Timothy's obsession with the enigmatic dead Other. But, as the creaturely and environmental imagery of a crowd, originating from the sea to attack the land suggests, the Other has taken up an ecological dimension. Next morning when he wakes up, Timothy finds the beach flooded by huge waves. Perran, meaning the 'little dark one', has become the dark ecology of climate change manifested by the sudden rise in the sea. The fish buried under the tree have been dug out to Timothy's surprise, and he buries them once again. When Timothy burns the old and new chemical-soaked furniture just outside his house, the fire speaks to the water in a dark silent dialogue. Perran is the sea. He is an embodiment of all the endangered fish in an increasingly resourceless sea. When Ethan observes the village landscape after the sea calms down, the place appears alien to him. All the elements of the place, be it the rocks at the mouth of the cove or the stones on the beach – everything is similar but not quite the same. He sees thin black lines on the surface of the beach, opening up like cracks. These lines appear from the water, barely perceptible, but caving in the place with them. He is unsure if this is happening inside his mind or in reality. He wants to have someone to witness the cracks. This is the affect of the environmental uncanny produced by climate change. It makes the unconscious ecological in its shared sense of vulnerability, endangerment and anxiety.

    The catastrophic hairline fractures continue well into the village, dividing buildings from the middle. The lines penetrate into human bodies and crack them up, making their dreams visible. Ethan is happy to imagine the container ships divided by the lines. He cannot communicate this psychic image of disaster to anyone. His words dry up. Others do not see these lines. The complex geometry of multiplying and intersecting lines coming out of the sea takes over the human habitations, but the sea is 'immune to them' (130). These lines resemble the multiple fish-like Perrans. They are yet another incarnation of the eco-psychic multitude of the 'many'– enactments of a divided ecological subjectivity. Ethan can hear a muffled voice coming from the cracks and stoops to hear the chthonic voice. Timothy's inter-subjective question, 'Who was Perran?' is echoed from these cracks (131). The novel ends with a strange enmeshing of the trio – Perran, Timothy and Ethan. The flashbacks reveal that Timothy and wife Lauren had a son named Perran who passed away as an infant. In the final chapter, Timothy watches Ethan, as if from within his body, through his eyes. Ethan jumps into the sea from the 'Great Hope', and cannot be seen among the waves. This is a spectral repetition of what had happened to Perran when he drowned in the sea. The container ships finally sail away and almost disappear into the horizon, clearing a greater space for fishing.

Does Ethan dive into the water for fish? Or does he commit suicide to be one with Perran? Do we read the extension of the fishing area as an optimistic conclusion? What about the white fish from outside the limit? Why were they different from the dogfish found inside? *The Many* does not answer these questions. It ends suspended between ecological hope and despondency. The directionless, abandoned ship in the sea is a reminder of the posthuman dimension of dark ecology, but the fishermen have a bigger place to try their luck now. What remains unambiguous in this ambivalent tale is an ecological characterisation of the unconscious psyche as the border between the inside and the outside. It is a psyche that follows ecology and merges with it in its inter-subjective sweep. What happens to deform the ecology resonates in the deformation of the psychic world. Death-drive, as a reflection of the unconscious, be it Perran's or Ethan's, matches up to the climate apocalypse. We could consider here psychoanalyst Julie Reshe's recent argument about 'nature' as an embodiment of death-drive in the context of climate-crisis.[4]

In *Ice* and *The Many* we have a convergence of the ecological with the psychic, or what could be called eco-psychic in its underlying political implications. The destruction of ecology is homologous to the death-drive that destroys the psyche. In Reshe's words, '[t]he material reality exists in the ruins of itself, with nothing existing outside of the ruins. Nature is continuously negating itself, repeating its own destruction' (172). As she observes, ecology (though Reshe uses the signifier 'nature', we will use 'ecology') as an incarnation of death-drive is related to a decentring of the mal-adapted human beings: 'The concept of the death drive, when applied to the process of evolution, functions as a proper dethronement of humankind. It implies that humans are not even exclusive in their shittiness, but are just random evolutionary shit, and just the same meaningless by-product of destructive and discontinuous forces' (176–77). Posthumanism or anti-anthropocentrism is not far from the concept of the death-drive when it is extended onto ecology. The ecological unconscious is a sign of our times when the death of ecology and the death of the psyche have become one and the same.

To sum up, this chapter examined environmental discourse in the context of anthropogenic climate change and arrived at fragmented posthuman ecologies. We committed ourselves to the ethico-political positions vital to thinking posthuman ecologies and pursued their nuances from Morton and Colebrook to Chakrabarty and Ghosh, not to mention Foster and Saito. Uncoupling ecology from both the romanticism of nature and the human-centric discourse of sustainability, emerged as important ethical directions. The political ethic of posthuman ecology led us to construct an ecological notion of the unconscious psyche from Lacanian psychoanalysis that goes beyond the human. The human psyche repeats what happens in the ecological world and not the other way. It is secondary to ecology. Anthropogenic climate change brings in a surge of the Real, teeming with hollows that manifest themselves in anxiety as the principal affect of the climate-crisis era. Finally, the chapter offered two literary case studies of the ecological unconscious that highlighted the uncanny reproduction of ecologies in the unconscious psyche and ramified our notion of the eco-political by intersecting the biopolitical discourse of governmentality with the psychical impact of climate destruction. The posthuman subject is embedded in ecology and their psyche mirrors ecological changes in such a way that we cannot talk about an exclusively human mind anymore.

We must rethink the psyche as a posthuman ecological entanglement. Subjectivity emerges as a collective multi-species assemblage, crafting its own unique death (*pace* Braidotti in Chapter 2). Posthuman subjectivity is this ecological principle of co-existence. The ecological unconscious takes the subject beyond the human. It emerges as a pluralistic and fragmented subject of shared vulnerability with other species. The posthuman divided subject exists at the cusp of the inside and the outside, between the self and the Other and between the one and the many. It is as an ontological multitude that we must negotiate the relation between ecology and politics, between the psyche and the world or the worldlessness of the Real.

NOTES

1. For more on this notion and its complex critique, see Foster, p. 15, 508. For a take on capitalist metabolism, see Saito's *Karl Marx's Ecosocialism*, pp. 99–137.

2. For more on this point, see John Michael Williams' 2000 paper on the subject, https://arxiv.org/vc/physics/papers/0008/0008228v1.pdf.

3. We may remember Sigmund Freud observing his grandson playing the *fort-da* game in *Beyond the Pleasure Principle* and D. W. Winnicott's work on child analysis in which games take centre stage.

4. For another approach to ecology and death-drive, see Lisa Baraitser's article, 'The maternal death drive: Greta Thunberg and the question of the future'.

REFERENCES

Baraitser, Lisa. "The maternal death drive: Greta Thunberg and the question of the future". *Psychoanalysis, Culture & Society*, vol. 25, 2020, pp. 499–517, https://doi.org/article/10.1057/s41282-020-00197-y. Accessed 14 November 2021.

Burnham, Clint, and Paul Kingsbury, editors. *Lacan and Environment*. Palgrave Macmillan, 2021.

Chakrabarty, Dipesh. *The Climate of History in a Planetary Age*. U of Chicago P, 2021.

Colebrook, Claire. *Death of the PostHuman: Essays on Extinction, Vol. 1*. Ann Open Humanities Press, 2014.

Foster, John Bellamy. *Marx's Ecology: Materialism and Nature*. Monthly Review Press, 2000.

---. *The Return of Nature: Socialism and Ecology*. Monthly Review Press, 2020.

Ghosh, Amitav. *The Great Derangement: Climate Change and the Unthinkable*. Penguin, 2016.

Ghosh, Ranjan. *The Plastic Turn*. Cornell UP, 2022.

Kavan, Anna. *Ice*. Penguin, 2017.

Lacan, Jacques. "Lituraterre". 1971. Translated by Beatrice Khiara-Foxton and Adrian Price, *Hurly-Burly*, vol. 9, 2013, pp. 29–38.

---. *The Seminar of Jacques Lacan: Book XVII; The Other Side of Psychoanalysis*. Translated by Russell Grigg, edited by Jacques Alain-Miller, Norton, 2017.

---. *The Triumph of Religion*. Translated by Bruce Fink, Polity Press, 2013.

Langford, Sasha J. "The Psychotopology of Climate". *Lacan and Environment*, edited by Clint Burnham and Paul Kingsbury, Palgrave Macmillan, 2021, pp. 97–116.

Menary, Richard, editor. *The Extended Mind*. MIT P, 2010.

Menmuir, Wyl. *The Many*. Salt, 2016.

Miller, Jacques-Alain. "A Real for the 21st Century". Translated by Roger Litten, *Lacan Quotidien*, 2012, https://lacanquotidien.fr/blog/2012/05/the-real-in-the-21st-century-by-jacques-alain-miller/. Accessed 14 November 2021.

Morton, Timothy. *The Ecological Thought*. Harvard UP, 2010.

---. *Ecology without Nature: Rethinking Environmental Aesthetics*. Harvard UP, 2009.

---. *Hyperobjects: Philosophy and Ecology after the End of the World*. U of Minnesota P, 2013.

Nixon, Rob. *Slow Violence and the Environmentalism of the Poor*. Harvard UP, 2011.

Orange, Dona M. *Climate Crisis, Psychoanalysis and Radical Ethics*. Routledge, 2016.

Reshe, Julie. "The Death Drive of Evolution (From the perspective of Depressive Realism)". *Nature and Philosophy*, vol. 11, no. 1, 2021, pp. 156–80, https://doi.org/10.33280/2310-3817-21-11-1-156-180. Accessed 14 November 2021.

Roszak, Theodore. *The Voice of the Earth: An Exploration of Ecopsychology*. Simon and Schuster, 1993.

Saito, Kohei. *Karl Marx's Ecosocialism: Capitalism, Nature and the Unfinished Critique of Political Economy*. Monthly Review Press, 2017.

---. *Marx in the Anthropocene: Towards the Idea of Degrowth Communism*. Cambridge UP, 2022.

Soler, Colette. *Humanisation? Psychoanalysis, Symbolization and the Body of the Unconscious*. Translated by Benjamin Farrow and Hugues d'Alascio, Routledge, 2018.

Williams, John Michael. "Entropy shows that global warming should cause increased variability in the weather". *Arxiv*, 2000, https://arxiv.org/vc/physics/papers/0008/0008228v1.pdf. Accessed 14 November 2021.

Wolfe, Cary. *Ecological Poetics; or, Wallace Stevens's Birds*. U of Chicago P, 2020.

Zeiher, Cindy. "Love Thy Enemy: Environment(al) Politics". *Lacan and Environment*, edited by Clint Burnham and Paul Kingsbury, Palgrave Macmillan, 2021, pp. 19–38.

Coda: Posthumanist Subjectivity

If there is a central argumentative programme that runs through this book, it is the ethico-political imperative to preserve the agonistic principle of subjectivity in posthumanism. Without the subject, there is no politics, agency or resistance. But, the posthuman agent cannot be the classical human subject of humanism or academic humanities. There is an inclination in posthumanism to push the subjectivity question toward citizenship, granting citizen status to nonhuman entities and taking the discussion in the direction of cloning, organ donation, prosthetic bodies, and so on. For instance, one could consider the robot Sophia, developed by a Hong Kong-based company, activated in 2016 and given citizenship by Saudi Arabia in 2017. One could ask what this citizenship means for Sophia's agency beyond representational tokenism. Can the posthuman subject be a citizen–subject is a question I have kept aside in this book, as I remain sceptical about the emancipatory potential of such a move. For me, the bio-ethics of posthuman citizenship is predominantly held captive within transhumanism if not ultrahumanism (Colebrook). It wants to make everything human and acts mostly as an ideological cover for the subjectless ontology that transhumanist discourses promote.

Chris Hables Gray is aware of the danger of giving up on the subject. In his 2001 book, *Cyborg Citizen*, he considers the citizen–subject as a composite entity or an assemblage where 'subjectivity can be constructed in large part by the choices we make about our own cyborgization' (190). The cyborg–subject needs to be given citizenship rights for the sake of justice and Gray formulates an elaborate cyborg bill of rights from right to life and death to the freedom to choose family, sexuality and gender. While I remain empathetic to the politics of posthuman rights, I am not sure if the statist idea of citizenship is the best platform for this politics. This is why Gray has to question the given idea of citizenship too (see Gray 25). Citizenship itself is a humanist idea. Though Gray doesn't take citizenship as a universal value, for pragmatic reasons he chooses to stay within this framework. My decision in this book has been otherwise. I have chosen to subtract citizenship from subjectivity to take it outside the nation–statist order. For me, there is a crucial gap between the subject and the citizen. We have to preserve this gap as it holds promises of resistance and insurrection. To abolish the gap will be counterrevolutionary. This gap is the site where the subject can protest the dominant ideology by subverting their statist taming through citizenship. There are subjective acts that remain irreducible to the statist and identitarian logic of citizenship. Posthumanism must be committed to these dissident subjectivities that transcend the humanist–statist notion of citizenship. The posthuman subject in its irreducibility to citizenship can be conceptualised beyond the state as a political entity.

To characterise the posthuman subject further, let me quote Vicky Kirby from *Quantum Anthropologies*: 'humankind emerges as an expression of the world's measured subjectivity' (39). The human is not the world. It is not a centre to the world. The world as matter pre-exists the human. The human subject is only a geomaterial expression of the world's subjectivity. This is an ecological materialist positioning of the human subject within a multi-species planetary entanglement. This posthuman subject is peripheral but significant to rethink the ethics and politics of posthumanism. To resist the capitalist transhumanism of machine fetishism; to resist the biopolitics of governmental control; to resist climate insensitivity; to resist atrocities on animals and to resist diverse forms of human exploitation that involve the nonhuman, we need to anchor ourselves on a politics that changes not just human life but all lives and the material world itself. This cannot be done only by the human or from the exceptionalist position of anthropocentrism. For this to happen, we have to situate political subjectivity as an ontological principle of the world that interconnects the human and the nonhuman. Unlike the individualist subject of conservative humanism, this would be a collective subject of posthuman political resistance: a radical democratic multitude, irreducible to the human. Let us look at one last literary micro-illustration. The ageing writer Elizabeth Costello in J. M. Coetzee's story 'The Glass Abattoir' (2017) could be seen as a posthuman subject. Though she ethically dedicates herself to writing about animals and the human cruelty brought upon them, there is no humanist hubris in this representation but a pluralist identification with the animals as ontological multitude. As she tells her son, Costello watches a TV programme about factory farming where they show artificial hatching of chickens – how the female chickens are put into a box for dispatch to the egg-laying plant and the male chicks are ground into a paste that becomes cattle-food or fertiliser. She empathises with a male chick on the conveyor belt about to face his fate and, though her account personifies the animal by giving him human language, the anthropomorphism builds a human–nonhuman kinship here. Costello tells her son about how she feels affected by the image of these animals, either kept alive or put to death, depending on whether their gender (binary) fits the business plan of the humans. Elizabeth Costello ontologically identifies with these chickens and uses her human tool of writing to extend her subjectivity onto the nonhuman multitude. These words to her son close the story:

> 'It is for them that I write. Their lives were so brief, so easily forgotten. I am the sole being in the universe who still remembers them, if we leave God aside. After I am gone there will be only blankness. It will be as if they had never existed. That is why I wrote about them, and why I wanted you to read about them. To pass on the memory of them, to you. That is all.' (Coetzee, 232)

We have a strong 'I' of the subject as human individual (only next to God) here. It may appear to be species-humanist but it's a self that feels akin to the nonhuman Other. This ethical subject writes for the Other. Though she, a human, wants to represent the chickens and their transient lives, the ethics of this writing is quite literally 'post' or 'after' the human writer insofar as it is oriented toward a future when Costello will cease to exist. But she doesn't want the chickens to be forgotten when she is dead. Her writing, serving as an archive for the nonhuman, has a futuristic testimonial function. It wants to preserve a memory of these neglected victims of human-made industrial capitalism. The aim of her ethical writing is a transgenerational transfer of the memory of nonhuman life in all its poignant richness. This is one human subject, feeling at one with many nonhuman subjects and writing about them from an ethical position. Though there is a flirtation with the representative humanist *cogito* in Costello's self-reflection, it is inclined toward a humble multi-species ethic. And yet it does not let go of human subjectivity. It is a posthuman humane subject we encounter in Elizabeth Costello.

Dipesh Chakrabarty in his recent book *One Planet, Many Worlds: The Climate Parallax* (2023) has argued that there is a dialectic of the one and the many between the differentiated (not-one) subject of politics and the planet, seen as one by the earth science system. In this dialectical space between planet and politics, we must construct a posthumanist subject that is both the one and the many. In this Platonic, numerical dialectic lies the possibility of thinking a collective but not necessarily unitary subject that goes beyond one species. We require a multispecies collective that refuses the dogma of unicity (one central species in this case) and totalisation (a closed subjective chain). This is a collective but a-central subject without totalisation. It is a political subject that admits multiplicity and collectivises itself without homogenising or creating a monolith. The point is to think subjectivity in relational terms. In his final comment on the problem of the one and the many, Chakrabarty writes: 'Yet the planet is one, at least for Earth system scientists. They regard the planet's climate system as one. Humans are many, divided in multiple ways and yet connected. Making kin is a way of forging connections around and across differences' (106).

Though I agree with his language of kinship as relation, Chakrabarty's political subject remains humanist – enclosed within the human species. I will argue for a human–nonhuman kinship that forges relations among different species and creates a collective that is open and infinite. The posthuman subject will synthesise the dialectic of the one and the many by ontologically inhabiting the place of the one-multiple – an antinomic, inter-subjective, inter-objective and inter-human assemblage. The one gives this posthuman constellation collectivity, and the many gives it multiplicity without a totalising unity. This idea of the subject as both the one and the many could offer the ontological principle for a posthuman subjectivity of politics in the twenty-first century.

Let me conclude by making a few brief points about this posthuman political subject. As I see it, the posthuman (both as posthumanisms and post-humanities) is an *event* that has *interrupted* the global humanist historical sequence. I use the term 'event' following the contemporary French philosopher Alain Badiou whose work situates the human subject as a product of events. Badiou doesn't engage with posthumanism but his work imbibes Althusser and Lacan's structural anti-humanism.[1] Badiou's evental ontology of subjectivity acknowledges that the events shaping our subjecthood can come from anywhere. The event for him is a chance encounter and politics is one of the basic evental truth processes. It is events that create subjects of truth and not the other way round. In this thesis of Badiou's, we glimpse a reversal of the classical humanist-Marxist thesis in which human beings create events to change the world. Badiou's collective political subject is a rethinking of Marx's 'generic humanity', shorn of all identitarian structures. In *The Immanence of Truths* (2022), Badiou writes, 'The word "generic" has a long history. It is the word by which Marx referred to the proletariat in the *1844 Manuscripts*. He said that the proletariat was the representation of generic humanity, that is to say, of humanity as such, not assignable to this or that identity' (230).

As Saumyabrata Choudhury has shown, Badiou's 'generic humanity' is homologous with what Babasaheb Ambedkar calls 'social humanity'.[2] The anti-caste social humanity of Ambedkar or the fundamental generic humanity of Badiou requires a push toward the nonhuman for it to become a posthuman political subjectivity. We can become as posthuman as we like, but we must preserve a residue of the human in the posthuman. The human co-constituted in a chain with the nonhuman will together construct a socio-political, collective form of subjectivity. To change the world, the nonhuman world needs to be changed, but it cannot be changed by the human alone or the human in any self-conscious, leading position.

I extend Badiou's notion of the event to think about the human as a multi-species (including matter as species) encounter that reorients the human subject and turns it into a posthuman object, part of a human–nonhuman chain. This is no great chain of being with inflexible species hierarchies. It is a relational, flat ontology of objects in a chain-like network. What Badiou calls the 'human animal's' (103) infinite, creative struggle for truths via eventual sequences in politics, art, science and love, must converge with nonhuman procedures that take their own course. The human subjective infinity he theorises must meet the infinity of the nonhuman in animals, plants, machines, tools, objects, matter, and the planet itself. Encountering the nonhuman in its own autonomous being produces an ontological cut in the humanist subject. Technology, machines, animals, plants, objects, and the materiality of the planetary world, divide the human subject and allow it to see itself as a tiny component of an enormous and multi-layered ecological matrix. This is indeed of the order of the event in Badiou that breaks ontological stasis and inaugurates new subjectivities. We need to envisage both the human and the nonhuman encountering each other in their mutual alterities and getting ontologically radicalised by one another. This will produce a posthuman chain-subject of ethico-political action. We must speculatively conjure this collective subject for the sake of social justice and political resistance. This is the ethico-political imperative of posthumanism in our times.

NOTES

1. For more on Badiou's idea of the human, see the chapter 'Alain Badiou: Formalised Inhumanism' in Christopher Watkin's book, *French Philosophy Today*.
2. For more on this, see Choudhury's book *Ambedkar and Other Immortals*.

REFERENCES

Badiou, Alain. *The Immanence of Truths: Being and Event III*. Translated by Susan Spitzer and Kenneth Reinhard, Bloomsbury, 2022.

Chakrabarty, Dipesh. *One Planet, Many Worlds: The Climate Parallax*. Brandeis UP, 2023.

Choudhury, Saumyabrata. *Ambedkar and Other Immortals: An Untouchable Research Programme*. Navayana Publishing, 2018.

Coetzee, J. M. "The Glass Abattoir". *The Pole and Other Stories*, Harvill Secker, 2023, pp. 208–32.

Gray, Chris Hables. *Cyborg Citizen: Politics in the Posthuman Age*. Routledge, 2001.

Kirby, Vicky. *Quantum Anthropologies: Life at Large*. Duke UP, 2011.

Watkin, Christopher. *French Philosophy Today: New Figures of the Human in Badiou, Meillassoux, Malabou, Serres and Latour*. Edinburgh UP, 2016.

Glossary

actor-network: Bruno Latour's theory of social and political networks that comprise multiple human and nonhuman actors in a set of heterogeneous relations.

accumulation: a notion in Tristan Garcia's object philosophy that refers to a process whereby objects relate to one another to produce meaning in societal structures.

anthropocentrism: a worldview or philosophy that places humans at the centre of the world.

anthropomorphism: a technique of humanising all that is not human.

Anthropocene: an era when humans become geological agents and can make serious changes in the environment.

assemblage: a concept from Gilles Deleuze that refers to a network of elements organised in an a-centrist way.

biopolitics: the way statist politics takes charge of *bios* or the biological body and the life of human citizens.

flat ontology: a philosophy that imagines human and nonhuman beings entangled in a non-hierarchical world.

humanism: species-humanism believes in human supremacy over other species on rationalist grounds.

hyperobject: Tim Morton's concept refers to objects that are stretched out in space-time in such a way that they may not be readily available to us in sensory experience.

mesh: Tim Morton's concept that signifies how multiple species are entangled with one another in an ecological web.

metabolic rift: this Marxist notion, reworked by John Bellamy Foster and Kohei Saito, refers to the process by which human-made capitalism alienates nature and capital as a form of metabolism and creates gaps between the human and the environment.

necro-politics: politics of and around death that brings in governmental control over bodies in both life and death. In posthumanism, death becomes a tool to flatten the supremacy of life as a divider between the human and the animal on the one hand, and the so-called inanimate matter on the other hand.

object-oriented-ontology: a contemporary school of continental philosophy that likes to think ontology (philosophical science of beings) from the perspective of objects and not human subjects.

overmining: Graham Harman's term for reducing an object to its relation with other objects.

planetarity: a term used often by Spivak which refers to a way of thinking about the planet as an agent in itself.

posthumanism: a philosophy of de-centring the human from all kinds of thinking, and seeing it as one among many elements in a larger system of thought.

poststructuralism: a twentieth-century school of Continental philosophy (Derrida, Foucault, Deleuze, Lacan, and so on) that attempts to think about language and discourse beyond the idea of a centralised structure.

real, symbolic and imaginary: the three orders of the unconscious for Lacan. Real is the impossible that is rejected from the Symbolic construction of reality. It is something inexpressible and yet of this world. The Symbolic is the realm of language and the Imaginary order refers to anything that is of the species of the image, not just visual but any other sensory image.

speciesism: a way of philosophical thinking that believes in a hierarchy of species and cannot think of them in egalitarian multi-species networks.

spectrality: a condition of ghosting between presence and absence that produces an uncanny feeling.

transhumanism: a philosophy that champions the capitalist acceleration which turns the human into the machine.

ultrahumanism: Claire Colebrook and others talk about a posthumanism that is nothing but a disguised form of humanism with all its supremacist agency.

undermining: Graham Harman's term for reducing an object to its constituent elements.

vegetal philosophy: a way of thinking about plants as autonomous ontological units.

zoe-politics: A posthuman idea of expanding politics beyond human life (*bios*) where it can include all life (*zoe*) – human, animal, plant and vibrant matter.

Further Reading

Boulter, Jonathan. *Parables of the Posthuman: Digital Realities, Gaming and the Player Experience.* Wayne State UP, 2015.

Castricano, Jodey. *Animal Subjects: An Ethical Reader in a Posthuman World.* Wilfrid Laurier UP, 2008.

Dinello, Daniel. *Technophobia!: Science Fiction Visions of Posthuman Technology.* U of Texas P, 2005.

Dixon, Joan Broadhurst, and Eric J. Cassidy. *Virtual Futures: Cyberotics, Technology and Post-Human Pragmatism.* Routledge, 2005.

Ezra, Elizabeth. *The Cinema of Things: Globalization and the Posthuman Object.* Bloomsbury, 2018.

Haney II, William S. *Cyberculture, Cyborgs and Science Fiction.* Rodopi, 2006.

Hauskeller, Michael. *Sex and the Posthuman Condition.* Palgrave Macmillan, 2014.

Heise-von der Lippe, Anya. *Posthuman Gothic.* U of Wales P, 2017.

Hofkirchner, Wolfgang, and Hans-Jörg Kreowski, editors. *Transhumanism: The Proper Guide to a Posthuman Condition or a Dangerous Idea?* Springer, 2021.

Jaques, Zoe. *Children's Literature and the Posthuman: Animal, Environment, Cyborg.* Routledge, 2015.

Lykke, Nina. *Vibrant Death: A Posthuman Phenomenology of Mourning.* Bloomsbury, 2022.

Malone, Karen, Marek Tesar, and Sonja Arndt, editors. *Theorising Posthuman Childhood Studies.* Springer, 2020.

Murray, Stuart. *Disability and the Posthuman: Bodies, Technology, and Cultural Futures* Liverpool UP, 2020.

Neimanis, Astrida. *Bodies of Water: Posthuman Feminist Phenomenology.* Bloomsbury, 2017.

Newman, Saul, and Tihomir Topuzovski, editors. *The Posthuman Pandemic*. Bloomsbury, 2022.

Norman, Jana. *Posthuman Legal Subjectivity: Reimagining the Human in the Anthropocene*. Routledge, 2022.

Pentaris, Panagiotis. *Dying in a Transhumanist and Posthuman Society*. Routledge, 2022.

Pinn, Anthony B., editor. *Humanism and Technology: Opportunities and Challenges*, Palgrave Macmillan, 2016.

Roden, David. *Posthuman Life: Philosophy at the Edge of the Human*. Routledge, 2015.

Shaw, Debra Benita. *Posthuman Urbanism: Mapping Bodies in Contemporary City Space*. Rowman and Littlefield, 2018.

Waldby, Catherine. *The Visible Human Project: Informatic Bodies and Posthuman Medicine*. Routledge, 2000.

Waters, Brent. *From Human to Posthuman: Christian Theology and Technology in a Postmodern World*. Ashgate, 2006.

Other Books in the Series

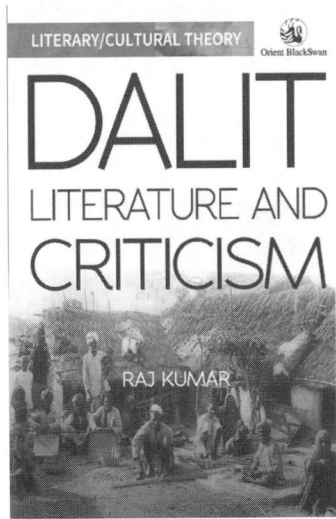

For more information, visit www.orientblackswan.com

Other Books in the Series

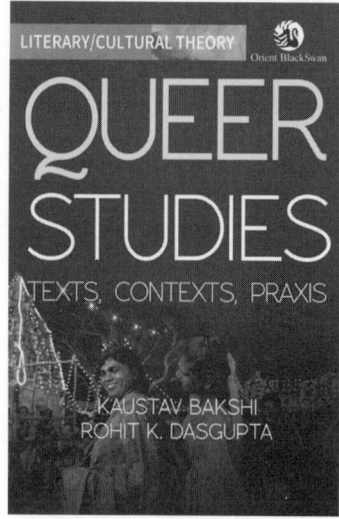
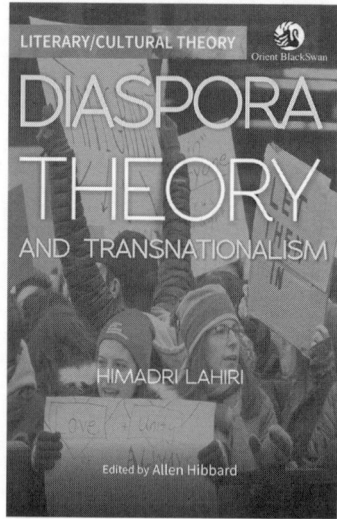

For more information, visit www.orientblackswan.com

Other Books in the Series

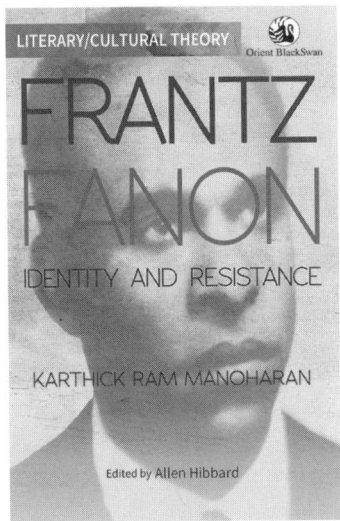
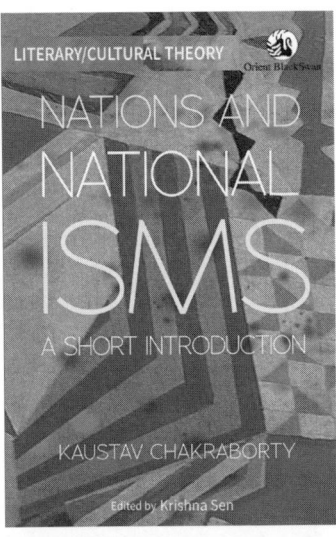
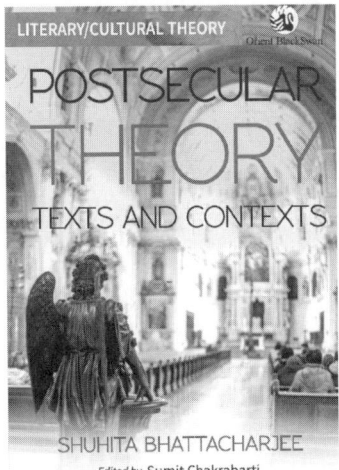

For more information, visit www.orientblackswan.com

Other Books in the Series

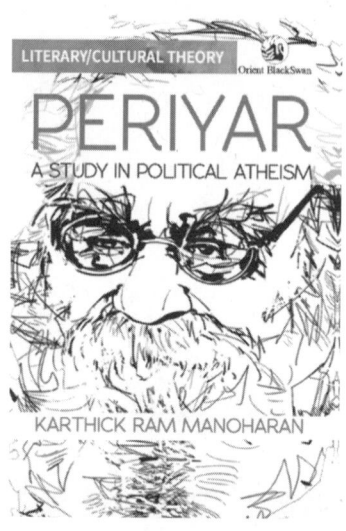

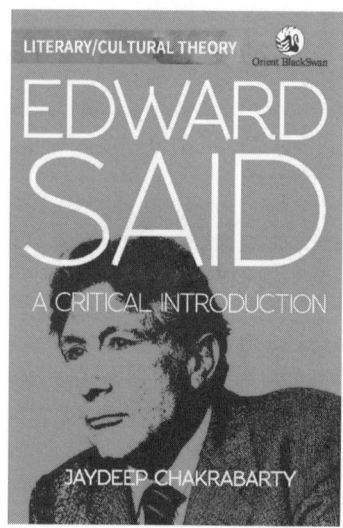

For more information, visit www.orientblackswan.com

Other Books in the Series

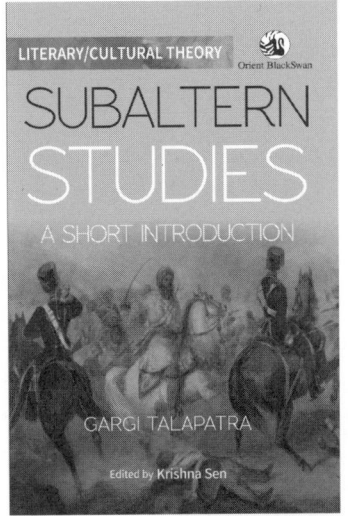

For more information, visit www.orientblackswan.com